CLARENDON

Edited
TONY HONORÉ AND JOSEPH RAZ

CLARENDON LAW SERIES

Some Recent Titles in this Series

PLAYING BY THE RULES

A Philosophical Examination of Rule-Based Decision-Making in Law and in Life

FREDERICK SCHAUER

Frank Stanton Professor of the First Amendment
John F. Kennedy School of Government
Harvard University

CLARENDON PRESS · OXFORD

Oxford University Press, Great Clarendon Street, Oxford OX2 6DP

Oxford New York
Athens Auckland Bangkok Bogota Bombay
Buenos Aires Calcutta Cape Town Chennai
Dar es Salaam Delhi Florence Hong Kong Istanbul
Karachi Kuala Lumpur Madras Madrid Melbourne
Mexico City Mumbai Nairobi Paris São Paolo
Singapore Taipei Tokyo Toronto

and associated companies in
Berlin Ibadan

Oxford is a trade mark of Oxford University Press

Published in the United States
by Oxford University Press Inc., New York

First published 1991
Reprinted new as paperback 1992
Paperback reprinted 1998

British Library Cataloguing in Publication Data
data available

Library of Congress Cataloging in Publication Data
Schauer, Frederick F.
Playing by the rules: a philosophical examination of rule-based
decision making in law and life / Frederick Schauer.
(Clarendon law series)
Includes bibliographical references and index.
1. Law—Decision making—Philosophy. 2. Decision-making—
Philosophy. 3. Social norms—Philosophy. I. Title II. Series.
K230.S315P56 1991 340´.1—dc20 91.13957
ISBN 0–19–825661–2
ISBN 0–19–825831–3 (pbk.)

Printed and bound in Great Britain by
Biddles Ltd, Guildford and King's Lynn

for
Virginia

this time, next time,
and for all time

PREFACE

THIS book is an exercise in *analytic isolation*, which is to say that it is deliberately and unashamedly 'unrealistic'. In examining any aspect of human life, an investigator may attempt to capture the full subtlety and intricacy of experience, seeking to understand and depict a complexity that is never absent from anything we do, individually or socially. Yet without denigrating such forms of inquiry, I choose to avoid them. Far too often such aspirations to comprehensive accuracy achieve their goals only by replicating the vagueness and the messiness of life. However faithful to reality these depictions may be, their accuracy often fails to increase our understanding.

In order to steer far wide of the dangers of vacuous accuracy, I wish artificially to wrench from the richness of reality just one among the myriad factors determining what we do, how we act, and what decisions we make. I select this course in the belief that careful analysis of individual components is often helpful in understanding, ultimately, the whole that those components constitute, and that careful analysis often proceeds best under conditions in which the phenomenon to be analysed is isolated, however artificial that isolation may seem. Just as scientists employ controlled experiments in order to exclude from their inquiries all factors but one, so too do I engage in this exercise with the full knowledge that the complexity of decision-making is far richer than I attempt to explore here. Instead, I hope the phenomenon I analyse can thereafter be returned to its more realistic home alongside other factors in actual decision-making, but returned in such a way that the analysis may then help those who study decision-making in greater breadth.

The phenomenon I subject to analytic isolation is the phenomenon of *rule*, the way in which prescriptive (or regulative) rules appear to play a large role in decision-making, most obviously in law but also in politics, in family governance, in religion, and in life in general. Rules appear all around us, but often our understanding of what they do and how they do it is a mystery, remaining mysterious even as we follow and break rules as part of our daily routine. Trying to figure out that mystery is what this book is all about.

In pursuit of some better understanding of the nature of prescriptive rules, I employ methods that are, broadly speaking, philosophical and analytic. I do not, however, claim these methods to be anywhere near exhaustive. Much that is interesting about rules can be said from the perspectives of psychology, economics, sociology, decision theory, anthropology, and a host of other disciplines. But my emphasis here on a philosophical approach is premised in part on a belief that it is important for any discipline to have some clear conception of what it is investigating before the investigation can begin. For much the same reasons, the aims of this book are only secondarily normative, and often I am unconcerned with whether rules are good things to have. I *am* concerned that consideration of that question proceed with as little confusion as possible, and thus much of this book is premised on the belief that it is often important to get things straight before we can think about getting them right.

I am by no means the first to consider prescriptive rules from a philosophical perspective. Yet part of the justification for this book is the very existence of varied literatures with too little intersection. A rich corpus of relatively modern scholarship has developed and examined the distinction between act- and rule-utilitarianism, and an older and even richer literature in legal theory has considered both the nature of rules and their role in legal decision-making. Recently, renewed attention to Wittgenstein's remarks on rule-following has developed into an industry of its own, at times supplementing and at times detached from what an eclectic collection of philosophers of language has written about the place of rules in understanding the functioning of language. And finally, there is also a valuable if somewhat less widely accessible technical literature addressing the logic of norms, focusing sometimes on individual norms and sometimes on the logic of full norm systems such as that of the law.

I draw on all of these literatures, but I do not see my task as one of synthesis. Instead, I pick and choose from among these diverse perspectives to say things about the nature of prescriptive rules that I hope will be of value in thinking both about law and about decision-making outside the legal system. If I can enrich all of the literatures on which I have drawn I will have partially repaid a large debt to those who have preceded me in thinking about rules. If in addition I can say things of interest to those who, although rule users themselves, have not thought philosophically about the nature of that phenomenon, then I will consider this enterprise a complete success.

Although this book is not a collection of previously published work, it owes its existence to a project that has occupied my professional life for some time, and which has produced, in addition to some number of published articles and reviews, frequent opportunities to present versions of the arguments that have culminated in this book. For all its loneliness and ultimate individual responsibility, scholarship remains a collective enterprise, and I am pleased to acknowledge my debt to audiences who by their hospitality and comments have assisted in an enterprise for which I alone will get an excessive amount of the credit if it is successful, although I willingly take all of the blame if it fails. With apologies for the omission of those who have participated in less formal exchanges that are more difficult to acknowledge, I wish still to thank audiences at the University of Alberta Faculty of Philosophy, American Philosophical Association (Eastern Division), American Philosophical Association (Pacific Division), American Society for Political and Legal Philosophy, Association of American Law Schools, Boston University School of Law, Brooklyn Law School, Case Western Reserve University School of Law, University of Chicago Law School, Columbia Law School, Cornell Law School, Dartmouth College Department of Philosophy, Georgetown Law School, Hamline University College of Law, Harvard Law School, Indiana University School of Law, New York Law School, New York University School of Law, University of San Diego School of Law, University of Southern California Law Center, Oxford–USC Institute of Legal Theory, University of Texas Law School, University of Toronto Faculty of Law, University of Virginia School of Law, Washington University Department of Philosophy, Wayne State University Department of Philosophy, College of William and Mary Department of Philosophy, University of Windsor Faculty of Law, and the Yale Law School.

In addition, I am delighted to acknowledge the support, partly financial but much more importantly personal and environmental, of the institution of which I was a member during the writing of this book, the University of Michigan Law School. Its resources provided the time and assistance necessary for completion of this project, and my students and colleagues provided an atmosphere in which I could feel that it was of some interest and some importance. I am also grateful to the University of Michigan Department of Philosophy, whose openness to me at all times and in many ways was essential to an auto-didactic philosopher. I learned much during the Winter Quarter 1990 as a Visiting Professor of Law at the University of Chicago, and during the Summer of 1988 the University of Washington School of Law was most generous in providing me an office and full use of its facilities in exchange for nothing whatsoever. In the final months of this project the resources and support of the Joan Shorenstein Barone Center on the Press, Politics and Public Policy, the John F. Kennedy School of Government, and Harvard University made easy and enjoyable the part of the process that is normally just the opposite.

Whatever my institutional debts, they are not nearly as great as the personal. Rita Rendell assisted in ways far beyond the typing of several versions of the manuscript. By cheerfully performing a multitude of frequently tedious tasks, and by calmly dealing with the urgencies of the moment, she made it possible for me to have the time to complete this book. Larry Alexander, Paul Bullen, Don Herzog, David Lyons, Mary Jane Morrison, Stanley Paulson, Richard Posner, Joseph Raz, Philip Soper, Terrance Sandalow, Marian Smiley, Jeremy Waldron, and Nicholas White took time out from their own work to comment on the entire manuscript, and Heidi Feldman, Brian Leiter, Margaret Radin, Virginia Wise, and Richard Zeckhauser offered highly useful critiques of parts of it. In the Spring of 1990 the University of San Diego School of Law sponsored a symposium centered around my work on rules, and the comments on that occasion of Larry Alexander, Jules Coleman, Ruth Gavison, Kenneth Kress, Michael Moore, Gerald Postema, and Margaret Radin provided critiques that were extraordinarily helpful. I have benefited as well from those who commented on drafts of articles and essays that stand in an ancestral relation to this book, and from extended conversations over the years with Sanford Levinson, Donald Regan, and numerous others. There is little doubt that many of the ideas in this book were spawned in all of the foregoing and countless other exchanges, and at this point it is difficult to determine which of my ideas are mine and which I owe largely to others. Yet if my idealism about the purpose of scholarly inquiry is justified, then perhaps in the final analysis it does not matter.

TABLE OF CONTENTS

PROSPECTUS

THE plan of this book is as follows. Chapter 1 is rather a *mélange*, offering some tentative definitions and distinctions, and locating this inquiry into the nature of prescriptive rules within the related philosophical and jurisprudential terrain. Although this chapter remains of necessity unsatisfyingly disjointed, the issues with which it deals may at least prevent some readers from being distracted into thinking about potentially related issues that are not within the scope of the project.

With some of the underbrush thus cleared, Chapter 2 introduces the central theme of the book, the importance of seeing rules as crude probabilistic generalizations that may thus when followed produce in particular instances decisions that are suboptimal or even plainly erroneous. First I take up *de*scriptive generalization, emphasizing its potential for focusing on the irrelevant and suppressing the relevant, and then show how *pre*scriptive rules also incorporate and thus hinge on descriptive generalizations still containing those potentially error-producing characteristics. Consequently, from the perspective of their background justifications, prescriptive rules are either actually or potentially (and here I introduce the idea of open texture into the analysis) under- and over-inclusive.

That prescriptive rules may be under- or over-inclusive, however, is only the beginning of the story. In Chapter 3 I distinguish between conversational and entrenchment models of generalization. Under the former, under- or over-inclusive generalizations are adaptable as the needs of the moment require, but under the latter those generalizations resist such continuous malleability. Rule-based decision-making can consequently be seen as a form of decision-making in which such entrenched generalizations provide reasons for decision *qua* generalizations, independent of the reasons supplied by their background justifications.

If the force of rules thus resides in the phenomenon of entrenchment, and indeed so I argue, then it becomes necessary to locate the sources of entrenchment. This is the theme of Chapter 4, examining the relationship among rules, rule-formulations, language, and meaning, and concluding that the meaning of a rule's actual or potential formulation is more central to understanding its power than is commonly supposed. I proceed to analyse the view about language that undergirds this conclusion, in the process explaining both the limited relevance of Wittgenstein's observations on rule-following and the mistakes of those whose conflation of semantics and pragmatics can explain neither the operation of language nor the operation of rules. This chapter generates a more precise definition of rule-based decision-making, focusing on the relationship between an instantiation and its background justification. Rule-based decision-making exists, I conclude, when the instantiation is entrenched, supplying a reason for decision even when it does not serve the goals established by its background justification.

Chapter 5 then pursues the distinction between rule-based and particularistic decision-making, focusing on the suboptimality of rules, and showing how the limited specificity and limited malleability of rules built into this account resists David Lyons's arguments of extensional equivalence between particularistic and rule-based decision procedures. I also compare my account of rules with several others, devoting a section to the analysis offered by Joseph Raz, another to the rule-sensitive particularism found in the act-consequentialist literature, and the final section challenges the traditional understanding of rules of thumb.

In Chapter 6 I examine just what it is for a rule to constitute a reason for decision. The inquiry starts by looking at the idea of an internal point of view, suggested in different but connected ways by Hart, Kelsen, and Wittgenstein. What emerges is a different way of thinking about the weight of a rule, its ability to resist the force of other reasons for decision indicating contrary results. In addition, focusing on internalization shows both the importance and the limitations of a sanction-based explanation of the process of internalization.

From these first six chapters emerges a clear but seemingly normatively unattractive picture of rule-based decision-making. In Chapter 7, however, I seek to show what might be said for such a suboptimizing decision procedure. Although I reject arguments couched in terms of fairness, and question the importance traditionally placed on reliance and efficiency, I offer a defence of rules that starts with a focus on distrust of certain classes of decision-makers with respect to certain kinds of decisions, showing how one of the chief virtues of rule-based decision-making stems from a desire to guard against decision-maker error in direct application of background justifications. But this account is only transitional to a fuller one that sees rules as devices for the allocation of power. Such an allocation among individuals and institutions may at times be based on concerns about accuracy and the avoidance of error, but may also be based on substantive determinations about who should be doing what in any multi-membered or multi-institutioned environment. These substantive determinations are only occasionally concerned with competence in the sense of ability, and are just as often the reflection of political, social, and moral determinations of who ought to make what kinds of decisions.

In Chapters 8 and 9 I develop the argument by exploring in greater depth the relationship between law and rule-based decision-making, a relationship that to this point in the book has been suggested but not analysed. Chapter 8 looks at the connection between rules and the common law, examines the rule-based presuppositions of the idea of precedent, considers the philosophical foundations of the Legal Realist challenge to rule-based constraint, and develops the idea of local priority among conflicting rules. This idea enables us to analyse the degree of ruleness in a decision-making system, and leads to the partially rule-based picture of legal decision-making I call 'presumptive positivism'. These same themes are pursued from a different direction in Chapter 9, where I focus on interpretive questions, and examine from a rule-oriented perspective the roles of purpose and intention in the interpretation of rules. I revisit the Hart–Fuller debate, and scrutinize more recent claims about interpretation made by Ronald Dworkin, arguing that legal decision-making and legal interpretation leave open more of a role for an admittedly formal use of constraining rules than is commonly recognized. I conclude in Chapter 10 by returning to the theme of rules and the allocation of power, observing in the process that the effect of rules is likely to be ignored or undervalued if we train our attention only on the cases a particular array of decision-makers actually decides. As devices for the allocation of power, rules are most effective not in determining the results in the cases on some decision-maker's agenda, but in determining at the outset what is on the agenda at all. This has significant implications for legal theory, for the contemporary focus on the decision of hard cases is seen to be far less important than the role that rules and our attitudes towards them play in determining just what *is* a hard case, and just which cases never wind up in court at all.

I

INTRODUCTION
THE VARIETIES OF RULES

1.1 *The Pressure of Rules*

'Speed Limit 55.' 'No Smoking.' 'Stand on the Right—Walk on the Left.' 'Honor Thy Father and Thy Mother.' 'Don't put your elbows on the table.' 'Littering Prohibited.' 'Never on Sunday.' 'Don't end a sentence with a preposition.' 'Never split an infinitive.' 'Play the national anthem before the beginning of the game.'

We think ourselves free, yet we are surrounded by rules. As we negotiate the maze of life, rules are recurring obstacles, foreclosing otherwise attractive paths and requiring otherwise unappealing ones. Our life plans are so often impeded by rules, large and small, that the very idea of a life plan independent of rules is scarcely imaginable.

But what are these things that so often stand in the way, and so often push us where we do not want to go? How is it that rules exert such great control over our lives, and how do they do it? And just what *are* rules, anyway?

This book is not about every phenomenon to which people attach the word 'rule', but instead about the narrower class of *regulative rules*. In order to clarify the scope of this enterprise, I must at the outset distinguish regulative from other sorts of rules, thereby focusing attention on the one type of rule I think sufficiently important to justify an entire book. Although it is awkward to begin an analytical work with a set of clarifying definitions, precise definition being more the product of analysis than precursor to it, it seems nevertheless important to commence with some tentative but still helpful distinctions.

Initially, regulative rules are members of the class of *prescriptive* rules, which are distinguished from *descriptive* rules, the latter usually being used to state an empirical regularity or generalization. 'As a rule the Alps are snow-covered in May.' 'German wine is sweeter than French.' Sometimes descriptive rules explain a mathematical or logical relationship, as in 'Descartes' Rule of Signs.'[1] But whether the identified regularity is mathematical or empirical, it is characteristic of descriptive rules that they are not used to change or channel behavior. Instead, like the *law* of gravity and the *principles* of physics, they are used to describe and explain the world rather than alter it.[2]

Unlike descriptive rules, prescriptive rules ordinarily have normative semantic content, and are used to guide, control, or change the behavior of agents with decision-making capacities. 'Thou shalt not kill.' 'Seat belts must be fastened at all times.' 'You are to be in bed by ten o'clock every evening unless I say otherwise.' Even when they take the form of declarative sentences—'Dogs will be leashed in this park'—prescriptive rules are not used to describe. 'No smoking until after the toast to the Queen' is not an empirical report of high table behavior. Prescriptive rules are employed not to reflect the world but to apply *pressure* to it.

Sometimes a prescriptive rule is used to apply pressure against a state of affairs existing prior to its imposition. Consider the typical 'Stop' sign, commonly placed where people would not have stopped absent the intervention of the rule (the sign). Rules addressed to children regarding bedtime or tidiness are similar; they are used in an attempt to change some pre-existing pattern of behavior by making a course of conduct an agent might otherwise have selected less eligible, or by making a course of conduct an agent might not otherwise have selected more eligible. Other rules, however, are employed not to change conduct, but to *prevent* such change. They are aimed at reinforcing patterns of behavior pre-existing the rule by preventing divergence from that pattern of behavior. Traditional honor codes in universities and in the military are of this sort, for they do not presuppose that prior to their existence people were dis-

---

[1] The example is from David Lewis, *Convention*, 101.

[2] I do not deny that description and explanation affect the world. Such effects, however, are different from the direct application of normative pressure.

Paul Ziff, after properly stressing the distinction between prescriptive rules and mere regularities, urges withholding the word 'rule' when there is no 'plan or policy'. Ziff, *Semantic Analysis*, 36–7. Although the now common distinction I offer does not differ fundamentally from Ziff's, our linguistic intuitions are plainly in conflict. Ziff would take 'As a rule the Alps are snow–covered in May' to be a linguistic mistake, inconsistent with ordinary usage of the word 'rule'. My linguistic intuitions to the contrary, intuitions that treat *this* sense of 'rule' as synonymous with 'regularity' and with *one* sense of 'law' or 'principle', appear to match those of *inter alia*, H. L. A. Hart, *The Concept of Law*, 9–11, 54–5, and Peter Winch, *The Idea of a Social Science*, 57–65, 84–94.

honorable as a matter of course. Instead, these rules attempt to maintain a norm, guarding the *status quo* against threats of individual deviation or widespread shift. But in both cases, whether to modify pre-existing behavior or forestall such modification, prescriptive rules are used to exert pressure against the inclinations of some agents to act inconsistently with the mandates of the rule.[3]

1.2 *Mandatory Rules*

The class of prescriptive rules must itself be subdivided. One sort is an *instruction*, used to provide directions for success in some enterprise or task. 'Check the seasoning before putting a casserole in the oven.' 'Start each paragraph with a topic sentence.' 'Do not turn the ignition key until you have pumped the accelerator pedal three times.' This type of rule, often called a 'formula' or 'recipe', is characterized by being *optional* in two ways. First, instructions apply only if an agent wishes to succeed in the pertinent task, and only if it is one that can plausibly be avoided. Unlike Kant's categorical imperative and rules such as 'No Parking from 9 a.m. to 6 p.m.' and 'Thou shalt not take the name of the Lord thy God in vain', instructions are hypothetical, containing an explicit or implicit 'if' clause limiting the application of the rule to those seeking success in some enterprise. '*If* you wish a joint to hold, apply glue lightly to both surfaces of wood.' '*If* you want to avoid a slice, hit the golf ball with a closed club face.' Of course the distinction between optional and non-optional activities, between the categorical and the hypothetical, should not be pressed too hard. 'No parking' could be interpreted as, '*If* you wish not to pay a twenty dollar fine, then do not park here.' Similarly, each of the Ten Commandments could, according to some religious traditions, be preceded by '*If* you wish to avoid eternal damnation, . . .'. Still, rules whose 'if' clause appears to restrict the applicability of the rule to some comparatively limited class of addressees, and rules whose

---

[3] Nothing I say in this preliminary chapter should be taken as suggesting that rules themselves are necessarily intrinsically prescriptive, or necessarily or intrinsically provide reasons for action. As I shall make clear in subsequent chapters, agents who *do* engage in rule-based decision-making take the existence of *some* rules as providing reasons for action independent of the reasons for action provided by the existence of the justifications behind those rules. It is too early to delve into why agents employ rule-based decision-making, and this footnote is designed only to deflect or at least postpone objections relating to this preliminary description. Thus, I defer considering the relation between a prescription, as speech act, and a prescriptive rule (which need not be a product of a prescriptive speech act) as understood by an agent making a decision based on that rule.

addressees seem likely to think there is a genuine choice whether to engage in the designated task, are usefully thought of as optional in a way that categorical prescriptions are not.

Instructions, however, are also optional in a second way, one that links with the central theme of this book. When we are addressees of instructions, we consider them optional in that we take their force to be congruent with our assessment of the likelihood they will produce the desired result. If we believe that in *this* case the instruction will *not* lead to that result, the rule's force evaporates and we feel free to ignore it. If we believe that a paragraph will better fit the flow of an argument if it discards the usual initial topic sentence, or that this particular type of car will start more quickly with one rather than three pumps of the accelerator, our allegiance to the rule comes to an end, and we do not take the existence of a rule to the contrary as an impediment to doing what is best in *this* instance. And that is because these are *rules of thumb*, providing useful guides for the routine case, but not taken by even those addressees who accept them to exert any normative pressure *qua* rule. I will have much more to say throughout this book about rules of thumb,[4] but for now it is important only to distinguish a rule of thumb from another sort of rule, one employed (or taken) to apply normative pressure because of its *status* as a rule, and not merely because of its indicative usefulness on this occasion.

A rule taken by an agent (or an enforcer) as exerting normative pressure *qua* rule is therefore not for the agent wholly optional. The fact of the rule's existence becomes a reason for action, and the rule's normative force is not exhausted by its value in a particular instance. When such an attitude towards a rule is in place, to disregard the mandates of the rule is to *violate* the rule even when it appears that it is better (and perhaps even when it *is* better) in this instance to disregard the rule than to follow it. The difference between 'Speed Limit 55' and 'It is unsafe to drive more than 55 miles per hour' is that only the former prohibits driving at greater than 55 miles per hour even when it would be safe to do so. If driving in excess of 55 miles per hour were under the circumstances safe, the former rule would still be violated by those who exceed that speed because, and only because, the fact of the rule being a rule provides a reason for driving no faster than 55 miles per hour.[5]

---

[4] See Chs. 3, 4, and 5, and particularly Chap. 5.7, which casts doubt on and complicates the claims in this paragraph.

[5] On rules as providing reasons for action, see Joseph Raz, *Practical Reason and Norms, passim*, and below, Sect. 4 and Chap. 6.

Thus, we must distinguish *rules of thumb*, which are useful guides but do not, even when accepted, provide reasons for action in themselves, from *mandatory rules*. Mandatory rules, when accepted, furnish reasons for action simply by virtue of their existence *qua* rules, and thus generate normative pressure even in those cases in which the justifications (rationales) underlying the rules indicate the contrary result. This is not to say that it is necessarily *wrong*, all things considered, to violate even a mandatory rule. What we have a reason to do is different from what, all things considered, we *should* do. Even when a mandatory rule supplies a reason for conforming to the indications of the rule, other features of the situation may provide reasons for acting in some other way. To exceed the speed limit in order to rush a critically injured person to the hospital is still to *break* the speed limit, however much other reasons for action may justify breaking it.[6]

This conception of the force of mandatory rules is often called 'prima facie', but that term is misleading.[7] First, it suggests that the reason supplied by a rule evaporates when overridden by a stronger reason. But there is no basis for supposing this, any more than there is for supposing that my sweater disappears when it is penetrated by an icy wind. It is simply that the protection of the sweater, like the reason supplied by the rule, is not always sufficient. Yet the rule's insufficiency in some cases is not inconsistent with its ongoing sufficiency for many, nor with its ability to raise the threshold of strength that *any* contrary reason must meet in order to prevail. Insofar as the term 'prima facie' obscures this ongoing force, it is more distracting than useful. Moreover, the term 'prima facie' suggests a reason of substantial weight. Some reasons may be so weighty, but they need not be *substantially* weighty in order to qualify as reasons. Weak reasons are still reasons, capable at least occasionally of generating outcomes different from those that would have been generated absent those reasons. It is better, therefore, to say a rule supplies a reason for action, thus being a mandatory rule

---

[6] The relationship I depict here parallels one prominent in the literature of rights. Some theorists properly identify a distinction between infringements of rights, which may at times be justifiable, and violations of rights, which are unjustifiable infringements, all things considered. See Alan Gewirth, 'Are There Any Absolute Rights?', 2; Robert Nozick, 'Moral Complications and Moral Structures', 33–41; Judith Thomson, 'Some Ruminations on Rights', 47–8.

[7] My thinking about the infelicity of 'prima facie' in this context has been influenced by John Searle, '*Prima Facie* Obligations', *passim*. The use of 'prima facie' in this way, now an unfortunate commonplace, is attributable to W. D. Ross, *The Right and the Good*, 19–47.

rather than a rule of thumb, when it tells us what to do, *ceteris paribus*, recognizing in so saying that a rule that is *ceteris paribus* dispositive can still have little power against contrary reasons. And best of all is to avoid the distraction of either term, settling instead for the sufficiently comprehensible proposition that identifying the ability of a factor to supply a reason for action is different from asking what, all things considered, ought to be done.

Pursuit of these themes is part of what this book is about, and I do not want to get ahead of myself at this preliminary stage. For now it is sufficient that within the class of prescriptive rules, mandatory rules differ from rules of thumb by virtue of the ability of mandatory rules, when accepted by an agent or enforcer, to supply normative pressure, or reasons for action, simply from their existence *qua* rules.[8]

1.3 *Constitutive and Regulative*

Philosophers commonly distinguish regulative from *constitutive* rules. According to the distinction, suggested by H. L. A. Hart,[9] Max Black,[10] and John Rawls,[11] and most prominently associated with John Searle,[12] regulative rules govern antecedently existing behavior—behavior defined without reference to the rule and therefore logically prior to the rule. Speed limits are a good example, for the capacity to drive an automobile at 65 miles per hour is independent of any rule governing that activity.

By contrast, constitutive rules create the very possibility of engaging in conduct of a certain kind. They define and thereby constitute activities that could not otherwise even exist. Rules of games are the archetypes, for the very possibility of winning a *trick* or *castling* or hitting a *home run* is created by rules. The rule providing, *inter alia*, that in order to castle a chess player must not previously have castled does not just control a process but constitutes it. Without the rules of chess you cannot castle at all.

---

[8] I will use the terms 'mandatory rule' and 'regulative rule' more or less interchangeably. Where I focus on the capacity of a rule to supply a reason for action solely from its status as a rule, I favor the former term; where other aspects of prescriptive rules are the object of the discussion, the latter is less confusing.

[9] Hart, 'Definition and Theory in Jurisprudence', 33–5.

[10] Max Black, 'The Analysis of Rules', 123–25.

[11] John Rawls, 'Two Concepts of Rules', and also B. J. Diggs, 'Rules and Utilitarianism', 40.

[12] Searle, *Speech Acts*, 33–42. An illuminating use of the distinction is Lewis, 'Scorekeeping in a Language Game', 236–44.

Although the distinction between regulative and constitutive rules is illuminating, it is also misleading, for many constitutive rules have their regulative side. Although sets of constitutive rules establish institutions such as games, universities, corporations, and language, these constitutive rules lose their constitutive character within those institutions, serving instead to regulate antecedently defined behavior. The rule has a double aspect—first defining the behavior and *then* regulating it. Take the rule prohibiting *clipping* in American football. Although it is possible to hit a person from behind without reference to the rules of football, clipping is different, being constituted by certain of those rules. Yet the same rules also *prohibit* clipping, and the prohibitory side of the rules about clipping operates in the same way within the institution of football as a rule prohibiting driving in excess of 55 miles per hour operates outside that institution.

Thus, regulative rules regulate behavior within rule-defined sets of practices just as they regulate behavior within environments whose definition is less rule-dependent. Rules against clipping in football resemble rules against driving at speeds greater than a specified rate, and rules limiting the occasions of castling in chess resemble rules limiting the occasions of purchasing alcoholic beverages. This is not to challenge the usefulness for some purposes of the distinction between the constitutive and the regulative.[13] But it is a mistake to assume that regulative rules are not part of the world of rule-created practices and institutions.

1.4 *The Logic of Norms*

Regulative rules apply pressure to human behavior, and initially it appears that such pressure can be applied in two directions—behavior can either be *prohibited* or *required*. But the logic of norms is not

[13] Joseph Raz does challenge the distinction (*Practical Reason and Norms*, 108–13), in part for reasons similar to those here, for Raz sees in every constitutive rule a regulative rule as well, and demonstrates that all regulative rules create otherwise impossible forms of behavior, viz. violating that rule. He accepts the distinction between normative and natural act-descriptions, but sees no warrant for supposing that this distinguishes types of *rules*. Yet if Searle's constitutive rules regulate as well, and if regulative rules create actions, then what distinguishes a *home run* from *eating*? The distinction, recognized by Raz in terms of types of act-descriptions and by Searle in terms of different types of rules, remains significant, for there are differences between terms whose meaning comes from a discrete normative system and those whose meaning does not. Thus, part of the issue is terminological, in that Searle is searching for a way to mark a distinction that is important whenever we try to define 'corporation' or 'tort' or 'unconstitutional'. But with Raz I believe that more is obscured than illuminated by thinking of this as a distinction between kinds of rules.

bivalent, for the negation of prohibition is not only compulsion but also *permission*. Within the universe of deontic statements, 'you may' is as significant as 'you must' or 'you must not', although it is not clear that 'you may' has normative force.[14]

Prohibition, compulsion (or obligation), and permission, however, are not three discrete points exhausting the totality of deontic space. Instead, the deontic universe is a continuum, on which prohibition and compulsion are the positive and negative poles of a continuous range containing the property of *strength*.[15] This continuum of strength, however, comes not from the logic of norms, but, as I shall explore in Chapter 6, from the *sanctions* (whether positive or negative) that attach to following or violating rules, or from *attitudes* about rules held by addressees of those rules. The extent to which the latter is a function of the former is important, and I also address that question in Chapter 6. Still, it is useful at the outset to see that the strength of a rule resides not so much in a rule's logical status or linguistic meaning as in the conditions surrounding its applicability, acceptance, and enforcement.

Consider a rule, issued by parents to their child, mandating that 'You must clean up your room before you leave for school each morning.' The rule appears to make certain conduct obligatory, but the way in which the conduct is obligatory is called into question once we compare this simple rule to more complex variations: 'If you do not clean up your room each morning before you leave for school, you will make us angry.'; 'If you do not clean up your room each morning before you leave for school, you will have no dessert at dinner.'; 'If you do not clean up your room each morning before you leave for school, you will be beaten without mercy.' At least for the child otherwise disinclined to treat the rule as a reason for action, the last of these rules makes the mandated behavior *more*

---

[14] I ignore a realm of complications. For example, although both obligation and permission entail the absence of prohibition, it is not apparent that absence of prohibition is necessarily *either* a permission *or* an obligation. See G. H. von Wright, 'On the Logic of Norms and Actions', 103–4. Instead, permission may involve something deontically stronger than the mere absence of prohibition. If this is so, there is likely a normative component in a permission and consequently still another deontic category representing *indifference*, almost like a deontic void.

[15] Viewing the deontic modalities of prohibition and compulsion as continuous is consistent with the views of those who see mandatory norms, encompassing both prohibition and obligation, as fundamentally different from permissions, and who see mandatory norms as the central deontic phenomenon. See Risto Hilpinen, 'Normative Conflicts and Legal Reasoning', 194–5; id. 'Conflict and Change in Norm Systems', 37.

obligatory than do the other two. In the last, from the perspective of the same addressees, the option of non-compliance is less available than in the other two cases.

It may appear that I am simply confusing a rule with the sanctions attaching to its violation. But consider the British Rail rule prohibiting, on pain of a £5 fine, use of the emergency stop cord in the absence of a genuine emergency. Observing the effect of that rule upon his own behavior, P. G. Wodehouse's Bertie Wooster opined that £5 was quite a reasonable price to pay for the thrill of bringing an entire train to an instant halt. Although Bertie presumably would have preferred to pay nothing at all (and that is questionable, if part of the thrill comes from the very illegality of the act), he can hardly be deemed to have viewed this rule, prohibitory in form, as prohibitory in fact.

Similar considerations surround permission and compulsion. Permissions may range from failure to prohibit to grudging acknowledgement to strong encouragement, and indeed permission in form may turn into compulsion in fact with a sufficient inducement. A rule giving the addressee a choice whether to comply or not but rewarding compliance with payment of one million dollars is a rule in which the formal option is in practice unavailable.[16] And just as sanctions may convert formal permissions into compulsions, so too may they convert formal obligations into options, obscuring the distinction between a price and a penalty. The obligation not to park in front of a fire hydrant (unless you pay twenty dollars) bears an interesting affinity to the obligation not to take a shirt out of the store (unless you pay twenty dollars). There are differences, to be sure, and I do not mean to suggest identity between a price for doing what is allowed and a penalty for doing what is disallowed. Still, it is important to stress that rules exist within complex systems of

---

[16] I intentionally skirt the debate about the extent to which inducements can be considered coercive. Those holding offers, rewards, benefits, and other inducements to be potentially coercive include Theodore Benditt, 'Threats and Offers', 382, and Virginia Held, 'Coercion and Coercive Offers', 54. To the contrary, believing coercion to be limited to threats, penalties, and burdens, are Michael Bayles, 'Coercive Offers and Public Benefits', 139, and John Garvey, 'Freedom and Equality in the Religion Clauses', 198–207. For useful clarification of the debate, see Daniel Lyons, 'Welcome Threats and Coercive Offers', *passim*, and Peter Westen, ' "Freedom" and "Coercion"—Virtue Words and Vice Words', 569–89. In large part this debate is about the consequences, whether moral or legal, of an attribution of coerciveness, and, consequently, of a lack of attribution of freedom or choice. My analysis precedes the attributive issues, however. I wish only to note the way in which the capacity of rules to influence human behavior is a function of more than is contained in the language of the rule.

communication and control that cannot be understood without reference to conditions external to the rules themselves.

These complications raise fundamental questions about the nature of a rule and the source of its normative force. Are rules linguistic entities or behavioral phenomena? Is the force of a rule located in its meaning or in its sanctions or in the attitude of its addressees? How does the nature of a rule relate to the rule-independent preferences of its addressees? Much that is to follow attempts to confront these questions, for they are centrally important in understanding the role occupied by rules in the much larger array of factors that influence and indeed constitute human decision-making. Initially, however, we get the enterprise off the ground by being temporarily satisfied with noting that mandatory rules make certain conduct *more or less eligible* than that conduct would have been absent the existence of the rule. This is sufficiently broad to accommodate all cases of prohibition and obligation, and maybe even some of permission, while also accommodating the possibility, which I have yet to argue, that ruleness is a variable dimension rather than a simple condition that either obtains or does not.

1.5 *Rules and Law*

It is worth underscoring that nothing in the conception of a regulative rule suggests either a natural affinity to, or exclusive location within, the political state's mechanisms of social control and dispute resolution. Thus the relationship between rules and a 'legal system' is contingent, for decision according to rules is but one among several sorts of decision-making. As a result, although empowering rules create the institutions of dispute resolution and empower certain officials to resolve certain sorts of disputes, disputes could still be resolved largely without reference to mandatory rules imposing substantive constraint on the content of the decisions. Having been empowered to resolve a dispute, the adjudicator would be authorized, as in Weber's description of the *qadi*, to come to a conclusion as open-endedly as appropriate in the circumstances.[17] Similarly, if rule-based decision-making is only one option among several, it need not be central to social control and co-

---

[17] I do not suggest that such an adjudicator needs no substantive theory of decision. The *qadi* does more than react to theoretically uninformed intuitions about particular outcomes. Still, as I argue in Chs. 2, 3, and 4, there is a fundamental distinction between a decision procedure employing direct application of a substantive theory of decision and one involving the application of rules derived from that same substantive theory.

ordination. Rather than rely largely on rules, governments could control and co-ordinate behavior through the discretionary acts of subordinate governmental officials whose particularized judgement was uncontrolled by rules.[18]

In creating these stylized alternatives to rule-based dispute resolution and social control, I do not intend to endorse them. Nor even do I want to suggest that such totally rule-sterile systems are socially possible. Yet although these ruleless alternatives are caricatures, the caricatures suggest less extreme and more pervasive manifestations of the fact that much of the mechanism that we call the 'legal system' need not operate according to the conception of rules I elaborate in this book. If we assume at the outset that law just *is* a system of rules, especially of mandatory rules, we may assume that legal decision-making is necessarily rule-based. Such an approach, however, will distort the analysis of rules, for rules would then need to be *defined* in conformity with the objectives of a legal system. Instead, however, some of those objectives may be ill-served by rule-bound decision-making. This is hardly implausible, and explains why modern legal systems often avoid the use of mandatory rules. Consider child custody determinations, in which an open-ended 'best interests of the child' standard, rather than any more constraining set of rules, provides guidance for the decision-maker; the system of equity, no less part of the legal system for embodying flexibility and particularity as its method; the traditional sentencing process, in which the range of factors permissibly relevant to the decision is virtually unlimited; and the increasing use of substantially rule-free arbitration, mediation, and conciliation procedures as adjuncts to or substitutes for formal adjudication. These are but a few among many examples of forms of legal decision-making that only with difficulty can be characterized as rule-based. Consequently, I want to start with the assumption that rule-governed decision-making is a subset of legal decision-making rather than being congruent with it.[19]

[18] Again, empowering rules would be necessary to establish the authority of those subordinate officials, but the necessity of such rules is consistent with distinguishing systems in which the rules that authorize subordinate officials to act prescribe nothing further about the substance of those actions from systems in which rules not only create authority, but attempt to guide the substance of the exercise of that authority. This distinction, to which I return in Chap. 8.1, tracks both the commonplace legal distinction between jurisdiction and substance and Stanley Paulson's interpretation of Kelsen as distinguishing formal from material authorization. See Paulson, 'Material and Formal Authorisation in Kelsen's PureTheory', *passim*.

[19] I focus here on rules as directives to officials, but, as shall become clear in

Rules not only under-explain the legal system, but they also explain much that takes place outside of the legal system. Indeed, decision-making based on regulative rules permeates much of our social existence. For one thing, many formal institutions, such as churches, clubs, and associations, are permeated with such rules. And even more pervasively, many less formal social practices, including the practices of morality, etiquette, and child-rearing (and family governance in general) appear to operate at least partially through the use of regulative rules. On closer inspection it may turn out that some of what look like rules, and are even called rules, are not rules at all. But my point is only that regulative rules intrude themselves into many corners of our lives, and it is thus simply mistaken to assume they are the peculiar province of that portion of our existence we describe as 'the law'.

Thus, to analyse the idea of a regulative rule is to analyse a form of decision-making and control that exists at numerous places within social life. Once we have isolated this form of decision-making and control, it is *then* appropriate to consider whether, and to what extent, it can or should be employed in those institutions of the political state we commonly call 'the legal system'. But this book proceeds in the order it does precisely because law is about more than rules, and because much about rules is not about law.

1.6 *Some Problems of Terminology*

Various philosophers who have written about rules have conspicuously avoided using the word 'rule'. R. M. Hare, for example, refers to 'principles', presumably to make clear that the precepts of morality need not be as detailed as those contained in the Internal Revenue Code.[20] Insofar as some understand the word 'rule' to imply a degree of precision or specificity, substituting 'principle' serves to dispel the expected misapprehension. Similarly, insofar as 'rule' suggests either a canonical or easily canonizable formulation,[21] the use of 'principle' may again prevent misunderstanding. The advantages of 'principle' in eliminating connotations of necessary

subsequent chapters, it is important to recognize that rules, including rules of law, are directives to 'subjects' as well as to the officials who are to enforce (and at times interpret) the rules.

[20] R. M. Hare, *Moral Thinking*, 30–43; id. 'Principles', 1–3. The same effort to avoid the connotations of necessary specificity suggested by the word 'rule' is even more explicit in David Gauthier, *Practical Reasoning*, 161.

[21] See Ziff, *Semantic Analysis*, 35, presuming that prescriptions, to be rules, must be 'laid down'.

canonicity or specificity, however, may come at the price of engendering exactly the opposite confusion. Just as 'rule' suggests to some the presence of specificity and canonicity, so too does 'principle' suggest to many (of the same) people the necessary *absence* of these features. For many, a principle is a principle and not something else just because it is general rather than specific, and just because it is not canonically formulated. I am no more satisfied with this artificial constriction at the outset to the general and non-canonical, however, than with an artificial constriction to the specific and canonical. Consequently, replacing 'rule' with 'principle' adds no clarity, but only substitutes one set of debatable assumptions for another.

Issues of specificity and canonicity are not the only ones surrounding the choice between the words 'rule' and 'principle'. Some normative theorists, most prominently Ronald Dworkin, distinguish rules, which Dworkin takes to be dispositive if applicable, from principles, which can be applicable yet not controlling.[22] Yet as Joseph Raz has noted, 'we do not normally use the rule/principle distinction to mark the difference between *prima facie* and conclusive reasons or between the standards which establish them'.[23] Moreover, the distinction Dworkin *does* desire to mark, between the conclusive (or categorical) and the prima facie, or between the absolute and the overridable, or between the closed and the defeasible, cuts across the distinctions between the specific and the general and between the canonical and the non-canonical. General prescriptions *can* be conclusive, and specific ones overridable. The Golden Rule is often thought general and categorical, but the equally general prohibitions of the Equal Protection Clause of the Fourteenth Amendment to the United States Constitution (mandating that no state shall 'deny to any person within its jurisdiction the equal protection of the laws') are subject to override in cases of 'compelling interest'. Philosophers debate whether a mandate to 'tell the truth' is conclusive or overridable, but none would deny that either is conceptually possible. Conversely, the specific prohibitions of the Jewish dietary laws are defeasible in cases of danger to life or health, but equivalently specific provisions of most tax laws more closely fit Dworkin's vision of rules as

---

[22] Ronald Dworkin, *Taking Rights Seriously*, 22–8, 72–80. Important critiques of Dworkin's distinction include Raz, 'Legal Principles and the Limits of Law', *passim*, and Colin Tapper, 'A Note on Principles', *passim*.

[23] Raz, 'Legal Principles and the Limits of Law' (revised), 82.

controlling if applicable.[24] That overridability is more common in general prescriptions is an empirical tendency and not a logical truth about rules. It thus seems best to hew to the distinction between conclusive and overridable rules, without suggesting that anything about either generality or canonicity necessarily relates to that distinction.

In order to avoid such confusions, I stipulate at the outset that I take neither specificity, conclusiveness, nor authoritative formulation as necessary conditions for the existence of a mandatory rule. Thus, a non-canonized, general, and (to some) overridable prescription such as 'Do Unto Others As You Would Have Them Do Unto You' is still, by this preliminary terminology, a 'rule'. As the analysis deepens, some of these definitional inclusions will turn out to be more problematic. But I do not want to beg important questions by artificially narrowing in advance the definition of a mandatory rule.

Although some writers substitute terminology such as 'principle' in order to avoid the connotation that rules must be specific, canonized, or conclusive, others seek a term that will distinguish prescriptive from descriptive rules. Interestingly, however, few candidates serve that sorting function effectively. Certainly 'principle' does not, for once again the same word is used to refer both to empirical regularities, like Newton's First Principle and the principles of economics, and to mandates with normative force, such as the principles of morality to which Hare and others frequently advert.

Much the same linguistic tolerance for both the descriptive and the prescriptive resides in words like 'law', 'precept', 'maxim', and 'norm'. Each of these is properly used to refer both to an empirical regularity and a normative requirement. Consider the difference between the law of gravity and the laws of Texas, or the way in which we use the word 'norm' to refer both to the *usual* form of behavior and to the prescriptions set forth by legal authority.[25] That

---

[24] This is not to say that a legal decision-maker might not import from some other area of law an exception in cases in which, say, a threat to life or health prevented compliance with the tax laws. This only shows, however, the way in which it is mistaken to incorporate into the *definition* of a rule the way in which various rules relate to each other within a complex *system* of rules. See below, Chap. 8.4.

[25] The word 'norm', in its prescriptive sense, has a special problem, in that it is sometimes (albeit usually technically) taken to often refer both to general prescriptions and to specific commands such as 'Jackie, take out the garbage now!' In part because the prescriptive use of 'norm' collapses the particular and the general, and in part despite that feature of the word, it is the term of choice in much of contemporary normative theory. See, e.g. Raz, *Practical Reason and Norms*, 49–50; George

each of these words, and others (consider the difference between 'You *ought* to obey your parents' and 'He *ought* to be arriving in town about now'; or between 'She is *supposed* to advise the patient of all the risks before performing surgery' and 'It is *supposed* to be windy in March'), has both a descriptive and a prescriptive side might be just a remarkable coincidence. Alternatively, the use of the same words to refer to descriptive and prescriptive modes might be a linguistic holdover from an ontology in which the active hand of God was thought equally responsible for guiding our behavior and establishing the regularities of existence. But there is a more intriguing alternative explanation. The seeming ambiguity might suggest that the philosopher's commonplace distinction between descriptive and prescriptive rules is, if no less a distinction, at least misleading insofar as it suggests that thought about prescriptive rules cannot be aided by consideration of descriptive rules. In fact, focusing on the shared features of descriptive and prescriptive rules will be the starting point for the central arguments of this book.

1.7 *The Limits of Ordinary Language*

It should now be plain that this enterprise is not an analysis of the use of the word 'rule'. There are reasons, some of which I have just explained, for preferring that word to 'norm', 'principle', 'law', 'prescription', 'precept', 'maxim', and a host of other candidates, but these reasons do not reflect an attempt to capture distinctions extant in ordinary language. Attention to the distinctions embedded in ordinary language is often analytically illuminating, but the techniques of ordinary language analysis, ones I occasionaly employ in this book, are hardly exclusive when the goal of the enterprise is other than analysing a particular word.

Thus my aim initially is to isolate a form of decision-making characterized by its reliance on entrenched but potentially under- and over-inclusive generalizations. In isolating this form of decision-making, I will be drawing a distinction crisper than that recognized by ordinary language, although the ordinary usage of 'rule' does have somewhat more affinity with what I call rule-based decision-making than it does with other forms of decision-making. But

---

Christie, *Law, Norms, and Authority*, 2–3. But because much of my argument focuses and indeed turns on the distinction between the particular and the general, use of a term that suppresses that distinction is directly at odds with the perspective offered in this book.

although the distinction I draw can be marked by selective deploy-
ment of the word 'rule', and although I will mark the distinction this
way, I do not want much to turn on my linguistic intuitions. I do not
deny that forms of decision-making that I will show to be distinct
from decision-making by mandatory rule are also commonly thought
to be rule-based, and are often described in those terms. But the
multiple uses of the word 'rule' are part of the problem, and thus my
arguably stipulative use is intentionally narrower than ordinary
talk. Perhaps I would be better off avoiding the tension between
how I will come to use the word 'rule' here and the looser array of
meanings now at large in ordinary language by inventing a new
term. But describing as, say, 'qule-based' the form of decision-
making that I will attempt to isolate would only compound what is
already a terminological morass. Instead, I will stick to the term
'rule' as clarified here, and as it is to be further clarified throughout
the ensuing chapters of this book.

2

RULES AS GENERALIZATIONS

2.1 The General and the Particular

The distinction between prescriptive and descriptive rules is a philosophical commonplace.[1] Indeed, distinguishing rules prescribing conduct from ones reporting an empirical regularity is thought so important that the two uses of the world 'rule' are often treated virtually as homonyms, bearing little in common but a shared spelling. Newton Garver, for example, takes the use of 'rule' to identify empirical regularities as no more germane to an analysis of rules than the use of that word to refer to a 'straight line or the reign of a monarch'.[2] Max Black also treats descriptive and prescriptive rules as foundationally unalike, viewing the former as rules only in a 'degenerate' sense.[3]

I do not want to challenge the distinction. There *are* differences between descriptive and prescriptive rules, just as there are differences between the laws of physics and those of Nebraska, and between the principles of economics and of morality. Nevertheless, the distinction obscures a revealing similarity between descriptive and prescriptive rules.

In employing descriptive rules, we report or explain a regularity or uniformity. The use of a descriptive rule thus presupposes a multiplicity of instances, making descriptive rules differ from singular observations in being general rather than particular. It is true that yesterday I walked to my office, but it is true in a different way that *as a rule* I walk to my office. Observing that 'as a rule the Alps are snow-covered in May' is not the same as observing a snow-covered Alp. To assert the existence of a descriptive rule is necessarily to generalize. There are no rules for particulars.

---

[1] See, e.g. R. M. Hare, *The Language of Morals*, 1–31; W. D. Ross, *The Right and the Good*, 1–3.
[2] Newton Garver, 'Rules', 231.
[3] Max Black, 'The Analysis of Rules', 114.

Interestingly, the logic of the prescriptive use of 'rule' is similar, with prescriptive rules also being necessarily general. We say there is a rule prohibiting people from walking on the lawn if a sign prohibits many people over time from walking on the lawn, but we would not describe as a 'rule' a particular instruction (rather than a reminder of a pre-existing rule) from a parent to a child not to walk on this lawn at this time. The order of a police officer to 'Get back!' is different from a rule requiring everyone to keep clear of a specified area, and the child's game of 'Simon Says' is not about rules (except the rules of the game itself), but precisely about the non-regularity of particularized commands.

Rules, descriptive *and* prescriptive, thus speak to *types* and not to particulars. Unless we mean to describe for multiple instances or prescribe for multiple actions it is simply mistaken to use the word 'rule'. Ordinary language thereby highlights a difference between the particular and the general that is as significant for prescriptions as for reports of empirical regularity. In order to explore this further, however, we must start with the descriptive, thereafter applying the fruits of that attention to the analysis of prescriptive generalization.

2.2 *Descriptive Generalization*

To generalize is to engage in a process that is part of life itself. Our confrontations are commonly with particulars—this person, that building, these rocks, those words—but we hold on to the world by organizing those particulars within larger groupings. The particulars we perceive are as a result not only particulars, but are particular x's, being instances or tokens of more encompassing categories.[4]

Some of the categories with which (or into which) we group our

---

[4] For my purposes, I take the words 'class' and 'category' to be synonymous, thus departing from the usage of the metaphysician, who reserves the word 'category' for those classes that are in some sense ultimate. Similarly, my distinction between the particular and the general is intended to track the distinction between token and type and between individual and species, all expressing much the same relationship.

I do not by referring to our perception of particulars deny that many of these perceptions are mediated through concepts. Moreover, I do not claim that the process of 'organizing' particular perceptions into categories is necessarily active or conscious, or even that the particular is logically or temporally prior to the general. I rely only on that which is relatively uncontroversial about the distinction between the particular and the general.

particular perceptions are natural kinds, such as leopards and silver. Others are artefacts, such as cars and books and telephones. And sometimes our categories are more institutional than physical, as with contracts and political parties, drawing lines around and through the physical particulars to reflect the culturally and temporally contingent social, moral, cultural, and political choices of a community. Categories consequently vary in malleability, but for now my concern is less with the source or rigidity of categories than with their relationship to each other. More specifically, I want to focus on the *simultaneity* of categories, the way in which a particular is simultaneously a member of numerous intersecting categories.

The categories we employ are neither mutually exclusive nor rigidly distinct, but instead overlap and are nested within each other, such that a particular object or event is commonly a member of many of them. Because of this, particular objects, actions, events, or perceptions cannot mechanically be placed into a unique category, for no one of the simultaneously applicable categories of which any particular is a member has a logical priority over another. Instead as we think and talk we make the choice to depart from the particular, and make a further choice when we select the category within which to locate that particular. I will refer to choosing to go from the particular to the general as *generalizing*, and the product of that process as a *generalization*. When we generalize we see particulars not in isolation but as examples of a type or members of a class.

Thus, the collection of chemicals sitting before me is not only a dog, but also a member of numerous other natural and non-natural classes. *This* dog, Angus, is simultaneously a Scottish Terrier, black, an animal, a mammal, a pet, a carrier of fleas, a possession of my friend Herb, and something located 300 miles from Chicago. But life is short and mental space is finite, so although it is perhaps theoretically possible to refer to a particular by identifying all of its properties (all of the categories of which it is a member), in practice we drastically truncate this list of categories as we describe any particular. Accordingly, communication involves incessant choice from among numerous classificatory candidates, all of which are empirically and logically correct generalizations, but only some of which fit the purposes of the moment. To refer to Angus as 'a dog' rather than 'Herb's' or 'a carrier of fleas' or 'something 300 miles from Chicago' involves a choice determined not by any of Angus's numerous properties, but by the discursive context in which Angus is being described.[5]

Each of the properties of a particular *extend* it in different and potentially conflicting directions. The class of particulars 300 miles from Chicago and the class of Herb's possessions may have few common members other than Angus. Generalizing in one direction calls forth all of the other members of the class constituting *that* generalization, but generalizing in another direction suggests a different collection of particulars. Saying that Angus is Herb's is different from saying that Angus is a Scottish Terrier because the same Angus is in quite different company depending on the property chosen for attention.

In addition to choosing directions of generalization, speakers select more or less exclusive generalizations within the same direction. Angus's membership in the class of dogs and in the class of Herb's possessions involve generalizations in different directions, in that there is no relationship (other than the happenstance of Angus) between the two categories. Other generalizations, however, nest within each other in the same direction. Consider the difference between Angus as 3-year-old male Scottish Terrier and Angus as dog. The latter generalization includes all members of the former, and is thus a larger generalization in the same direction, admitting additional members (e.g. bulldogs and female Scottish Terriers) but excluding none from the smaller class. The range of choices with respect to the *degree of generalization* is of course larger, for Angus could also have been described as a 3-year-old male Scottish Terrier, as a male Scottish Terrier, as a Scottish Terrier, as a dog, as a mammal, or as an animal. As we proceed from one nested class to the next, we generalize in increasingly larger categories, each of which includes all members of its constituent classes. Generalizations are thus relative, for the particular in one domain can be general in another.

Choosing a direction and a degree of generalization are both subsequent to the decision to generalize in the first place. It is always in theory (at least if location in space and time are included) and usually in practice possible to refer to some particular with

---

[5] The point in the text can be seen as a variant on the principle that explanation is underdetermined by the particulars to be explained. See Pierre Duhem, *The Aim and Structure of Physical Theory*; Willard v. O. Quine, *Word and Object*, 26–30, 78–9. Just as multiple particular observations do not uniquely determine their own explanation, so too do the multiple properties of any particular not uniquely determine its description.

sufficient richness of detail that the particular becomes unique. This rich description of a particular would, to be sure, involve the use of general terms. Still, most of the particulars that we comprehend exist at the unique intersection of an array of non-unique properties, each of which is a general term, but all of which together describe the complete profile of this and only this particular.[6] Angus is a particular, a collection of chemicals at a time and place certain, and Angus, even putting spatio-temporal location aside, is extraordinarily unlikely to be identical in every respect to any other collection of chemicals. Were we to describe every property of Angus, at some point in the process of listing additional properties only Angus would meet the description. We rarely specify to this extent, but it remains useful to acknowledge the availability of a particularizing description, for the possibility reminds us that describing a particular in a way that strips it of its uniqueness is itself a discursive choice.

Because one who seeks to describe must make these choices of whether to generalize and if so in what direction and to what degree, generalization is a contingent process. In saying that I do not intend to commit to a nominalist metaphysics. It may or may not be true that we could as easily have grouped black birds together with black cars as members of the category 'blacks', and placed antelopes and two-tined forks within the same category of 'biprongs'. But even if there are natural kinds, and even if our apprehension of them shapes and limits the process of generalization, most of the categories of our conceptual existence are neither natural nor ultimate. As a result everyday language use poses numerous generalizing options at every turn. The user may still choose not to generalize, deploying a sufficiently large number of properties in a description so that only one item is described. And when the language user does decide to generalize, she then must choose a direction of generalization and a level of generality, in the process rejecting an array of equally accurate but extensionally divergent descriptions of the identified particular. The choice of one correct description rather than another consequently highlights the chosen properties for special attention.

2.3 *Generalizations as Suppressions*

Generalizations are thus selective, but as selective inclusions generalizations are also selective *ex*clusions. In focusing on a limited

[6] I owe the term 'complete profile' to Steven Yablo, 'Identity, Essence, and Indiscernibility', 296.

number of properties, a generalization simultaneously *suppresses* others, including those marking real differences among the particulars treated as similar by the selected properties. Describing the *Queen Elizabeth* as a 'ship' *simpliciter*, calling up associations with battleships and supertankers, simultaneously masks from active consideration those features of the *Queen Elizabeth* distinguishing it from battleships and supertankers, such as its casinos and ballrooms. These properties distinguishing the *Queen Elizabeth* from other ships are no less its properties than the ones its shares with other ships, but the description of the *Queen Elizabeth* as a 'ship' rather than, say, a 'resort', focuses on some of its properties and suppresses others. Suppression is important precisely because it is not negation. Saying that the *Queen Elizabeth* is a ship suppresses that it has ballrooms, but does not deny that it has ballrooms. When I refer to the robin I spot only as a 'bird', I suppress the differences between robins and penguins, however real they may be. Generalization as a form of discourse thus involves the suppression in some contexts of differences that would be germane in others. Among the numerous available generalizations, the one a speaker chooses will suppress differences that would have been highlighted by others, just as the chosen generalization will call forth similarities that would have been suppressed by others.[7]

The suppression of properties by selective generalization is particularly striking when events and institutions are being described. Speakers' Corner at Hyde Park in London can with equal accuracy be described as a forum for free speech or as a tourist attraction, but the two generalizations say different things and include a widely divergent range of particulars. The incident at a traffic intersection that is a tort to the lawyer is a traffic violation to the police officer and an upper back injury to the physician. Different observers of the same event, generalizing in different directions for different purposes, suppress properties of the event that might be relevant for other people, purposes, and times.

---

[7] 'Suppression' is perhaps a stronger than desirable word here, in that the degree of negative implication from that which is omitted varies from context to context. If I see you on the street and compliment you on the suit you are wearing I have not suppressed the fact that you are a wonderful public speaker in the same way that I would were I to compliment you on your suit immediately subsequent to your delivery of a lengthy lecture. Still, that which is omitted is less available, and the strength of the word I use to describe this comparative unavailability is most apt given what is to follow.

2.4 *Generalization and the Structure of Rules*

We are now ready to analyse prescriptive rules, a task that will be facilitated by disassembling such rules to observe their characteristic structure and component parts. When we observe the components of prescriptive rules, we will see that generalization, with its necessary selection and suppression, is as central to prescribing by rule as it is to the process of description.

One part of any rule, which some writers refer to as the *protasis*[8] and others call the *operative facts*,[9] specifies the scope of the rule, the factual conditions triggering the application of the rule. This component of a rule, which I will refer to as its *factual predicate*, can be understood as its *hypothesis*, for prescriptive rules can be formulated in a way such that they commence with 'If x', where x is a descriptive statement the truth of which is both a necessary and a sufficient condition for the applicability of the rule. '*If a person drives in excess of 55 miles per hour*, then that person must pay a fine of fifty dollars.' '*If you stay out after ten o'clock*, then your parents will no longer permit you to use the car.'

Rules also contain what I call the *consequent*, prescribing what is to happen when the conditions specified in the factual predicate obtain.[10] 'If a person drives in excess of 55 miles per hour, *then* that person shall pay a fifty dollar fine.' 'If a person is 21 years old or older, *then* that person is permitted to purchase alcoholic beverages.'

Rules are not ordinarily formulated so that the separation of the factual predicate from the consequent is as sharp as in these examples. Indeed, one or the other part may not be explicit at all. Nevertheless, any rule can be reformulated to take the canonical form of a hypothetical factual predicate followed by a consequent. 'Keep off the grass' is equivalent to 'If you are on the grass, then you will be told to leave', and 'Jackets required for gentlemen' means the same as 'If you are male and wish to enter this restaurant, then you must wear a jacket.' Moreover, there is some potential looseness with respect to which facts are located in the factual predicate and which are in the consequent. The immediately preceding rule could also be formulated as 'If you are male and wish to enter the

---

[8] Gidon Gottlieb, *The Logic of Choice*, 39, 43–7; William Twining and David Miers, *How to Do Things With Rules*, 137–40.

[9] Neil MacCormick, *Legal Reasoning and Legal Theory*, 43, 45.

[10] Those who refer to the factual predicate as the protasis refer to what I call the 'consequent' as the *apodosis*, e.g. Gottlieb, *The Logic of Choice*, 36, 39.

restaurant, and if you are not wearing a jacket, then you may not enter the restaurant.' Similarly, almost any rule can be so formulated such that the consequent is only a naked deontic operator, with everything other than an assertion of obligation, prohibition, or permission appearing in the factual predicate. Exploring how and why this is the case is not at the moment germane, however. For now all that matters is the basic distinction between factual predicate and consequent.

Once we separate a prescriptive rule's factual predicate from its consequent, we see the factual predicate as a generalization just like the descriptive generalizations examined above. Consider again Angus the Scottish Terrier. 'Angus shall not come into this restaurant at this time' is not a rule but a *command*, a term I use to refer only to *particular* prohibitions and compulsions, and not to rules.[11] Its factual predicate—'Angus (this dog) in restaurant (this place) at this time'—is not general but particular. But compare this with the factual predicate contained in a rule such as 'No dogs allowed'. This rule's factual predicate can be stated as 'dog in restaurant', or, more explicitly, 'any dog in this restaurant at any time'.[12] Note the difference between this and 'Angus in this restaurant at this time'. Unlike the command, the rule hinges on a generalization, prohibiting *all* dogs at *all* times. And the essential 'allness' of any generalization persists even when the generalizations are narrower. A different rule might prohibit only Scottish Terriers, only 3-year-old Scottish Terriers, or only dogs weighing less than thirty pounds, but such rules would still restrict, respectively, *all* Scottish Terriers, *all* 3-year-old Scottish Terriers, or *all* dogs weighing less than thirty pounds. Regardless of scope, any rule uses its generalizing factual predicate to make it applicable to *all* of something.[13]

[11] My usage, employing the word 'command' to demarcate particular from general prescriptions, resembles that of John Austin, *The Province of Jurisprudence Determined*, 21–3. This usage is by no means universal. Compare Gottlieb, *The Logic of Choice*, 115–19, using 'command' to refer to any prescription, particular or general, in which the addressee is precluded from inquiring into the purpose behind the prescription, and Alf Ross, *Directives and Norms*, 48–51, taking a 'command' to be any particular or general prescription that is backed by personal authority. H. L. A. Hart's usage in *The Concept of Law*, 19–20, appears close to Ross's.

[12] If the rule were a municipal ordinance instead of a sign in front of a restaurant, then all three components might be generalized, with the rule then prohibiting *any* dog from being in *any* restaurant at *any* time.

[13] I am not now concerned with the empirical generality of a logical generalization. It is useful to bear in mind, however, that a logically unlimited generalization, such as 'all women who are Justices of the Supreme Court of the United States', may in fact pick out only one particular.

2.5 *Prescriptive Generalization*

Although rules prescribe for *all* of some category, here too no one category uniquely emerges from a particular. Moving from particular event to general prescription accordingly requires making choices of the same sort made when engaging in descriptive generalization. Rule-making in response to a particular event, and indeed most rule-making of any kind, involves the use of generalizations *chosen* from among numerous equally logical candidates.

Suppose I enter a restaurant with Angus, who then proceeds to bark, run around, jump up on patrons, and eat food scraps from the floor. The proprietor of the restaurant, seeking to prevent a recurrence, proposes excluding not only Angus now, but future events *of the same kind*. Consequently, the proprietor must generalize from the particular event of Angus barking, running, jumping, and eating at time t (and place p). Angus is black, so the proprietor might establish a rule excluding from the restaurant everything black, consequently excluding not only black Scottish Terriers such as Angus, but also black cats, black shoes, black ties, black dresses, and black hair. Such a generalization from the precipitating event would be logically impeccable, for that event is correctly described as a problem caused by a black agent, and the exclusion of black agents would ensure that no event exactly like this ever recurred. Yet this logically legitimate generalization is absurd, and that is because Angus' blackness is causally irrelevant to the occurrence of the events inspiring the initial decision to exclude. We know that Angus's blackness is causally irrelevant, or spurious, with respect to barking, running, jumping, and eating because of what we know about the world, our empirical knowledge justifying the conclusion that these acts, even when committed by Angus, are not causally the consequence of Angus's blackness.

Suppose that Angus's interference with the patrons' enjoyment of their dinner was not a consequence of his barking, running, jumping, or eating, but instead resulted from allergic reactions to concentrated blackness. Whenever some people were near something black, they would sneeze, itch, and develop rashes. If blackness rather than the annoyance resulting from Angus's barking, running, jumping, and eating were thus a causally relevant feature of the precipitating event, the generalization from that event to everything black would no longer be absurd.

As with description, therefore, prescriptive generalization

commonly starts with a particular, takes it as an exemplar of some more general category, and then searches for the property of the particular that is causally relevant to the occurrence of the more general category. From now on I will refer to the more general category as the *justification*, the evil sought to be eradicated or the goal sought to be served. Thus, the desire to eliminate annoyance of the patrons in the restaurant constitutes the justification leading the proprietor to generalize from the particular event. (Justifications may exist at different levels. Eliminating patron annoyance may itself be justified by the goal of increasing patron happiness, which might in turn be justified by the goal of maximizing the welfare of the proprietor.[14] I will have more to say later about different levels of justification, but for now I want to stick to the simple relationship between a rule and its most immediate first-order justification.)

The justification thus determines which among logically equivalent generalizations from some particular precipitating event will be selected as the factual predicate of the ensuing rule. The justification of preventing patron annoyance, for example, guides the rule-maker in generalizing from the particular precipitating event of Angus barking, running, jumping, and eating. Blackness failed as a factual predicate because that generalization was not causally relevant to the presence of annoying distractions, but what if we

---

[14] I do not intend by using a utilitarian example to maintain that all ultimate justification is necessarily utilitarian or consequentialist. Nor do I intend to *deny* that all ultimate justification is consequentialist. Throughout this book I remain agnostic on questions of foundational moral theory, including the question whether there must be foundational justifications at all. I adopt this course because much of what I have to say about rules is applicable within numerous non-moral decisional domains, and is applicable to various theories even within the domain of the moral.

This is not to deny that the picture of justification I employ appears largely linear. Still, a few caveats are in order for the reader sceptical about linear justification. First, to say that a justification lies behind or generates a rule is not to make a temporal claim. As in the restaurant example, the particular may temporally precede the general, and a rule may precede its more general justification, with the latter being constructed only when the rule is applied or its application troublesome.

Moreover, much that I say is compatible even with coherence models of justification. If a particular outcome is justified only insofar as it coheres with other particular outcomes, the single outcome still stands in a relationship to the coherent whole that is similar to the relationship that a particular bears to a justification lying behind it. And even if the relationship between a whole and its parts is more circular than linear (as with Rawlsian reflective equilibrium), the part that is most narrowly applicable to the case at hand still bears a relationship to the whole that again resembles in useful ways the relationship between rule and justification.

Much of this will become plainer as I proceed, but I add these caveats now only in an attempt to persuade those whose sympathies are with anti-foundationalism or coherence theories of justification that it may still be useful to read on.

generalize from Angus not to blackness but to dogness? Prohibiting dogs appears to be less absurd, because we know from experience that dogness is causally relevant to the incidence of annoying distractions in a way that blackness is not. An agent possessing the property of dogness is especially likely to engage in annoying behavior, but an agent possessing the property of blackness is no more likely because of being black to engage in annoying behavior than anything else. Moreover, we know that annoying behavior is unlikely to be concentrated within the category of dogs by breed or age, and thus Angus's status as a Scottish Terrier and as a 3-year-old, just like his status of being black, 300 miles from Chicago, and a possession of Herb's, are causally irrelevant in light of the rule's justification. The factual predicate of the proposed rule barring dogs is thus a generalization from the particular precipitating event that caused the problem on this one occasion to that property (or those properties) of the particular that appears to be, *as a type*, causally relevant to the incidence of the problem, as a type.[15]

Neither Angus nor the event in which he was the primary actor are necessary to rule-creation. Particular occurrences often precipitate the creation of a rule, but they are not necessary. Frequently the impetus is an accumulation of experiences or perceptions, with that accumulation rather than one event precipitating a desire to prescribe for properties having causal propensities *vis-à-vis* certain justifications.[16] But whether emanating from a single event or a less focused empirical assessment, a rule's factual predicate consists of a generalization perceived to be causally relevant to some goal sought to be achieved or evil sought to be avoided. Prescription of that goal, or proscription of that evil, constitutes the justification which then determines which generalization will constitute the rule's factual predicate.

2.6 *Generalization and Probability*

Although only those generalizations causally related to a rule's justification qualify as non-spurious factual predicates for that rule,

---

[15] The intricacies of determining the appropriate normative class for some particular are discussed illuminatingly in David Lyons, *Forms and Limits of Utilitarianism*, 30–118; Marcus Singer, *Generalization in Ethics*, *passim*; Jonathan Harrison, 'Utilitarianism, Universalisation, and Our Duty to be Just', 114–16.

[16] And although for my purposes right here the inductive process of rule-creation is more illuminating, I do not want to suggest that a deductive process (see Hare, *Freedom and Reason*) is impossible. Often rules emerge not from particulars but from other rules, although the rules that so emerge still share the same characteristics of contingent generalization I discuss in this section.

this conclusion rests on a particular conception of causation that must be explored. What is it for a generalization to be *causally* relevant to some goal sought to be achieved, or some mischief sought to be avoided? Consider again Angus barking, running, jumping, and eating at time *t*. Plainly Angus's dogness is not a sufficient condition for the occurrence of these annoying events. Even adding the qualification 'in restaurant', the presence of 'dog in restaurant' would not necessarily produce the annoying behaviors. Some dogs are perfectly well behaved, displaying (when appropriately instructed) none of the feared behaviors. In order for those behaviors to occur, numerous factors in addition to 'dog' and 'in restaurant' must exist. To say that the property of dogness, or even dogness in restaurant, is causally relevant to the occurrence of annoying behavior appears at least misleading, and more likely just erroneous.

Not only is Angus's dogness not a sufficient condition for the occurrence of the annoying behaviors, but it is also not a necessary condition. Other animals or small children might likewise make noise (although probably not bark), run, jump, and eat food scraps off the floor. The property of dogness, at any level of justification, is thus not a necessary condition for the occurrence of the events constituting the justification for the rule.

If dogness is neither a necessary nor a sufficient condition for the occurrence of annoyance in a restaurant, then how is dogness causally relevant to that consequence? One possibility is that dogness is merely shorthand for a larger array of conditions and properties, *all* of which are individually necessary and jointly sufficient for the occurrence of the annoying behavior. But then dogness would no longer be a satisfactory factual predicate for the rule. A satisfactory (causally relevant) factual predicate would be more complex, consisting of all the properties and conditions that together would ensure the occurrence of the feared behavior. The 'No dogs allowed' rule would then be discarded in favor of 'No badly behaved dogs whose owners cannot control them allowed in this restaurant.'[17] Even this rule, with its more complex factual predicate, is likely to be excessively simple, and an accurate statement of all of the individually necessary and jointly sufficient conditions for the occurrence of the feared consequences would be substantially more lengthy. Still,

---

[17] Note that these are different rules. Why this is so (as opposed to the former merely being the shorthand form of the latter) will be apparent by the end of Chapter 3.

even this somewhat more complex specification enables us to see quite a contrast between it and the simple 'No dogs allowed'.

If 'No dogs allowed' and not something more intricate is itself the rule, then the factual predicate of the rule, dogness *simpliciter*, is not a statement of the individually necessary and jointly sufficient conditions for the production of the feared consequences. Rather, the factual predicate—dog in restaurant—represents a set of facts standing in a relationship of *probabilistic causation* to the justification.[18] If 'dog in restaurant' is the factual predicate of the rule, and 'annoying disruption in restaurant' is the justification for the rule, then 'dog in restaurant', although neither a necessary nor a sufficient condition for the occurrence of 'annoying disruption in restaurant', is still causally related to 'annoying disruption in restaurant' in a probabilistic way. To say that a relation of probabilistic causation exists between a property and a consequence is not to say that the occurence of the property is necessarily followed by the occurrence of the consequence, nor is it to say that the occurrence of the consequence requires occurrence of the property. It is to say only that the incidence of the consequence will be higher in a population possessing the property than it is in an otherwise identical population in which the property is absent.

This probabilistic conception of causation shows the 'No dogs allowed' rule to be premised on the belief that dogness probabilistically causes annoying behavior. The rule builds on the expectation of finding a higher incidence of annoying disruptions when dogs are permitted than when they are not. To say the same thing in a different way, the requisite probabilistic relationship exists when the likelihood of an annoying disruption is greater given the presence of a dog than it would be were there no dog.[19]

---

[18] My discussion of probabilistic causation is no more sophisticated than necessary for the purpose at hand. As a result, I ignore many qualifications and complications. Among the classics on which I draw are Patrick Suppes, *A Probabilistic Theory of Causality*; Nancy Cartwright, 'Causal Laws and Effective Strategies'; I. J. Good, 'A Causal Calculus'; Deborah Rosen, 'In Defence of a Probabilistic Theory of Causality'; Wesley Salmon, 'Probabilistic Causality'. Important modern contributions to our understanding of probabilistic causation include Ellery Eels, 'Probabilistic Causal Interaction'; David Papineau, 'Probabilities and Causes'; Elliot Sober, 'Apportioning Causal Responsibility'.

Those convinced of the soundness of a deterministic account of causation may find the phrase 'probabilistic causation' either meaningless or oxymoronic. If so, rejecting that phrase and substituting, *mutatis mutandis*, 'the probability that one thing will cause another' should be easier to swallow without detracting from the central point I wish to make.

[19] I need not deal here with the process of determining, as a question of fact, that

Thus a probabilistic conception of the relationship between cause and effect, and therefore between factual predicate and justification, is compatible with some annoying disruptions being caused by agents other than dogs, and with dogs not causing some annoying disruptions. The factual predicate thus represents a set of facts whose existence indicates an increased likelihood of the occurrence of the justification, and whose (effective) prohibition will consequently decrease the likelihood (or incidence) of the evil against which the rule is aimed.[20] Similarly, if the rule is seen to have been established in pursuit of a positive goal rather than diminution of an evil, the existence of the condition represented by the factual predicate will, when the probabilistic relationship exists, increase the likelihood of the positive goal toward which the rule is targeted. The key in either case is the probabilistic relationship, explaining why 'No dogs

such a relationship exists. Still, it is important to note that such a process will, if operating properly, distinguish cases of causation from cases of mere correlation. The distinction between causation and correlation, however, goes not to the conceptual validity of the idea of probabilistic causation, but only to its identification. Controlled experimentation, or non-laboratory approximation of that process, can still produce probabilistic causal conclusions purged of the possibility of mere correlation, as when scientists conclude that smoking causes cancer, or when ordinary people conclude that icy roads cause accidents.

It may appear that causation, even probabilistic causation, is a stronger relationship than is necessary to explain the emergence of rules, for in many areas of life we take the existence of mere correlation to be a sufficient condition for the creation of a rule. Take as an example a law prohibiting possession of firearms by those convicted of a felony. The empirical claim undergirding such a rule is not that conviction of a felony *causes* people to engage in certain forms of anti-social behavior, but rather that conviction of a felony probabilistically *indicates* the existence of certain other characteristics, characteristics that do bear a causal relationship to the propensity to commit anti-social acts. Although it thus appears that it is common for rules to be premised on mere correlative indication, even in such cases there is a causal claim behind the rule. The causal agent is not specified in the factual predicate of the rule, but instead the rule turns on the presence of certain properties thought to indicate the existence of the causal agent. In cases such as this, the probabilistic relationship is twofold. The property identified by the rule bears only a probabilistic relationship to the presence of the causal agent, and the causal agent bears only a probabilistic relationship to the incidence of the rule's justification.

[20] Nothing in this conception requires that the probabilistic relationship be the relationship with the highest probability. The necessary probabilistic relationship exists when the likelihood of the consequence is greater given the presence of the property than it is absent the presence of the property, and this increased likelihood may exist even if the likelihood would be increased by a greater amount with the presence of other properties. Just as it is sound to conclude that smoking probabilistically causes (or, as the cigarette companies would have it, indicates) heart disease even though the increase in the likelihood of heart disease is greater for, say, obeseness than for smoking, so too is it sound to identify the probabilistically causal relationship between dogness and annoyance even if the presence of other agents might increase the likelihood of annoyance to an even greater degree.

allowed' is an appropriate response to the Anguses of the future, while at the same time recognizing both that not all dogs will cause annoying disruptions, and that not all annoying disruptions will be caused by dogs.

2.7 *The Under- and Over-Inclusiveness of Rules*

A rule's factual predicate is a generalization not only in the sense that it includes all of some type. When we say of some statement, slightly pejoratively, that it is 'only a generalization', we mean that, however true that statement might be for *some* or *most* cases, it is not necessarily true for *all* cases. In theory, we could exclude such probabilistic generalizations from our linguistic life, employing the language of generalization when, and only when, the generalization represented, as far as we then knew, a universal truth. In order to do that, however, we would have to speak a language impossibly cumbersome to serve the purposes of ordinary talk. The limits of time and understanding make it impossible to restrict our assessments of cause and effect, or our reports of empirical truth, to universally correct statements, and so we frequently employ generalizations that are only probabilistic. We say that smoking causes cancer, that dogs have fleas, that Mexican food is spicy, and that Scots are dour without supposing that in saying so we are stating invariable universal truths.[21] Instead, we generalize probabilistically and not inexorably, allowing the use of descriptive generalizations as long as they are statistically justifiable.[22] But the conventions of everyday linguistic behavior require nothing more than this statistically justified relationship between cause and effect, or between the property and the class within which it appears, and one does not misspeak in saying that German wine is sweet, Norway is cold, smoking causes cancer, or philosophers are clever. So long as the identified generalization (German wine, Norway, smoking,

---

[21] This distinction is sometimes marked by the difference between a descriptive rule and a descriptive *law*. The laws of science are commonly thought to be necessarily universal, and both scientists and laypeople appear to withhold use of the word 'law' unless universality is present.

[22] I say 'statistically justifiable' in order to encompass, as discussed above, both the case of direct probabilistic causation and the case of probabilistically justified *indication*. 'Statistically justifiable' is thus linked with that sense of 'relevant' in which an item of evidence is relevant to the acceptance of a proposition if the truth of the proposition is more likely with that item of evidence than without it. This relationship is commonly identified by use of the words 'tend' or 'tendency'. See, for example, A. Quinton, *Utilitarian Ethics*, 47–8; J. O. Urmson, 'The Interpretation of the Moral Philosophy of J. S. Mill', 37.

philosopher) has some predictive or indicative value in terms of the
ultimate concern (sweetness, coldness, cancer, cleverness), the
generalization is conversationally permissible, even though some
German wine is dry, Norway is sometimes warm, some smokers do
not contract cancer, and some philosophers are dim.

The factual predicate of a *pre*scriptive rule is commonly just this
sort of probabilistic generalization. Whether it be 'No dogs allowed',
'Speed Limit 55', 'No one under the age of 21 shall consume
alcoholic beverages', or 'Thou shalt not kill', the factual predicate
of a rule is a probabilistic generalization with respect to some
(usually but not necessarily unstated) justification. Insofar as some
dogs would not create annoying disturbances, some driving at
greater than 55 miles per hour is not dangerous, some people under
the age of 21 can use alcohol responsibly, and some killing might be
morally justifiable, the generalization of the rule's factual predicate
is *over-inclusive*. It encompasses states of affairs that might in
particular instances not produce the consequence representing the
rule's justification, even though the state of affairs, *as a type*, is
probabilistically related to the likelihood or incidence of the justification. A rule's factual predicate bears a probabilistic relationship
to the concerns of the rule, but that relationship leaves open the
possibility that in particular cases the connection between the
justification and the consequence is absent.

The 'No dogs allowed' example allowed us to see not only that
some dogs might not cause annoying disturbances, but also that
some annoying disturbances might be caused by agents other than
dogs. The factual predicate is thus *under-inclusive* as well as over-
inclusive. Just as the factual predicate may sometimes indicate the
presence of the justification in cases in which it is absent, so too can
the factual predicate occasionally fail to indicate the justification in
cases in which it is present. Thus, under-inclusiveness exists when
we recognize that some people *over* the age of 21 might be unable to
use alcohol responsibly, and that hazardous driving is often the
consequence of conditions other than excessive speed. Many rules
are of this sort, incorporating factual predicates not covering some
states of affairs that would produce in particular cases the consequence representing the justification for the rule.[23]

[23] I should stress here that there is nothing *wrong* with under- or over-inclusive
rules, and these terms should not be taken to indicate defects that ought to be
corrected. Shortly it will become apparent that *all* rules are either actually or

Unlike over-inclusive generalizations, under-inclusive ones need not be merely probabilistic in order to be under-inclusive. 'All Xs are Y' is compatible with some non-Xs being Y. But of course it follows from this, *a fortiori*, that under-inclusiveness can exist even when the factual predicate of a rule is only probabilistically related to the justification. The existence of the probabilistic relationship between factual predicate and justification is just as compatible with the existence of cases in which the justification is neither caused nor indicated by the generalization constituting the factual predicate.[24]

Rules thus hinge on factual predicates that are (usually) probabilistic and under-inclusive generalizations with respect to the justifications for the rule.[25] Because generalizations are necessarily selective, probabilistic generalizations will include some properties that will in particular cases be irrelevant, and all generalizations, whether probalistic or not, will exclude some properties that will in particular cases be relevant. Factual predicates will therefore in some cases turn on features of the case that do not serve the rule's justification, and in others fail to recognize features of the case whose recognition *would* serve the rule's justification.

potentially under- and over-inclusive, and starting with Chapter 5.7, and to a great extent in Chapter 7, I will explore just why decision-making according to under- and over-inclusive rules is frequently desirable. Unlike an undersized tomato, there is nothing inherently or necessarily wrong with an under-inclusive rule.

[24] Thus, the parallel between under- and over-inclusiveness is a function of the relation between generalization and justification, and does not hold as a general linguistic or logical matter. The proposition that philosophers are clever, if taken to mean all philosophers, is falsified by the occurrence of a dim philosopher but not by the occurrence of a clever carpenter. Except in certain special contexts, 'philosophers' is plausibly taken to mean 'all philosophers' but not 'all and only philosophers'. This lack of a logical or linguistic parallel is potentially relevant to thinking about prescriptive rules, for it need not be the case that 'No dogs allowed', as the rule emanating out of a concern with annoyance of patrons, must treat the cases of non-annoying dogs and annoying non-dogs as equivalent. Or to put it somewhat more technically, the American maxim of statutory construction *expressio unius est alterio exclusius* (the expression of one thing implies the exclusion of another) is a view about the parallelism of under- and over-inclusion that could be otherwise. But all of this anticipates what is to come, and at this stage I only want to note the way in which generalizations may be both under- and over-inclusive when under- and over-inclusion is measured by and only by the rule's justification. Whether that measurement is the correct way of *interpreting* a rule is quite another matter.

[25] I say 'usually' in order to acknowledge that rules are occasionally crafted with a factual predicate that might *then* appear to be a perfect fit, neither under- nor over-inclusive. Even in such cases, however, a currently universal factual predicate is potentially only probabilistic or potentially under-inclusive. This is the lesson of *open texture*, which I introduce into the analysis in the following section.

Because the factual predicate of a rule is consequently (either actually or potentially, as I shall discuss in the following section) under-inclusive or over-inclusive (or both) from the perspective of the justification for the rule, that factual predicate may at times not so much further the justification for the rule as impede it. If a rule applies even when its application would not serve the rule's justification, and if a rule does not apply even when application would serve that justification, is it a bad rule? Or have we just misapplied the rule? Or is this just part of what rules are all about? After the necessary qualification in the following section, it is to these questions that I will turn.

2.8 *The Open Texture of Rules*

I have been discussing generalizations that from the moment of conception are probabilistic or under-inclusive rather than universal or exclusive. These less than perfectly fitting generalizations, when used descriptively, are those in which the user knows at the outset either that not all of the particulars encompassed by the generalization are consistent with the generalization, or that some particulars not encompassed by the generalization are consistent with the generalization, or both. When used prescriptively, these loose-fitting generalizations can sometimes indicate outcomes other than those that would be indicated by direct application of the justification lying behind the generalization.

Yet such a preoccupation with the probabilistic or the currently under-inclusive appears at first to ignore many generalizations that are more precisely tailored. 'All American Presidents have been men' is true for all and not merely most American Presidents, and 'diamonds are harder than butter' is true for every diamond and every pat of butter. This is in contrast to the syntactically similar 'German wine is sweeter than French', true only for most and not all of its extensions. Congruence equivalent to universally true generalization is also available with respect to under-inclusiveness, as with 'men have been American Presidents'.

Just as descriptive generalization that is neither under- nor over-inclusive is possible, so too does it appear that we can have similarly close-fitting factual predicates in prescriptive rules. Suppose all human beings were known to have a violent allergic reaction to dogs, a reaction produced by no agent other than a dog, and a reaction that interfered with digestion in a way that no other allergic reaction did. Now, if prevention of *that* reaction were the justification for the 'No dogs allowed' rule, the rule would be neither under- nor over-inclusive. It would fit perfectly, prohibiting everything that caused the feared harm and nothing that did not.

This 'No dogs allowed' rule appears to be an example of a type of rule—one neither under- nor over-inclusive—that is fundamentally different from the ill-fitting specimens we have heretofore been considering. A more careful look, however, reveals that this difference is of less consequence than it seems. When the relationship between rule and justification is seen to be universal and exclusive rather than probabilistic and non-exclusive, this perception is premised on the empirical conclusions that all and only dogs would cause this type of allergic reaction in all human beings. These empirical conclusions, however, are based on current perception of the current world, and something about that world could change tomorrow, or we could tomorrow discover something previously unknown about today's world. In either case, this new knowledge would falsify the previously presumed precision of the rule. A hitherto undiscovered breed of dog, for example, might not possess the reaction-producing agent, or people might be found who had an immunity to the reactions previously thought to affect everyone. However remote the prospect of such unanticipated events or discoveries may be, the possibility remains, as does the possibility of further exceptions not now even imaginable. In part because human beings are fallible, in part because they have imperfect knowledge of a changing future, and in part because the world itself is variable, rules premised on the empirical relationship between generalization and justification remain vulnerable to future discoveries or events that would falsify what had previously been thought to be a universal or exclusive truth. Thus even rules that seem now to be neither under- nor over-inclusive with respect to their background justifications retain the prospect of becoming so. The most precise of rules is potentially imprecise.

The foregoing is merely an adaptation of the phenomenon of *open texture* identified by Friedrich Waismann.[26] Open texture is

---

[26] Friedrich Waismann, 'Verifiability', *passim*. For a useful elaboration of the idea, see Avishai Margalit, 'Open Texture', *passim*. Hart applies the concept to legal rules in *The Concept of Law*, 120, 124–32, but his notion seems slightly broader and in one way less helpful than Waismann's original conception. Hart identifies open texture as being an ineliminable feature of language, and thus of linguistically articulated rules, but he equates open texture with the fringe of vagueness surrounding the core (settled) meaning of most terms. It is true that the bulk of the terms we confront have both a core of settled meaning and a penumbra of uncertainty, but

distinct from vagueness. In contrast to currently identifiable vagueness, open texture according to Waismann is the possibility that even the *least* vague, the most precise, term will turn out to be vague as a consequence of our imperfect knowledge of the world and our limited ability to foresee the future. Open texture is the ineliminable possibility of vagueness, the ineradicable contingency that even the most seemingly precise term might, when it confronts an instance unanticipated when the term was defined, become vague with respect to that instance. No matter how carefully we may try to be maximally precise in our definitions, and therefore in the generalizations that those definitions both reflect and create, some unanticipated event may always confound us. Waismann asks us to recognize that although we may have thought that we had a precise definition covering all cases when we established that if something has properties a, b, c, and d, it is an x, and if something does not have each of those properties, it is not-x; yet when we are confronted with something that has, say, only $\frac{2}{3}$ b, this unanticipated contingency creates a vagueness where none had hitherto existed. Open texture is this indelible feature of language, a consequence of the confrontation between fixed language and a continuously changing and unknown world.

Waismann's point was captured perfectly by J. L. Austin's exploding goldfinch: Suppose we saw a bird that by all accounts was a goldfinch—it appeared to have all of the properties necessary for goldfinchness—but then it exploded before our eyes?[27] 'We just wouldn't know what to say', says Austin, and we wouldn't know what to say because possessing (or not possessing) the ability to explode was never contemplated by the linguistic community as

some terms, based on our *current* knowledge, appear to have no realistic penumbra of uncertainty. Although we are *now* unsure whether a bicycle is a 'vehicle', and whether bridge is a 'sport', we do not have the same kind of uncertainty about any now-known extension of the word 'platypus'. We might imagine penumbras for even that word, for in some context the question might arise whether a dead platypus or a picture of a platypus was a 'platypus'. But even those possibilities could be determined in advance, although it might take a sentence or a paragraph rather than a single word. It is Waismann's point, however, that even after we finish doing all of this to the best of our ability, foresight, and imagination, it remains the case that human fallibility and our imperfect knowledge of the future might *still* confound us, rendering vague that which we had previously taken to be maximally precise. Hart's conflation of the currently known with the currently unknown obscures a distinction likely to be of substantial assistance as we try to understand the nature of rule-based decision-making.

[27] Austin, 'Other Minds', 88.

there developed a definition limited by that community's existing knowledge of the world and the goldfinches that inhabited it.

Both Waismann and Austin were concerned with definitions, and in this realm the view that *every* term is open-textured is highly controversial. From the perspective of, for example, possible worlds semantics, it is just not the case that every term is open-textured, retaining the possibility of indeterminacy in the face of now-unknown empirical facts.[28] But these controversies within semantic theory are not especially relevant here. Little if anything in the analysis of regulative rules turns on whether all terms are of necessity open-textured, although a great deal turns on the non-controversial position I sketch here—that empirical generalizations, whether of cause and effect or otherwise, that we now believe to be universal or exclusive will frequently turn out to be merely probabilistic or merely exemplary. Regardless of the truth of his more global claims about language, we learn from Waismann that a seemingly universal and maximally precise definition may turn out to be less than universal. This enables us to see that universal or exclusive generalizations may frequently turn out to be otherwise. When this happens, the failure in the face of new knowledge of a previously universal or exclusive generalization and the failure in particular cases of a probabilistic or non-exclusive generalization are similar, for both represent situations in which a generalization is now inapt for the case at hand. This inaptness may be occasioned by a generalization previously known to be either under-or over-inclusive (or both), or it may be occasioned by the phenomenon of open texture. Whatever the cause, however, it is precisely in such cases that the central questions about the role of rules arise.

---

[28] See, e.g., Rudolf Carnap, *Meaning and Necessity*, *passim*.

3
THE ENTRENCHMENT OF GENERALIZATIONS

3.1 The Model of Conversation

We have seen that to generalize is not necessarily to universalize. Insofar as generalizations about *types* are premised on probabilistic rather than universal truths—Swiss cheese has holes—those generalizations are under- and over-inclusive, encompassing instances in which the generalization fails. And although there are times when generalizations will appear universal rather than probabilistic, even such seemingly universal generalizations are susceptible to the phenomenon of open texture, leaving open the possibility that apparently universal generalizations will be found with the unfolding of experience not to obtain on some occasions. When that occurs, a generalization formerly thought universal becomes equivalent to one known from the outset to be merely probabilistic.

In addition to the probabilistic generalization not true in this case and the universal generalization that becomes probabilistic when its open texture is manifested, a third type of 'bad fit' exists as well. Because generalizations are selective emphases on some of the properties of any particular and selective suppressions of others, the particulars collected by a generalization are similar with respect to the generalizing property but likely different in most other respects. The totality of Herb's possessions, including Angus, are similar by virtue of all being Herb's, but they are potentially different in every other way. All Scottish Terriers, including Angus, diverge in many of their properties (such as ownership) except the property of being Scottish Terriers. Because the particulars collected by any generalization diverge with respect to most properties except the generalizing one, the selectivity of generalization can produce a bad fit in a particular case. Some fact suppressed by a certain generalization as irrelevent may turn out in the circumstances to be germane. In such a case something about *now* falsifies our previous determinations of relevance, but the suppressing generalization renders inaccessible the now-important property.

Let us label all three types of ill-fitting generalizations—the first in which a probabilistically warranted generalization is incorrect on this occasion, the second in which a supposedly universal generalization turns out not to be universal, and the third in which a suppressed property is now germane—as *recalcitrant experiences*. These are the events that call into question in particular cases the generalizations that normally serve us quite well.

What happens when a recalcitrant experience occurs? How do we react when a statistically justifiable but non-universal generalization confronts an occasion in which the generalization does not hold? By what method does linguistic life accommodate the necessity of generalization to the reality of the recalcitrant experience?

Consider first the occurrence of recalcitrant experiences in *conversation*, marked as it is by the ability of the participants to adapt almost instantly to confusions, misstatements, and questions arising in the course of the conversation. Ideally, each participant in a conversation resonates to the needs of the other, and the necessary imperfections and over-simplifications of language present little more than temporary impediments to understanding and communication. Discourse in the conversational mode is thus maximally tolerant of, for example, the under- and over-inclusiveness of probabilistically sound generalizations that do not state universal truths. When in conversation the circumstances require more precision than some generalization offers, the participants can supply the requisite qualification or refinement as and when needed. When I observe, say, that driving at speeds in excess of 55 miles per hour is dangerous, I am not precluded from appending qualifications if the nature of the conversation demands it. I can add that driving over 55 miles per hour is not dangerous under ideal conditions, that especially skilled drivers can drive faster than 55 without danger, or that it is sometimes necessary to drive in excess of 55 even if it is dangerous to do so. I can also assert, if appropriate, that under some conditions driving at some speed less than 55 is still dangerously fast, or that forms of driving other than speeding are dangerous as well.

The conversational mode of communication, with its give-and-take plasticity, thus has a tolerance for over-simplification. This tolerance is the product of the way in which conversation can assume from the context certain unspoken qualifications ('I don't mean that *everyone* who drives greater than 55 is in danger'), or can affix those qualifications when the circumstances demand it. In either case, however, whether assumed or appended, the qualifications occupy the area of under- or over-inclusiveness of a generalization. It is precisely in the difference between 'most' and 'all', or between 'these' and 'only these', that the looseness of a generalization, however useful that loose generalization may be, demands contextual augmentation. The special beauty of conversation, when working optimally, is that it is able to provide the necessary supplementation. Conversation can thus simultaneously employ non-universal generalizations while avoiding the confusions that come from taking those generalizations to be either universal or exclusive.

Consider Wittgenstein's famous example: 'Someone says to me: "Shew the children a game". I teach them gaming with dice, and the other says "I didn't mean that sort of game." '[1] Wittgenstein's interlocutor has used a generalization—'game'—which under the circumstances is over-inclusive. Its extension includes some instances, e.g. gaming with dice, not within the scope of the interlocutor's purpose.[2] Although Wittgenstein's interlocutor was presumably elsewhere when the actual instruction in gambling was taking place, similar misunderstandings are frequently remediable in conversation. Indeed, that is what appears to have happened in this example (although perhaps too late), for the interlocutor attempted to cure the over-inclusiveness by observing that some activities within the extension of the instruction were nevertheless not within the interlocutor's intentions.

Were we required as we talk to add all conceivable qualifications at every turn, conversation would be impossible. Conversation takes place with the facility we take for granted only because its participants continuously over-simplify, abbreviate, and deploy under- and over-inclusive generalizations.[3] Participants in a con-

---

[1] Ludwig Wittgenstein, *Philosophical Investigations*, para. 70. I do not claim that my use of this example is faithful to Wittgenstein's project. See G. P. Baker and P. M. S. Hacker, *Wittgenstein: Understanding and Meaning*, 356–7.

[2] Note that the force of the example resides precisely in the fact that gaming with dice instantiates 'game' in ordinary talk. For those tempted to conclude that the example demonstrates that gaming with dice is not under the circumstances an instance of a game, consider the pointlessness of the following variant: ' "Shew the children an octopus." I teach them gaming with dice. "I didn't mean that sort of octopus".'

[3] As noted in Chap. 2, I do not claim that under- and over-inclusion are semantically equivalent. An over-inclusive generalization is false with respect to some of its extensions, but an under-inclusive generalization is not literally false with

versation can do this because they have the means at their disposal to remedy the negative side-effects of such logically loose talk. It is precisely the ability to clarify when—but only when—necessary that marks the special character of conversation, its contextual plasticity.

The plasticity of conversation also permits managing the phenomenon of open texture. Consider again Austin's exploding goldfinch. Perhaps at first 'we don't know what to say', but that would not compel permanent muteness in the face of the newly discovered species. We might say, 'That's an exploding goldfinch. There must be two kinds of goldfinch, the exploding kind and the non-exploding kind, and we ought in the future to specify which kind we mean.' Or instead, 'That is a goldfinch in every respect except that it explodes, and therefore we need some new name for it. Let us call these things "explofinches".' And so on. The point is that our language can and does change to adapt to exactly these kinds of previously unanticipated observations. We are left speechless, but not for long.[4]

Finally, the conversational mode is also potentially sensitive to the problems created by the third variety of recalcitrant experience, those suppressions that turn out to be mistaken because of the selectivity of generalization. If some fact about a particular, such as Herb's ownership of Angus, is suppressed by referring to this particular as a 'Scottish Terrier', it remains available for recall should the circumstances demand. If someone asks, 'But whose Scottish Terrier is it?', the answer, 'Herb's', is readily at hand. Similarly, facts highlighted by a generalization can be ignored, and different generalizations substituted. Generalizations make conversation possible, but conversation makes it possible for generalizations to be tools for understanding rather than obstacles to it.

---

respect to any of its extensions. It may still be, however, that in some contexts to say p is to imply only p. In such cases a speaker must resort to conversational supple- mentation or qualification if she wishes to avoid that implication.

[4] Austin himself recognized this. 'What the future can always do, is to make us revise our ideas about goldfinches or real goldfinches or anything else'. J. L. Austin, 'Other Minds', 89. Similarly, when scientists state a scientific law, and then through further observation or experimentation discover exceptions to that law, the law is then modified to take account of the new data. The law, as well as the statement of that law, are thus capable of continuous modification in order accurately to reflect the world, and the style of scientific discourse tolerates and even encourages continuous reformulation.

3.2 The Model of Entrenchment

The conversational model stresses the adaptability inherent in any context in which users of language continuously clarify, explain, and embellish what they say in order to accommodate to failures in understanding, to changes in the world, or to changes in their perception of that world. Recalcitrant experiences, the occasions on which the generalizations of the past prove unsuitable for the needs of the present, are the precipitating events for the accommodations which represent the primary characteristic of a pure conversational mode.

However attractive the conversational model may be as an ideal, it is hardly a wholly accurate rendition of the realities of linguistic life. Instead of being continuously malleable in the service of changing circumstances, generalizations become *entrenched*, and the entrenchment of past generalizations impedes the possibility of an infinitely sensitive and adaptable language.

The entrenchment of generalizations, which so limits the adaptability and precision of language, is in large part a psychological phenomenon. Consider, to take a shop-worn but still serviceable example, the numerous words in the Inuit language for different types of snow. Once we learn from the Inuit and their language (or from elsewhere) that there *are* various sorts of snow, we recognize that our word 'snow', equally applicable to all kinds of snow, is a generalization, gathering up different types of snow and suppressing differences among them. We *could*, of course, make certain that we always specified, when relevant, the properties of snow other than those necessary for its being snow.[5] But our minds rarely operate this nicely. The generalization 'snow' will ordinarily make it more difficult, albeit not impossible, to think and talk about the heterogeneity of snow than would have been the case had the generalization 'snow' not been so entrenched in our language and in our conceptual apparatus. The particulars suppressed by psychologically and con-

---

[5] The point in the text does not depend on the ability of a term to be defined by reference to essential properties. Even if 'game' is a family resemblance term applicable to a range of particulars holding no essence in common (Wittgenstein, *Philosophical Investigations*, para. 66), to refer to solitaire as a 'game' *simpliciter* suppresses its individual quality, just as referring to football as a 'game' suppresses its violence, and calling cricket a 'game' suppresses its complexity. What marks the family resemblance term (if indeed there are such terms) is that nothing *other* than the term can collect its various instances, but that does not mean that those instances are not collectible, nor that the process of collection will not suppress differences among collected particulars.

ceptually entrenched generalizations are likely in practice to be far less accessible than the pure conversational model supposes. Entrenchment makes the properties suppressed by a generalization less subject to recall on demand, and entrenched generalizations mould our imagination and apprehension in such a way that methods of thinking that would focus on different properties become comparatively inaccessible.

The phenomenon of entrenchment increases in importance when we recognize that most generalizations are open-ended. It *is* logically possible to generalize about a closed and known set of particulars. 'All American Presidents of the nineteenth century were men.' 'The streets of London are in need of repair.' 'James Mill had intelligent children.' Still, it is just as logically possible and far more common to generalize about a set of particulars that is temporally and spatially open. The term 'Scottish Terrier' applies to the Scottish Terriers of tomorrow as well as to those of today, we assume that the laws of gravity will apply to the balls we drop in the future along with those we have dropped in the past, and 'as a rule the Alps are snow-covered in May' is a statement that applies as fully to next May as it does to last.

Generalizations thus commonly draw on then-relevant similarities and *project* those similarities in time and space beyond the particulars which served as archetypes for the construction of the generalization. Conversely, the same generalizations suppress potentially relevant differences, projecting these suppressions as well. To the extent that generalizations become entrenched, the inclusions of past generalizations facilitate dealing with the future when it is like the past, but the suppressions of past generalizations impede dealing with the future when that future departs from our prior expectations.

3.3 *The Entrenchment of Prescriptive Generalizations*

We now have in place the foundations of a distinction between conversational and entrenchment models of description. Under the conversational model, the generalizations of the past are a useful and frequently necessary shorthand, providing a way of organizing the complexities of existence in light of the finite constraints of time and mental space. Nevertheless, under a conversational model these generalizations are continuously adaptable to the needs of the moment. Insofar as the generalizations of the past are probabilistic and inapplicable to the case at hand, or are universal but falsified by some previously unanticipated state of affairs, or suppress properties now relevant, the conversational model allows a speaker to adapt to any of the three types of recalcitrant experience at the moment of occurrence.

Under the entrenchment model, however, descriptive possibilities that may exist in theory are blocked in practice by the way in which existing generalizations steer understanding and observation in some directions and away from others. The generalizations channel our perceptions, making it difficult to jump the channels of existing apprehension. Insofar as available generalizations are entrenched, some descriptive options will never be seen, others will become substantially harder to express, and still others will become less understandable than they would have been had not certain generalizations been entrenched. The observer of Austin's exploding goldfinch is left speechless primarily because departing from existing categories, definitions, and generalizations in the face of new experiences is substantially stickier than the pure conversational model supposes.

The distinction between the conversational and the entrenchment models is fully applicable to prescriptive generalization. Because all factual predicates are generalizations, rules come in or can be transposed into the form, 'All x's must (must not) (may) ϕ.' For a prescriptive rule, prescribing for what is yet to happen rather than for what has already occurred, the generalization 'all x's' is projected onto an unknown future. When yesterday's generalization is hurled into tomorrow, however, any of the three recalcitrant experiences identified above may occur. First, the 'All x's must ϕ' rule may be based on the probabilistic conclusion that *most x*'s should ϕ. This probabilistic conclusion, when hardened into the *rule* that 'All x's must ϕ', still leaves open the possibility that this is one of the cases in which a particular x should not ϕ.[6] Secondly, although it might have been thought at the time of creating the rule that all x's should ϕ, some new and unexpected variety of x might now materialize, such that for this sort of x, although not for any previous x, it appears that x should not ϕ. Finally, there may arise a situation in which some feature of a particular x, suppressed by the 'all x's' generalization, is now relevant in determining whether this particular x should ϕ or not.

---

[6] Or, conversely, this may be a case of under-inclusion, in which some not-x *should* ϕ. Although this varies with the governing conventions of interpretation, a rule requiring x to ϕ is more susceptible to an 'only x must ϕ' interpretation than a statement that x ϕs is susceptible to an 'only x ϕs' interpretation.

Suppose that recalcitrant experience arose in a prescriptive mode resembling the conversational model. Were that the case, the generalization constituting the factual predicate of a prescriptive rule would when the recalcitrant experience manifested itself be modified to take account of the problem. The presence of the 'minority' x, in the case of probabilistic generalization, or the presence of an unexpectedly different x, in the case of open texture, or the presence of a now relevant non-x property of a particular x, in the case of suppression of potentially relevant properties, would each be the occasion for *modifying* the generalization. Often we say instead that an *exception* to the prior generalization is created at the time that that generalization became troublesome, in effect producing a new and narrower generalization.[7] Whether described as a modification or an exception, the effect of treating prescriptive generalizations as if they occurred in conversation is the same. The existence of the prior generalization does not constitute *qua* generalization a barrier to what ought to be *done* now, any more than the existence of a prior generalization constituted a barrier in the conversational model to what we wanted to *say* now.

But now contrast this malleable conversational model of prescriptive rules with an entrenchment model. Under an entrenchment model of prescriptive rules, the occurrence of a recalcitrant experience, although conflicting with the prior generalization in any of the foregoing ways, would not prompt reformulating the generalization. Even in the face of a recalcitrant experience, an entrenched generalization would still *qua* generalization control the decision.[8]

[7] Although not central at this point to the argument in the text, my intentional denigration of the phenomenon of the *exception* is worth amplifying. I down-play the idea of the exception because, of course, a rule with an exception is still a rule. The difference between a rule with an exception and a rule operating in the same way but without something that looks like an exception is often the product only of linguistic fortuity. 'No dogs except seeing eye dogs' looks different from 'Thou shalt not commit adultery' only because there is a word—'adultery'—for sexual-intercourse-except-with-one's-wife, but there is no one word for dogs-except-seeing-eye-dogs. Thus, the difference between a rule with exceptions and simply a narrower rule is semantic and not structural, and there is no difference that matters between modifying a rule and adding an exception. The difference that *does* matter is the difference between a modification (or exception) that applies only in future cases and one that is applied to the very case that prompted it. This difference, as will become increasingly apparent as the argument proceeds, is central to distinguishing rule-based decision-making from forms of decision-making not so constrained.

[8] My reference to 'control' in the text should not be taken too literally. Nothing but stylistic felicity would be lost by substituting, as explained in Chap. 1.2, something like 'provide a reason in opposition to' or any other formulation of non-conclusive effect.

The fact of entrenchment would cause the recalcitrant experience to be resolved in favor of the result indicated by the generalization instead of the contrary result appropriate for the case at hand.

Consider the effect of entrenchment on each type of recalcitrant experience. The consequence for the first kind, the probabilistic generalization, is the conversion of a probability into a universal. '*All x*'s will φ' is the entrenched prescription even though it is the case that only *most x*'s should φ. Were one of the *x*'s that should not φ to arise under the conversational model of prescriptive generalization, the 'all *x*'s' factual predicate would then be modified, producing a revised factual predicate indicating that *this x* need not φ. But under the entrenchment model the option of revising and fine tuning the factual predicate at the moment of application is unavailable. Where entrenchment prevails, 'all *x*'s' means *all x*'s, and thus if an *x* arises it is φ'd even though it would not be φ'd in the absence of an entrenched generalization as the factual predicate for the rule.[9]

With respect to the second type of recalcitrant experience, the case of open texture, the 'all *x*'s should φ' rule might have been thought to be a universal prescription, promulgated in the belief that every then-known or predicted *x* ought to φ. But now some new sort of *x* is discovered that we do not believe ought to φ, and as to which, had we known about it at the time of saying 'all *x*'s should φ', would have led to a different rule, one whose factual predicate did not encompass this kind of *x*. Under the conversational model, the rule is now modified to exclude this *x*, but under the entrenchment model the fact that we have just discovered an *x* that ought not to φ is insufficient to overcome the entrenched generalization, the result being that all *x*'s, even this *x*, must still φ.

Finally, the *x* now before us may also be a *y*, and *x*'s *y*-ness, suppressed by the 'all *x*'s' generalization, could now be relevant in determining whether this *x* ought to φ. Under the conversational model, the suppression of *y* is defeasible, and *y* can be brought forth

---

[9] 'It seems, then, that with regard to any rule which is *generally* useful, we may assert that it ought *always* to be observed, not on the ground that in *every* particular case it will be useful, but on the ground that in *any* particular case the probability of its being so is greater than that of our being likely to decide rightly that we have before us an instance of its disutility. In short, though we may be sure that there are cases where the rule should be broken, we can never know which those cases are, and ought, therefore, never to break it'. G. E. Moore, *Principia Ethica*, 162 (sect. 99). J. O. Urmson, in my view correctly, takes this passage as calling into question the standard interpretation of Moore as an unalloyed act-utilitarian: Moore's 'Utilitarianism', *passim*.

to control the decision when and as necessary. But under the entrenchment model, x's y-ness remains suppressed, and the entrenchment of the 'all x's' generalization, with its consequent suppression of y, enables 'all x's' to control even in those cases in which y now appears important.[10]

3.4 *Rules as Entrenched Generalizations*

By extending from description to prescription the contrast between the conversational and entrenchment models, we see a duality of prescriptive postures which can be illustrated by a concrete example embellishing the previous abstract and symbolic discussion. Consider again a 'No dogs allowed' rule posted on a restaurant door. The rule's factual predicate gathers *all* dogs, not merely those whose actions might cause the consequence that prompted the making of the rule. The rule thus appears literally to bar from the restaurant every dog, regardless of size, shape, breed, or disposition. It bars the well-behaved in addition to the troublesome, the clean along with the dirty, and the healthy as well as the diseased. Moreover, the factual predicate includes, and therefore the rule prohibits (or at least by its terms appears to prohibit), seeing eye dogs, police-dogs searching for illegal narcotics or the scent of a suspect, and corgis accompanying the Queen of England.[11] Yet notwithstanding that there are persuasive reasons for excising from the application of the rule each of these and other varieties of dog, the rule's generalization is indiscriminate, embracing the entire universe of dogs, bad and good, annoying and helpful, troublesome and obedient.

---

[10] As may now be evident, this third type of recalcitrant experience is parasitic on the first two. We can imagine circumstances under which the rule-maker knows she is suppressing some occasionally relevant property, but wishes to do so anyway, for reasons paralleling those justifying the use of probabilistic generalizations; and we can also imagine circumstances under which the rule-maker intends to suppress only the non-relevant, but it turns out, paralleling instead the phenomenon of open texture, that what had been predicted always to be irrelevant is now in this case relevant. Because the suppression of the relevant can thus be divided into cases of pre-determined non-universality and cases of open texture, the structure of recalcitrant experiences, when applied to prescriptive generalization, is perhaps less complex than presented in the text. Still, the third case, involving suppression of some property that now appears germane, seems often to be phenomenologically distinct from the first two, and little is lost by presenting a structure of recalcitrant experiences that may be slightly more complex than necessary.

[11] The parenthetical in the text is included to forestall concerns that I have conflated the meaning of a rule with the meaning of its terms. In fact I *do* intend so to conflate the two, but that conflation will be the product of the argument in this and the ensuing three chapters, rather than a simple assertion at this point.

The factual predicate of the 'No dogs allowed' rule thus appears to suppress a host of potentially relevant factual differences among various types of dog. As we discovered above, relevance is determined by a rule's justification, but this rule suppresses differences that its justification would recognize. Suppose again that the rule is justified by the probabilistic conclusion that many dogs are badly behaved, thereby creating disturbances that annoy other patrons in the restaurant. With the avoidance of patron annoyance constituting the rule's justification, the resultant rule is premised on a probabilistic generalization—possession of the property of dogness probabilistically indicates the property of annoyance. Yet the rule that this probabilistic generalization yields—'No dogs allowed'—is over-inclusive, for it prohibits *all* dogs. The rule prohibits seeing eye dogs, which (in addition to being useful) are specially trained to be particularly well-behaved, perhaps better behaved than many children and some adults. Moreover, the 'No dogs allowed' rule bars both police-dogs searching for criminals and corgis in the company of the Queen, although in each of these cases some property of those particular dogs appears relevant to determining whether they ought to be kept out.[12]

Were the 'No dogs allowed' rule to be understood as existing in conformity with the conversational model, then the appearance at the door of the restaurant of a seeing eye dog, a police-dog, or the Queen's corgis would occasion an adaptation of the over-inclusive rule *at that point*. Because these events are all situations in which the rule's generalization does not serve its justification, the rule, if conceived conversationally, would be adapted at the point at which this disjunction emerged, at the point at which the recalcitrant experience became manifest. And if the rule, conversationally, were to be modified or clarified or fine-tuned when the recalcitrant experience arose, the applications of the rule need never diverge from the rule's justification. Over-inclusiveness would be but a temporary impediment, correctible with respect to the very instance in which that over-inclusiveness appeared problematic.

---

[12] There is a way in which these latter two examples (police dogs and the Queen's corgis) appear at first to be different from the seeing eye dog example, but the similarities are, as I discuss in n. 13 below, more significant than the differences. For those inclined to quarrel with the examples themselves, consider a patron entering the restaurant with a small dog contained in a sealed and sound-proof box containing an internal supply of food, water, and air sufficient to keep the dog alive and healthy, despite the fact that from the outside the box containing the dog is no more likely to create a disturbance than a briefcase or a pocket-book.

Under the entrenchment model, however, the pre-existing generalization would be treated as just that—entrenched. The generalization would by its terms control the decision *even in those cases in which that generalization failed to serve its underlying justification.* Seeing eye dogs, which are undeniably dogs, would be prohibited whenever the factual predicate—'dogs'—was understood to be entrenched, even though that outcome is not one that would result from direct application of the justification underlying the rule. Were we directly to apply the 'no annoying disturbances' justification to this case, the seeing eye dog would be admitted to and not excluded from the restaurant. Similarly, under an entrenchment mode police-dogs and the Queen's corgis would also be kept out, although once again direct application of the justification precipitating and supporting the rule would produce a different result.[13]

Seeing eye dogs, police dogs, and the Queen's corgis represent cases of over-inclusion, but entrenchment has similar consequences with respect to under-inclusion. Suppose someone desired to enter the restaurant with his pet bear. If the rule's factual predicate were treated as entrenched, bears, not being dogs and therefore not encompassed within that predicate, would not be excluded from the restaurant (or at least would not be excluded by this rule). The non-exclusion of bears, however, would plainly not be the result indicated by direct application of the rule's underlying justification. Unlike the result generated by a rule encompassing only dogs, the result generated by direct application of the 'no annoying disturbances' justification would exclude bears as well, assuming the likelihood of

---

[13] The situations involving the police dog and the Queen's corgis are actually somewhat more complicated. Police dogs and the Queen's corgis could be unruly and consequently annoy the patrons in the restaurant, despite the fact that there are *other* reasons, were we making a totally particularized decision, not to exclude either the police dogs or the corgis. Thus, the reason not to apply the rule may be external to both the rule and its justification, meaning that prohibition *would* serve the rule's justification, even though it might frustrate some other justification that the decision-maker also thought important. Still, we could take the justification behind the 'No dogs allowed' rule to be more complex than simply the prevention of annoyance to patrons. Such a more complex justification, incorporating not only the goals of preventing patron annoyance but also the goals of assisting the police and showing respect for the Queen, could warrant, say, prohibition of only those annoying dogs not serving useful public functions. If that were the case, then all of my examples, as well as an even simpler one in which we knew that some particular dog did not happen to be ill-behaved, would equally illustrate the way in which a particular selected by the rule's generalization may be one that would not have been selected by direct application of the rule's (simple or complex) background justification.

unruliness and consequent annoyance to be at least as great for a bear as it is for a dog.

Now we can appreciate why rules are often described as under- and over-inclusive with respect to their generating justifications.[14] When the generalization necessarily part of any rule is entrenched, that entrenched generalization will (currently or potentially) cover particulars not covered by direct application of the justification lying behind the rule, and will not cover particulars that would be covered by direct application of the rule's justifications.

This under- and over-inclusiveness, it is important to note, is largely ineliminable, the product of entrenchment and not simply of how specific or how general a rule happens to be. Reminded of seeing eye dogs, sniffing police-dogs, and corgis in the company of the Queen, the proprietor of our restaurant might then choose to modify the rule so as to prohibit not *all* dogs, but only dogs *other* than those in the just-mentioned categories. 'No dogsexceptseeing-eyedogspolicedogsanddogsinthecompanyoftheQueen allowed'. The rule is now different, yet the category left after incorporating the exceptions is itself still a generalization, and still as subject to recalcitrant experiences as any other generalization. The factual predicate of the modified rule is a generalization about all dogs not seeing eye dogs, police-dogs, or in the company of the Queen, and *that* generalization suppresses some facts about particular dogs in the new and more limited category. For example, the newly narrowed factual predicate excludes consideration of whether some particular non-seeing eye, non-police, and non-Queen-accompanied dog is well-behaved and thus not potentially annoying to patrons. And even if the factual predicate were still more precise, covering every agent that was then thought to be annoying and none that was not, the phenomenon of open-texture remains, leaving open the contingency that even a precisely tailored rule will turn out to be under- or over-inclusive with respect to its underlying justification.[15]

---

[14] See, e.g., Gerald Postema, *Bentham and the Common Law Tradition*, 410, 446–8. 'But rules achieve clarity, certainty, and determinateness, at the price of including either more or fewer cases in the legal categories defined by the rules than the rationale underlying the rule calls for' (p. 447).

[15] Some rules, however, guarantee their maximal precision *vis-à-vis* their justifications by being couched exactly in terms *of* their justifications, as for example a rule prohibiting 'all annoying agents'. Such a rule, one that wears its justification on its sleeve, does eliminate the possibility of under- or over-inclusion with respect to the rule's justification because the rule essentially *is* the justification. Yet some annoying agent might still appear that called into question the categorical exclusion of all annoying agents. See below, Chap. 4.5.

We are finally in a position to distinguish two modes of decision-making. Although in many cases the two modes will indicate identical decisions, their difference emerges at just the moment when a recalcitrant experience arises. When an applicable rule does not produce the correct (as measured by the rule's justification) result, the two decision-making modes diverge. Under one mode, the decision-maker treats the pre-existing generalization of a rule as if it arose in conversation, modifying it when and as it is unfaithful to the rule's underlying justifications. The existing generalization operates merely as the defeasible marker of a deeper reality. It is transparent rather than opaque, and a decision-maker operating in this mode is expected to look through that transparent generalization to something deeper when recalcitrant experiences present themselves.[16] Under this view, the articulated generalization—'dogs'— is solely an indicator, but when that indicator does not indicate what we know from direct consultation of the justification to be the correct result, the indicator exerts no normative pressure of its own. That something is a dog is no reason to exclude it pursuant to the 'No dogs allowed' sign unless the exclusion of that dog would serve the underlying justifications of the 'No dogs allowed' rule.

By contrast, an alternative mode of decision-making would see a decision-maker treat the generalization of a rule as entrenched, prescribing (although not necessarily conclusively) the decision to be made even in cases in which the resultant decision is not one that would have been reached by direct application of the rule's justification. Under this decisional mode, the decision-maker treats the generalizations as more than mere indicators, but as supplying reasons for decision independent of those supplied by the generalization's underlying justification.[17] It is this latter form of

[16] A good example of this view, and one about which I will have much more to say in Chs. 8 and 9, is Ronald Dworkin, *Law's Empire*, 16–17, where Dworkin describes this deeper reality as the 'real' rule that the decision-maker must discover or construct. Little is served, however, by imagining a real rule undergirding a false one, and I would prefer to stick to the distinction between a rule and its justification. If we employ my terminology rather than his, Dworkin can be seen as both describing and justifying a mode of decision-making one feature of which is that the generalizations constituting a rule offer little if any resistance to the rule's justification whenever a recalcitrant experience presents itself.

[17] As I shall develop at greater length below, particularly in Ch. 6.1, I take the phrase 'rules as reasons for action' or its equivalent to be based on the premise that reasons for action, in general, are *facts*. Consequently, it would be possible for some decision-maker to treat the fact of the existence of a rule, or the fact of the existence of some generalization, as a reason for making the decision indicated by the generalization. This should make clear that it is not the rule itself that *is* the reason

decision-making, decision-making by entrenched generalization, that I refer to, with I believe only minimal definitional stipulation, as rule-governed, or rule-based, decision-making.[18]

We now have in place the distinction central to this book. Decision-making almost always proceeds from a prescriptive generalization, but it may proceed in two different directions. In one direction, the decision-maker treats the prescriptive generalization conversationally, as but the malleable indicator of the justification lying behind it. When decision-making proceeds in the other direction, however, the direction I refer to as 'rule-based', the decision-maker rejects the conversational treatment of those generalizations constituting the factual predicate of the prescription. Instead the decision-maker treats those generalizations as entrenched, and takes the fact of their existence as constituting a reason for action (or decision) even when recalcitrant experiences serve to drive a wedge between generalizations and the justifications that generated them.

for action, but rather the treatment by some decision-maker of the fact of the rule's existence as the reason for action. When and why decision-makers do or should treat the fact of the existence of some rules as reasons for action will be dealt with thoroughly below.

[18] Obviously my definition is narrower than ordinary language, for ordinary language applies the word 'rule' to a much larger range of phenomena, including a mode of decision-making in which normative generalizations *are* malleable at the moment of application. Still, having distinguished a mode of decision-making in which extant generalizations are subject to modification at the moment of application from a mode of decision-making in which they are not (or at least in which the existence of the generalization *qua* generalization impedes the ease of modification), I am confident that even ordinary language would find the word 'rule' to be a more comfortable fit with the latter than the former.

4

THE SOURCES OF ENTRENCHMENT

4.1 *Entrenchment and Semantic Autonomy*

Behind every generalization is a justification. Sometimes called goals, sometimes purposes, or sometimes even (confusingly) reasons,[1] justifications exist because normative generalizations are ordinarily instrumental and not ultimate, and justifications are what they are instrumental to. Dogs are excluded from a restaurant in order to serve a deeper purpose like protecting patrons from annoying disturbances. Driving in excess of the posted speed limit is prohibited so that safety might better be accomplished. And the 'No vehicles in the park' rule, in H. L. A. Hart's famous example,[2] does not exclude vehicles because they are intrinsically evil. Instead, the exclusion instrumentally fosters a background reason such as preventing noise or preserving order. I will continue to refer to this goal, purpose, or reason as the *justification* lying behind the rule, a relationship independent of whether the justification is temporally prior to the rule.

Among the most significant aspects of the relationship between generalization and justification is that a generalization *narrows* the array of facts that would otherwise indicate the applicability of the justification. Although determining the cause of disturbance in a restaurant is a complex and relatively unbounded task, determining what is a dog is more straightforward, requiring the identification of a narrower array of facts. In that sense the generalization—dogs— is a *simplification*, and it is also a *specification*. Generalizations *specify* the result that will usually be obtained from direct application of their justifications. Consequently, a generalization serves to

---

[1] The confusion to which I allude is one to which I have contributed. See Frederick Schauer, 'The Jurisprudence of Reasons', which I now wish I had entitled 'The Jurisprudence of Justification'.

[2] H. L. A. Hart, 'Positivism and the Separation of Law and Morals', 607. See also id. *The Concept of Law*, 123.

make a justification more specific, or more concrete, in the same way that the result of a calculation is more concrete or more specific than the formula indicating the way in which the calculation is to be performed.[3] 'No dogs allowed' is more specific than 'No annoying disturbances', 'Speed Limit 55' more specific than 'Drive safely', and 'No vehicles in the park' more specific than 'Peace and quiet shall be preserved'. Because generalizations apply and specify their justifications, I will at times refer to the generalization constituting a rule as the *instantiation* of that rule's background justification.[4]

The preceding chapter concluded by distinguishing two forms of decision-making. Recasting the terminology in light of the previous paragraph, the distinction between the conversational and entrenchment models of decision-making starts from the premise that instantiations may encounter recalcitrant experiences when those instantiations indicate results other than the results indicated by direct application of their background justifications. In the form of decision-making tracking the conversational model, such recalcitrant experiences are resolved in favor of the justification, with the instantiation modified at the moment of application to conform to the justification. In rule-based decision-making, however, tracking the entrenchment model, the instantiation persists, and a decision-maker who follows this method of decision-making treats the fact of the existence of the instantiation as providing a reason for reaching a decision in accord with its mandates even when the indicated decision differs from that which would be reached by direct application of the instantiation's justification.

---

[3] To make a justification more specific is not necessarily to narrow its scope. Although the word 'specific' connotes narrowness, what is narrowed is the range of factors to be considered, and not the size of the included class. When rules are over-inclusive, such as when all apples are quarantined because some carry a disease, the coverage of the rule is larger than the coverage of the justification even though the process of applying the rule, compared to the process of applying the justification directly, is simpler and more specific.

[4] An instantiation operates in much the same way with respect to its justification as a sharp distinction operates with respect to a continuum. At times we need more precision than vague predicates such as bald, short, or dark can provide, and our response is to specify, somewhat arbitrarily, a point on what would otherwise have been a continuum at which we will apply the predicate or some variation of it. When we sharpen a vague predicate, however, we in effect create a rule. The newly sharpened predicate is likely both under- and over-inclusive with respect to the original predicate. The sharpened predicate will exclude applications that would plausibly have been included by the original predicate, and it will include applications that would earlier have been plausibly excluded.

I want to concentrate on the point of divergence between the two decision-making modes. Logically, the possibility of extensional divergence between instantiation and justification presupposes that the extension of the instantiation is determinable without reference to the justification behind it. This in turn presupposes that the *meaning* of the instantiation is not coextensive with that of its background justification. If the meaning of the instantiation just *is* the justification as applied to the case at hand, then there can never be divergence between instantiation and justification. Hence situating the concept of a rule at the point of divergence between instantiation and justification is premised on the meaning of an instantiation not being found solely in the instantiation's justification. This premise itself relies on a view of language I believe to be plainly correct, but which should still be brought to the surface for closer inspection.

When we conclude that the meaning of an instantiation is not totally determined by its justification as applied to the case at hand, we necessarily take meaning to be something other than the use of particular language at a particular time by a particular speaker for a particular purpose. Although language is invariably used for a purpose, meaning is not reducible to that purpose, at least not to the purpose for which language is used on a particular occasion. My analysis of the concept of a rule is incompatible with such a particularistic understanding of meaning, and assumes instead that the meaning of language is not wholly explained by the unformulated purposes for which a speaker employs that language, nor wholly explained by the particular context in which that language is used. In other words, the potential divergence between rule and justification assumes that both language and meaning are at least partially acontextual. But is that assumption correct?

The contrast between the conversational and the entrenchment models focuses our attention on the *semantic autonomy* of language, the ability of symbols—words, phrases, sentences, paragraphs—to carry meaning independent of the communicative goals on particular occasions of the users of those symbols. Some would explain the basis of semantic autonomy in terms of rules of language, others in terms of conventions, others in terms of socially determined reference, and still others in yet different ways. But neither the name nor even the source of the phenomenon is germane here. For whatever the source of semantic autonomy is, or whatever name we give it, there is at least something, call it what you will, shared by all speakers of a

language that enables one speaker of that language to be understood
by another speaker of that language even in circumstances in which
the speaker and understander share nothing in common but their
mutual language. Whatever makes it possible for me to understand
some of what is written in an Australian newspaper of 1836 and
none of what might be written in Chinese in 1991 by some 45-year-
old American legal academic interested in rules is something located
in the understandings about the uses of symbols that is not totally
reducible to what a speaker might wish to communicate on a
particular occasion.[5]

Suppose I go to the ocean and while there notice a group of shells
washed up on the beach in a pattern that looks something like C-A-T.
I will think then of small furry house pets and not of zeppelins or
zebras, despite the fact that in this case there is no user of language
whatsoever. My ability to think cat when I see 'C-A-T', and the fact
that all speakers of English would have a rather closely grouped
array of reactions to that same shell pattern, demonstrates the
phenomenon I call semantic autonomy, the way in which language
carries something by itself, independent of those who use it on
particular occasions.

Although this view of language sees meaning as partly *acontextual*,
saying that meaning is acontextual is saying only that the meaning of
a piece of language is not totally determined by the circumstances,
or immediate context, in which that language is employed on a
particular occasion. In referring to this characteristic of language as
its acontextuality, I emphasize the way in which meaning is larger
than the context of a particular occasion of utterance. The description
of this characteristic as 'acontextual', however, cannot be taken too
literally. To identify the phenomenon of acontextual meaning is not
to deny that contextual factors are presupposed in attributing even
the barest amount of meaning to an utterance. I understand what
someone else says not simply because I understand the literal

---

[5] 'The meaning of an expression cannot be identified with the object it is used, on a
particular occasion, to refer to. The meaning of a sentence cannot be identified with
the assertion it is used, on a particular occasion, to make. For to talk about the
meaning of an expression or sentence is not to talk about its use on a particular
occasion, but about the rules, habits, conventions governing its correct use, on all
occasions, to refer or to assert.' P. F. Strawson, 'On Referring', 327. To the same
effect, see Paul Ziff, 'On H. P. Grice's Account of Meaning', 7, referring to the
'projective' character of meaning, and Y. Bar-Hillel, 'Indexical Expressions', distinguishing meaning (semantics) from the particular purpose on a particular occasion
for using language (pragmatics). The point is applied to normative language in
Michael Moore, 'The Semantics of Judging', 248, 274–8.

meaning of the words she uses, but also because I interpret those words in light of numerous contextual understandings not contained in the definitions of those words. But some number of these contextual understandings, a number sufficient for communication to take place, are similarly understood by both speaker and listener just because they inhabit the same planet and speak the same language. The identification of acontextual meaning involves not the denial of the necessity of context, but the recognition that a large number of contextual understandings will be assumed by all speakers of a language.[6] These aspects of context might be thought of as a *universal context*, or *baseline context*, precisely because, however much these widely shared components of context may be temporally and culturally contingent, they are largely invariant across English speakers at a given time. Thus, the universal context is to be distinguished from the particular context, those specific aspects of the occasion on which language is used, including but not limited to a speaker's communicative goals in using that language. The distinction I want to draw, therefore, is one between the context that is understood by (and partly constitutes) the linguistic community at a given time, and the context that is the specific occasion of utterance.[7]

[6] Here I follow John Searle, 'Literal Meaning', *passim*. To the same effect is Moore, 'A Natural Law Theory of Interpretation', 304–7. Searle's views are not without detractors (see, e.g. Jerrold Katz, 'Literal Meaning and Logical Theory', *passim*), but the challenge commonly comes from those who would claim that meaning is even less context-dependent than Searle and others suppose. These challenges, consequently, do not call into question my assertions in the text, except to question whether even my limited accommodations to context are necessary at all.

[7] Nothing here turns on a resolution of the dispute about a different kind of context. The substantive and exegetical controversy surrounding Frege's adage that 'only in the context of a sentence do words have any meaning' (Gottlob Frege, *The Foundations of Arithmetic*, x, 71, 73, 116) involves the question whether meaning is conveyed primarily by sentences or instead by smaller sub-sentential components. Little if anything about rules or their formulations turns on how this controversy is resolved, for no interpretation of the context principle would hold it to deny that meaning exists independent of the particular context in which either a word or a sentence is used. 'The context principle does not say that a word may have one meaning in one context and a different meaning in another; it says that it may be said to have a meaning at all only as occurring in *some* context. . . . [I]t is plain that it is a principle concerning what it is for a word to have meaning, and does not imply that its meaning may legitimately vary from one occurrence to another.' Michael Dummett, *The Interpretation of Frege's Philosophy*, 364. G. P. Baker and P. M. S. Hacker, *Frege: Logical Excavations*, 197, appear to agree with the foregoing statement, although denying that the statement is a fair interpretation of Frege. Thus, my point in the text requires only that some meaning reside in a unit no larger than a sentence, a conclusion contested by virtually no one.

The meaning I refer to as 'acontextual' can also be called 'literal' or 'plain'. It is often called 'utterance meaning' as distinguished from 'speaker's meaning'. And nothing in any of these notions, I stress, suggests anything essential or natural or inexorable about utterance, literal, plain, or acontextual meaning.[8] Nor would I wish to deny that such meaning incorporates substantive moral, social, and political presuppositions that could be and may yet be otherwise. Literal meaning can and does vary with time, changing as the language of which it is a component changes. Yet the ability of one English speaker to talk to another about whom she knows nothing is the best proof of the fact that at a particular time *some* meaning exists that can be discerned through access only to those skills and understandings that are definitional of linguistic competence.

The acontextual meaning of an utterance does not fully exhaust what a speaker *means* on a given occasion of utterance, or what a listener perceives a speaker to have meant.[9] Acontextual meaning may be quite thin in any particular communicative context, and would be especially thin in a face-to-face conversational context. Much of the particular context embellishes and enriches the process of communication, making it possible for speakers to communicate far more effectively than they would if their discourse were restricted to literal or acontextual meaning. Still, the phenomenon of literal or plain meaning remains the foundation of linguistic communication, and a totally particularist theory of meaning, under which the meaning of an utterance is completely a function of what that utterance is designed to accomplish on a particular occasion, cannot explain how it is that communication is possible. If the meaning of an utterance were entirely a function of how it was *then* used (as opposed to how the word is used within a language), it would be impossible to explain how meaning is conveyed, and why it is that we pick one word rather than another to serve a particular communicative task.

All this seems commonplace, or even banal, yet it is worth making these linguistic claims explicit, in part because what appears

---

[8] Nor do these locutions preclude the possibility of relevant linguistic subcommunities, employing their own terms, or their own plain or literal meanings for terms that have different plain or literal meanings in the larger linguistic community. A rule containing the word 'bug' might operate differently when addressed to entomologists than when addressed to ordinary folk, but the fact that technical meaning within some environment does not entail the conclusion that meaning varies from decisional occasion to decisional occasion.

[9] See Searle, *Intentionality: An Essay in the Philosophy of Mind*, 26–9, 160–79.

to me as obvious appears to others as obviously confused. More specifically, resistance to claims about semantic autonomy has a significant presence within the universe of those who write about the theory of law or the theory of adjudication. The most prominent example is Lon Fuller, who argued, against Hart, that terms (such as 'vehicle') cannot have even core meanings independent of the particular purposes for which those terms are employed.[10] The impetus for such a view seems plain. If meaning can diverge from purpose, then application of that meaning may produce results inconsistent with that purpose, even to the extent of absurdity. This was the point of Fuller's example about the statue of a vehicle, the exclusion of which from the park seems inconsistent with any sensible purpose behind the 'No vehicles in the park' rule. But one could say the same about the 'No dogs allowed' sign as it confronts a well-behaved or even an anaesthetized dog. Yet whatever we might say about well-behaved or anaesthetized dogs, they are still dogs, and thus still literally within the semantic scope of a 'No dogs allowed' prohibition. It may be that in such circumstances a decision-maker, such as a judge, should then refuse to apply the rule, or should revise the rule, but the (arguable) desirability of such an approach, and the (arguable) desirability of saving the legal system from occasional absurd results, ought not to be disguised in an implausible theory of meaning. The absurdity of excluding a seeing eye dog does not make it something other than a dog. This confusion between what language means and what we (might) want our legal system to do often parades under a Wittgensteinian banner, and indeed Fuller and his followers all take their challenges to be both inspired and supported by Wittgenstein. But even apart from the intrinsic implausibility of the argument, conscripting Wittgenstein in its service is confused, based perhaps on a too-easy borrowing of the 'meaning is use' slogan. It is one thing to say that the meaning of a word (or phrase, or sentence) is a function of how it is used by the community of speakers of a language. It is another to say (and Wittgenstein did not say it) that meaning is a function of how an item of language is used on a particular occasion by a particular speaker.[11] Indeed, were we searching for a renowned philosopher

---

[10] Lon Fuller, 'Positivism and Fidelity to Law—A Reply to Professor Hart', 176–7, To the same effect is James Boyle, 'The Politics of Reason', 708–13; Drucilla Cornell, 'Institutionalization of Meaning', 1137–8; Robert Moles, *Definition and Rule in Legal Theory*, 176–206.

[11] See William Alston, 'Meaning and Use', *passim*. As noted n. 8 above, the community of speakers of English need not be the only relevant community, and

some of whose less guarded statements might support this implausible theory of meaning, it would seem that William James rather than Wittgenstein would be the appropriate citation.[12] Yet even viewing this theory of meaning as inspired by James, Dewey, and pragmatism in general,[13] the use of that inspiration appears still mistaken, for it is a large leap from pragmatism to situation-specific pragmatism, and an equally large leap from a pragmatist theory of meaning to a particularistic one.

A somewhat more plausible challenge is grounded in realist theories of meaning commonly associated with philosophers such as Keith Donellan, Saul Kripke, Leonard Linsky, and Hilary Putnam.[14] According to this challenge, the factual predicate of a rule is not to be defined conventionally, but instead according to the best current understanding of the terms involved. With respect to factual predicates referring either to natural kinds or artefacts, a realist theory of meaning appears compatible with what I have been arguing, for even a realist theory would not have the terms vary with the pragmatics of their particular application. That the meaning of words like 'vehicle' or 'dog' or 'water' may vary as our understanding (or that of those to whom we may have assigned some of the burden of linguistic labor) of their real nature varies does not entail the conclusion that the meaning of those terms varies from particular

nothing I say denies the possibility of linguistic sub-communities within the community of English speakers. But even though we must acknowledge the existence of linguistic sub-communities speaking their own technical language, it is almost always the case that that technical language is parasitic on ordinary language. 'Technical language is . . . a part of some language like English or French and a part defined only by reference to some particular discipline or occupation or activity among the practitioners of which it is current.' Charles Caton, 'Introduction', vii. Once we acknowledge the existence of linguistic sub-communities, however, it is tempting to think about the possibility that every speech act environment is its own linguistic community, and that speakers constantly make and remake the rules of language, at least as applied to this particular context, as they are speaking. But this possibility, even if true, has its limits, for it remains the case that the communicative context in which rules of language are modified for this occasion only can get off the ground only if the communicative participants are members of a larger linguistic community and thus at the outset share a language whose rules they can then choose to modify.

[12] e.g., William James, *The Meaning of Truth*, 23–4: 'Before I can think you to mean my world, you must affect my world; before I can think you to mean much of it, you must affect much of it; and before I can be sure you mean it *as I do*, you must affect it *just as I should* if I were in your place'.

[13] See Kenneth Winston, Book Review, 754–5.

[14] Examples of such realist-based challenges include David Brink, 'Legal Theory, Legal Interpretation, and Judicial Review', 112–24; Katz, *Bad Acts and Guilty Minds*, 82–96; Moore, 'A Natural Law Theory of Interpretation', *passim*.

context to particular context. Where the factual predicate incorporates a term that is more obviously theory-laden, however, such as 'life', 'death', or 'cause', the realist challenge would say that such terms presuppose the purposes of the enterprise, such as law, within which the rules operate.[15] *If* one of those purposes is itself the avoidance of results inconsistent with the substantive justifications undergirding a rule, then the meaning of a rule using those terms will collapse into the meaning of the justification. Such a result, however, is by no means inevitable, and all I claim here is that it *could* linguistically be otherwise. At least with respect to terms such as 'life', 'death', and 'cause', which at any given time have meanings outside some decisional environment, it is contingent and not necessary that the meanings they are given in that environment diverge from the meanings they have outside it, and contingent and not necessary that even any transformation of meaning must be one in which the desirability of avoiding absurd results is incorporated. Thus, although presented in a much more sophisticated form, the realist challenge, in the hands of some of its exponents, suffers from the same flaws as the particularist challenge—it fails to distinguish an admittedly variable universal context from the particular context, and, more importantly, embeds in a theory of meaning what turns out to be a substantive theory of the goals of a particular kind of decision-making environment.[16]

I belabor all of this not only because objections to semantic autonomy have a surprising persistence, but also because the view of language I employ is central to my analysis. The divergence between rule and justification, a divergence I take to be crucial to understanding the idea of a rule, is possible only if formulated generalizations can have meanings differing from the result that a direct application of the justification behind a rule would generate on a particular occasion. My focus on the entrenched generalization is a focus on this divergence, and is consequently a focus on the possibility that a form of decision-making could conceivably be

[15] See, e.g., Brink, 'Semantics and Legal Interpretation (Further Thoughts)', 189–90, arguing that disagreements about the meaning of American constitutional terms such as 'due process of law' and 'cruel and unusual punishment' and 'right of privacy' are not disagreements about the fuzzy edges of semantically determinate terms, but are rather criterial disagreements not resolvable by recourse to conventional non-legal meaning. The point is even plainer with respect to terms like 'habeas corpus' and 'assumpsit' and 'final judgment' that exist *only* within the legal enterprise.

[16] The interpretive theories I discuss in this paragraph are treated at greater length in Chap. 9.3.

guided by the meaning of the formulated generalization rather than by the optimal particularized application of the justification behind that formulation.

4.2 *Rule and Rule-Formulation*

The careful reader will have noticed that at the conclusion of the previous section I ceased referring simply to generalizations and referred instead to *formulated* generalizations. Behind this shift is an attempt to focus on the *source* of entrenchment. Having explored the distinction between a conversational and an entrenchment model, and having seen that decision-making according to entrenched generalizations is different from decision-making according to continuously malleable ones, we must examine more carefully this phenomenon of entrenchment. Entrenchment is what enables a rule to resist the impetus to modify in the face of recalcitrant experiences, but where does entrenchment come from, and how does it operate? What is it about what I am now calling a 'rule' that prevents its generalization from being subject, as in the conversational model, to adaptation at the moment of application?

Examining the semantic roots of the distinction between the conversational and entrenchment models enables us to consider the possibility that the source of entrenchment, and therefore an essential component of a rule's ruleness, is more closely related to its verbal formulation than is commonly supposed. Thus, if the formulation of a generalization, or instantiation, is important to the entrenchment of that instantiation, then the formulation of a rule is equally important to what makes a rule a rule.

This suggestion appears to be in some tension with the generally accepted view of rule-formulations. Many of those who have written about prescriptive rules, including Max Black, David Shwayder, G. H. von Wright, and G. J. Warnock, distinguish rules from their formulations, maintaining that failure to hold to this distinction is evidence of a fundamental confusion.[17] Inspiring this view are certain unassailable propositions. 'No vehicles in the park', 'Vehicles are prohibited from the park', and a 'Vehicles keep out' sign at the entrance to the park are three different formulations of one rule, rather than being three different rules. We do not change a rule by

---

[17] Max Black, 'The Analysis of Rules', 100–2; David Shwayder, *The Stratification of Behavior*, 241–2; G. H. von Wright, 'The Foundation of Norms and Normative Statements', 68; id. *Norm and Action*, 93–106; G. J. Warnock, *The Object of Morality*, 36.

translating its formulation from English to German, nor do we make a rule narrower by writing it in smaller letters.[18] We can ask what the Golden Rule is, but we ask something very different when we ask how many words it has.

Examples like these make it clear that rules and their formulations *are* different, but that difference may be more trivial than central. The three different formulations of the 'No vehicles in the park' rule are syntactically divergent, but what makes them three formulations of one rule, rather than three different rules, is precisely the fact that they are semantically equivalent. This does not have to be the case. We *could* say that semantically equivalent but differently formulated rules were different rules, but this conception of a rule seems odd, focusing on something other than the behavior the rule seeks to affect. Instead, we commonly distinguish different rules according to what they do, rather than how they say it, and thus the three rules are the same just because they all have the same meaning. Conversely, when two different formulations are semantically divergent with respect to any particular application, when they generate different results in at least one (actual or potential) case, it is appropriate to describe them as being formulations of two different rules.

Consider again the 'No dogs allowed' rule-formulation. Starting with the justification of prohibiting boisterous and annoying agents, 'No dogs allowed' instantiates that justification on the basis of the probabilistic conclusion that many dogs are boisterous and annoying. As we have seen, the resultant 'No dogs allowed' rule-formulation, if treated as entrenched, excludes from the restaurant well-behaved seeing eye dogs as well as dogs that are boisterous and annoying, and this is because the extension of 'dog', taken literally, is broader than the extension of 'boisterous and annoying dog', taken literally. 'No boisterous and annoying dogs allowed' is simply a different rule from 'No dogs allowed', the former (by its terms) permitting entry by some dogs that would be excluded by the latter. If, because the justification behind the exclusion of all dogs was the desire to exclude boisterous and annoying dogs, we were to exclude under the 'No dogs allowed' rule only boisterous and annoying dogs, we would in effect be unentrenching the generalization, causing the rule to collapse into its underlying justification. This may often, or

---

[18] Baker and Hacker, *Wittgenstein: Rules, Grammar and Necessity*, 41. I assume in the text a simpler notion of translation than would be acceptable for other purposes.

even always, be a wise decision procedure. But the desirability of such a decision procedure should not obscure the difference between a malleable decision procedure and one in which the generalization, however under- and over-inclusive it may be, is entrenched. Decision-making by entrenched generalization differs from a form of decision-making in which generalizations can be adapted to conform to their background justifications because the meaning of the formulation creates the entrenchment, and thus gives rule-based decision-making the very characteristic that distinguishes it from particularistic decision-making.

Thus, although it is often important to distinguish rules from their formulations, the implications of that lesson are limited, and likely to be exaggerated.[19] Rules stand in relation to their formulations as propositions stand to sentences. If we change the sentence, 'The cat is on the mat', to 'The cat is under the mat', we have changed the underlying proposition, and similarly if we change the meaning of a rule-formulation we have changed to a different rule. It is now possible, therefore, to see that rules lie much more in rather than behind their formulations,[20] for it is the meaning of the formulation that is capable of being entrenched. Consequently, the question of whether there is a rule (for a given decision-maker or within a decision-making environment) appears now to be the question whether the meaning of a rule-formulation is treated as entrenched (by that decision-maker or in that environment).

4.3 *The Foundations of Rule-Following*

It thus appears that following a rule is explainable in terms of a paired relationship between a behavior within the extension of a rule-formulation and the behavior that takes place. But this is not yet a satisfactory explanation of what it is to *follow* (and also to break) a rule. Although it is superficially plausible to see rule-

---

[19] Thus Ronald Dworkin appears in *Law's Empire* at pp. 16–17 to view the formulation of a rule as but a transparent indicator of the 'real' rule, even in circumstances in which the meaning of the formulation diverges from the meaning of that 'real' rule. Contrast the following from Searle, *Minds, Brains, and Science*, 46: '[W]henever we follow a rule, we are being guided by the actual content or the meaning of the rule. In the case of human rule-following, meanings cause behavior. Now of course, they don't cause the behavior all by themselves, but they certainly play a causal role in the production of the behavior. . . . To say that I am obeying [a] rule is to say that the meaning of that rule, that is, its semantic content, plays some kind of causal role in the production of what I actually do.'

[20] For a compatible suggestion, see G. P. Baker, 'Following Wittgenstein: Some Signposts for *Philosophical Investigations* §§ *143–242*', 59–61.

following as constituted by a congruence between behavior within the extension of a rule and behavior that takes place,[21] this account is incomplete in many ways. Most significantly, a simple congruence model does not appear to have taken into account a range of questions about rule-following that start with the heuristic posing of seemingly sceptical challenges to the possibility of following a rule at all. These challenges, most prominently presented in Wittgenstein's various reflections on rule-following (primarily in the *Philosophical Investigations* and *Remarks on the Foundations of Mathematics*), are not Wittgenstein's challenges, or even those of his interpreters.[22] Rather, Wittgenstein offers us the sceptical interlocutor, much like Plato offers us Thrasymachus, for the purpose of answering him, although there is much debate about just what Wittgenstein's answer was, and just as much debate about what answer is correct, whether it be Wittgenstein's or not.

Consider as an example, one based on but not identical to those that Wittgenstein uses in the *Investigations* and the *Foundations of Mathematics*, the question, 'What number comes next in the series 1000, 1002, 1004, 1006, ——?' It is part of the Wittgensteinian point, as well as part of what has passed into the commonplace of mathematical theory, that there is no uniquely correct answer to this question. A rule could be constructed to make any answer to the question correct.[23] For example, the rule, 'If n is less than 1006, add 2, but if n is equal to or greater than 1006, add 13', would explain all members of the existing series, but would generate and justify the answer 1019, rather than the answer 1008. The point of this, of course, is that something other than the prior numbers in the series makes 1008 correct and 1019 incorrect, with the debate being about just what that 'something other' is.[24]

---

[21] See Paolo Leonardi, Book Review, 621–2.

[22] Among the most important works in the recent tradition are Baker and Hacker, *Scepticism, Rules and Language*; Robert Fogelin, *Wittgenstein*; Holtzman and Leich (eds.), *Wittgenstein: to Follow a Rule*; Saul Kripke, *Wittgenstein on Rules and Private Language*; Colin McGinn, *Wittgenstein on Meaning*; Crispin Wright, *Wittgenstein on the Foundations of Mathematics*; G. E. M. Anscombe, 'Wittgenstein on Rules and Private Language'. As will become apparent, resolving or even taking a position on the competing positions in the modern debate is not necessary for my purposes.

[23] It was in fact Leibniz who first made this point: '[I]f someone draws an uninterrupted curve which is now straight, now circular, and now of some other nature, it is possible to find a concept, a rule, or an equation common to all the points of the line, in accordance with which the very changes must take place. . . . Thus we may say that no matter how God might have created the world, it would have always been regular and in a certain general order' *Discourse on Metaphysics*, 304.

[24] No one but the sceptic claims that there is nothing that serves this purpose, for

But now suppose that the same question—'What number comes next in the series 1000, 1002, 1004, 1006, ——?'—were accompanied by the verbally formulated instruction, 'always add 2'. If 'always add 2' is an *instruction* incorporated within the question, then 1008 becomes the right answer, and 1019 is simply wrong. 'If n is less than 1006, add 2, but if n is equal to or greater than 1006, add 13' is a permissible rule extracted from the series standing by itself, but it is not a permissible interpretation of 'always add 2', and it is thus not a permissible rule if 'always add 2' is one of the parameters determining which results are permissible.

At first it appears that what I have just said misses the point entirely. Why is it, Wittgenstein's sceptical interlocutor asks, that 'always add 2' is inconsistent with 'If n is less than 1006, add 2, but if n is equal to or greater than 1006, add 13'? Why couldn't the word 'always' mean 'in every case except those in which a series ending in a number equal to or greater than 1006 is involved, in which case all instructions inconsistent with 'add 13' are void'? The reason it couldn't, of course, is again the topic of the debate about what it is that supplies the benchmark for following or breaking a rule *of language*, where the very characterization of that bedrock question makes it circular and question-begging to answer the question in terms of the existence of rules of language. Community practices or agreement, to refer (without endorsement) to just one possible answer to the sceptic, are what and only what make 'always' mean always, just as community practices or agreement are what and only what make '+' refer to addition and not quaddition. Yet once something, whatever it is, *has* determined that 'always' means always, the word 'always' can *then* be used to refer to always. That is, questions about the foundations of language and the foundations of mathematics, even if taken as sceptical questions, do not suggest that the techniques of language or of mathematics are non-existent, nor even that those techniques cannot themselves provide the foundations for practices other than those of language or mathematics. A practice of following rules articulated *in* language is thus not rendered problematic by the difficulty of explaining why it is that language operates in the way in which it plainly does operate. Our difficulty, to use Kripke's example, in explaining *why* 68 + 57

'if it were *always* possible to give a rule to justify any answer, a rule to make any answer *correct*, then there is no sense of the idea of "incorrect", and thus no sense of operating according to a rule at all'. Guy Stock, 'Leibniz and Kripke's Sceptical Paradox', 326.

equals 125 and not 5 does not mean that the right answer to the question, $68 + 57 = ?$, today, is not 125. And if $68 + 57$ does in fact, today in this culture, $= 125$, then *that* fact can provide the basis, today in this culture, for some number of other practices, such as building bridges, calculating bank balances, and making change at the supermarket.

The question about rules other than the rules of language, therefore, is not why the rules of language work, but whether the rules of language, which *do* work (whether we can explain why or not), enable *other* rules to work. If we presuppose the ability of the rules of language to generate meaning, then '1000, 1002, 1004, 1006, ——?', supplemented by the formulated instruction 'always add 2', is crucially different from the question '1000, 1002, 1004, 1006, ——?', without that linguistically formulated direction. Adding the specific instruction in language eliminates the problem that exists without the linguistic instruction, or within a domain in which such instructions are unimaginable. Thus, the question whether 'No dogs allowed' excludes seeing eye dogs is not a question whose answer requires direct reference, even according to Kripke and Wright, to community practices. Instead, the rule builds on and refers the rule-follower to the meaning of the phrase 'No dogs allowed', a phrase whose meaning exists apart from the question whether the community believes that seeing eye dogs should be allowed in this restaurant.

That a theory of formulated prescriptive rules *builds on* the existence of language, and therefore does not itself engender the same kind of questions as do theories that seek to explain the existence of language, does not mean that this form of Wittgensteinian inquiry has little relevance for us. On the contrary, Wittgenstein's imaginary sceptic compels us to wonder what it takes to constrain or at least to guide future behavior, and the message is now clear: The ability to explain the constraints *of an unformulated or unformulatable rule* is a difficult task, and one quite different from the task of explaining the potential constraint of a formulated rule. All agree that if *any* answer is correct to the question, '1000, 1002, 1004, 1006, ——?', then there is no rule. Suppose, analogously, that a restaurant had in the past excluded a Scottish terrier, a bulldog, and a cocker spaniel. When the question arises whether an Irish wolfhound is to be excluded, the past instances do not logically force the first rather than the second and third of the following three rules, any of which would explain all of the previous decisions: 'No dogs allowed'; 'No short dogs allowed'; 'No animals weighing less than 60 pounds allowed'. The authoritative formulation of the rule is sufficient to privilege the first over the others, and thus an authoritative formulation of a rule enables us to say that some acts conform to the rule and others do not. The 'No dogs allowed' rule, when formulated, acts just as 'always add 2', when formulated, acts, building on the workability of language to exclude some otherwise eligible candidates as successors in the series.

All of this is to say that a rule-formulation appears to be a sufficient condition (or, more accurately, as I will explore at length in Chapter 5, at least one of a set of sufficient conditions) for the capacity of a rule to guide, and therefore for the ability of people to follow (or break) rules. It remains possible, however, that a rule-formulation is not a necessary condition for rule following. If unformulated rules of language and mathematics can still be followed or broken, even if we are not sure of exactly why, then so too might it be possible for other sorts of unformulated rules to guide in analogous ways. But this is getting ahead of things. We have seen in this section that formulated rules can guide because the formulation provides the semantic content by virtue of which we can say that a rule is followed or broken. Perhaps, however, this semantic content may come from something other than a canonically inscribed rule-formulation, and it is to this that I now turn.

4.4 Formulation and Canonicity

Although the force of a rule is tied more closely to the meaning of a rule-formulation than is commonly supposed, it remains important to distinguish the idea of a rule-formulation from the canonical inscription of that formulation. Although a rule cannot have semantic content without there being some authoritative formulation of that rule, some way of determining that 'No dogs allowed' *is* the rule and 'No annoying agents' is not, an authoritative formulation may be authoritative without canonical and textual imprinting in written form.

As should by now be plain, generalizations become entrenched by the fixing of meaning, but meaning can be fixed in ways other than the setting out of a single written set of words from a single source. We have seen the problems created in trying to explain the constraints of unformulatable rules, and we have seen as well that these problems diminish once we consider specifically formulated rules which presuppose and build on the reality of meaning. But once we see that it is meaning that supplies the force of such specifically formulated rules, we can consider the possibility that formulatable but not canonically formulated rules can have the same force, and thus operate in that same way as do those rules that are canonically formulated.

Consider Hart's example of the rule requiring men to take off their hats in church,[25] or the rule prohibiting smoking prior to toasting the Queen, or the rule by virtue of which I do not teach my classes in short pants even in the warmest of weather. None of these rules has a canonical formulation. Although some rules of etiquette are collected and reinforced by books written by influential authors (Emily Post, Amy Vanderbilt, Miss Manners, etc.), these texts are hardly canonical in the same way that we conceive codified laws the official rule-books of certain sports and games, and the prescriptions set forth in the Bible or in the Talmud, to be canonical. One who follows a rule of etiquette; or one who criticizes another for breaking one, does not point to any authoritative language, as one commonly does when the rules of law, the rules of a game, or the rules of the Talmud are concerned. Still, there *are* rules of etiquette, and the rules to which Hart refers are hardly non-existent. We follow such rules all the time, even when we might think it best not to. But from where, if rule-formulations are so central to the idea of a rule, do these non-canonical rules derive their force?

Let us focus on the hats-off-in-church rule, translatable into 'hat in church (forbidden)'.[26] If this rule were canonically formulated, we might imagine, as in the dog-in-restaurant example, a sign on the front of the church saying 'No hats may be worn inside'. As we have seen, such a sign might be treated as a mandatory rule, entrenching the generalization 'hat in church (forbidden)' even under circumstances in which that result was unfaithful to the justifications behind the rule. I now want to suggest that the same result might follow even absent the sign. A community of putative rule-followers, even without a sign, could still all have in mind the same meaning, and all treat it as entrenched. This could happen by virtue of the convergence of a series of linguistic but non-canonical instructions, as when all parents, in somewhat different language, tell their

---

[25] Hart, *The Concept of Law*, 121–2.

[26] On this translation, see R. M. Hare, *The Language of Morals*, 17–31. My particular deontic specification of Hare's *neustic* is compatible with but not attributable to Hare.

children not to wear hats in church. As a result, the children would as adults think of the rule in terms of what they had been told by their parents, and the point of semantic convergence among the various instructions, as understood, might then become the rule that the community of previously instructed children now enforces by sanctions or otherwise. If, for example, the various instructions produce uniform condemnation of those who wear hats inside a church building, but less than uniform condemnation of those who wear their hats on the front steps of the church, then these behavioral stimuli might assist in reinforcing the convergent and dissipating the divergent features of the various instructions, such that the semantic content of the rule becomes more consistently understood. As a consequence of this reinforcement of some but not all under-standings of what the rule is, if at some point each member of the community were asked to write down the rule about hats in church, they might write down pretty much the same thing, or at least write down sentences with approximately the same meaning. And as long as we can suppose that many rule-subjects and rule-enforcers could if asked articulate the same rule, there is no reason to believe that the fact they have not yet done so, or that no one has written down one authoritative version, eliminates the existence of the common understanding of meaning upon which any rule rests.

Although I have just been talking in the context of instructions once received, the same process of generating shared understandings of a rule's semantic content could take place inductively. If because of existing community patterns of perception, members of a com-munity group the instances they observe in more or less the same way, then they might again come individually to assimilate rules that are quite similar across that community. If everyone took cocker spaniel, bulldog, and dalmatian to be instances of the category dog rather than instances of the category living things weighing less than 100 pounds, then if asked everyone could write down 'No dogs allowed' or something close to that as the rule explaining the prohibition of each of those three kinds of dog. Here of course the questions become even closer to those asked with respect to the rules of language and mathematics, except that once again the ability, if asked, to write down some rule makes the questions different and in some ways easier. This is not to suggest that there are not difficult Wittgensteinian questions involved in asking how it is that the category dogs rather than the category animals weighing less than 100 pounds comes to be the accepted generalization from these three instances, and what the accepted generalization is will again likely incorporate various cultural determinations that could be otherwise. But if at some time most members of the community would be able inductively to create the same rule from the same instances, and if those members behave as if that rule did exist, then that rule exists in the same way for that community as does a rule that actually has a canonical inscription.

Thus, insofar as some number of people have internalized the same rule, a rule with the same meaning, and have all treated that meaning as entrenched, the rule can be said to exist, for those people, even without any one canonical formulation.[27] The rule against wearing hats in church, therefore, exists (provides a reason for action, independent of its background justifications, for some set of putative rule-followers) insofar as 'hat in church (forbidden)' is treated *as if* it were canonically formulated, and this treatment does not require that the formulation appear as marks on a sign, on a printed page, or anywhere else. We might say, therefore, that the phenomenon of entrenchment is in the final analysis about common understandings, where those understandings have semantic content, rather than about inscribed rule-formulations. Inscribed rule-formulations will facilitate the development of common understandings with common semantic content but are not necessary for them, and thus entrenchment exists insofar as a decision-maker treats a generalization or instantiation as itself providing a reason for action even when there are good reasons not to. This generalization may be gleaned from the marks on a page, and the canonical formulation may foster the mental entrenchment, but it is not necessary for it.[28]

Although rules can therefore exist without canonically inscribed formulations, entrenchment of such rules is likely to be significantly weaker. As we have seen, the consequences of entrenchment are such that rules will be either currently or potentially under- and over-inclusive with respect to their generating justifications. When no recalcitrant experience, occupying the area of under- or over-inclusiveness, is presented, the existence of a regulative rule will be

---

[27] For an agent to internalize a rule is simply for that agent to treat the existence of the rule as a reason for action. *Why* an agent would treat a rule as a reason for action is not at the moment germane, although it will presently become so.

[28] And this is why, in some environments, 'Scottish terrier, bulldog, cocker spaniel, ——?' is like '1000, 1002, 1004, ——?' In both cases there *is* a rule—'add any dog' and 'add 2', respectively—even though in neither case does the rule emerge uniquely from the series itself.

neither problematic nor interesting. When a particular application of a rule does not lie within the area of under- or over-inclusion, the decision-maker could just as easily have applied the justification directly, and the rule is superfluous. Rules get interesting, however, when we are in the region of under- or over-inclusiveness, when a particular application of a rule generates a result divergent from that which would have been generated by direct application of the rule's justification.

In these interesting cases, the ones in which the application inhabits the area of under- or over-inclusiveness, the pressure on the entrenched generalization is likely to be enormous. After all, it is only the generalization and not its underlying justification that inclines in the direction of enforcement rather than avoidance of the rule. Only the instantiation *qua* instantiation, rather than anything deeper, provides a reason for decision in accordance with the rule. When in such cases the formulation exists only in the mind and not on paper, the pressures to avoid the under- or over-inclusiveness by reformulating at the moment of application will be considerable. Nevertheless, these pressures are in theory resistable, and a person could be imagined saying to himself, 'Even though the reasons for having the rule against wearing hats in church is inapplicable to this situation, the rule as I understand it refers to "hats" *simpliciter*, and thus I must take off my hat.' In such cases the addressee's understanding of a rule equivalent in meaning to 'No hats in church' operates as if it were canonically formulated, because in both cases the rule-proposition, 'Hats in church (forbidden)' is sufficiently entrenched to resist attempts to change its meaning by substituting, at the instant of application, 'Hats in church (forbidden), except . . .'.

Thus, although I have attempted to demonstrate that the distinction between a rule and its formulation is less of a chasm than is commonly believed, I want to locate a rule not so much in its canonical formulation as in its entrenched meaning. This entrenchment will ordinarily be the product of a rule-formulation in a fixed set of words, and such fixed sets of words will usually make entrenchment both more likely and more durable. Nevertheless, a fixed verbal form, as in the United States Code or the Official Rules of Chess, is not a necessary condition for the existence of the entrenched generalization that is an essential component of a rule.

4.5 *The Layers of Rules*

Divorcing the idea of a rule from its most specific and canonized formulation makes it possible to appreciate the intriguing way in which there may be stacked layers of rules, and the way in which the concept of a rule may be seen to be more of a *relationship* than an isolated entity.

Until now I have been operating with a model of decision-making involving only formulated or formulatable rules and the justifications that lie behind them. Those background justifications themselves, however, do not appear from thin air, nor can the kinds of justifications I have been considering be thought to be in any sense foundational or ultimate. Rather, these comparatively specific justifications (peace and quiet in the park; no dangerous driving; no annoyance of patrons in the restaurant) are themselves instantiations of deeper and yet more abstract justifications. For example, we have been treating the 'No dogs allowed' rule as the instantiation of the justification of excluding from the restaurant agents that are boisterous and annoying. With respect to this justification, the categorical exclusion of dogs is both under- and over-inclusive, but that categorical exclusion still serves the justification insofar as the troublesome properties are probabilistically if not inexorably located in dogs.

But the justification of excluding boisterous and annoying agents has in turn its own justification, say, increasing the enjoyment of the patrons in the restaurant. And if then we ask why *this* justification is to be valued, the answer is that something even deeper exists as the justification for this justification, such as increasing the profitability of the restaurant. We could go further, asking why profitability is to be pursued, and so on, until we arrived at a level of bedrock justification.[29]

Once we see that justifications exist on different levels, we can appreciate that what is a justification with respect to *its* instantiation is usually itself also the instantiation of a deeper justification. And just as the most particular instantiations, the formulated rules, can be seen as entrenched or not, then so too can instantiations be

---

[29] I employ here a model of multiple justification that is a simple one-dimensional linear regress. Justification is commonly more complex than this, but what I say here applies to any less linear form of justification with justifications existing at different levels of generality, and applies as well, as I discuss at greater length above in Chap. 2, n. 14, to coherence or constructive models of justification.

entrenched (or not) on different levels. Insofar as an instantiation of some justification is so entrenched at any level, and insofar as such an instantiation may also serve as the justification for a lower-level instantiation, it appears that justifications can themselves operate as entrenched generalizations—rules—with respect to *their* generating justifications.

Let us again use as an example the 'No vehicles in the park' rule as it formed the centerpiece of Hart's debate with Fuller.[30] In response to Hart's claim that such a rule has a core of settled meaning and a penumbra of uncertainty requiring discretion by the decision-maker, Fuller offered a counterexample, designed to show that the notion of core meaning was incoherent without reference to the unformulated purpose of the rule. He asked us to consider a Second World War military truck mounted on a pedestal as part of a war memorial.[31] Fuller's point was that something, the statue of a vehicle, might be within the letter of a rule but yet not within its purpose, in which case the letter should yield to the purpose. Fuller can thus be seen as arguing against the entrenchment of the generalization, viewing generalizations as defeasible when they do not serve the purposes of their underlying justifications.[32] Rule-based decision-making, on the other hand, takes the generalization 'vehicle' as entrenched, thus excluding from the park even those vehicles, such as vehicles incorporated into war memorials, whose exclusion does not serve the justifications behind the rule.

Suppose, however, that the justification for the 'No vehicles in the park' rule is the preservation of peace and quiet in the park. Fuller's argument for exclusion of the statue-vehicle from the

---

[30] Hart, 'Positivism and the Separation of Law and Morals', 607; Fuller, 'Positivism and Fidelity to Law—A Reply to Professor Hart', 669.

[31] Fuller's counterexample turns out to make the example itself slightly inapt for the point of the debate, for it is arguable that the lack of current mobility disqualifies the truck from being a vehicle. But this is a defect in the example and not the central claim, for there are numerous general terms whose correct application requires no reference to function or to success in performing it. As a result, let me stipulate in advance that it is *not* definitional of the word 'vehicle' that the vehicle be currently operable. Just as caged lions are still lions, and just as seeing eye dogs are still dogs, so too can we stipulate that immobile vehicles are still vehicles.

[32] Fuller also makes the case in terms of meaning, arguing at times (e.g. 668–9) that the meaning of a term cannot be divorced either from the specific context in which it is used, nor from 'some specific intention in the use of it'. I have dealt with this claim above (Chap. 4.1), and I am now discussing an alternative characterization of the Fullerian claim, one that recognizes that meaning is different from and can therefore conflict with speaker's intention, but argues that in such cases intention or purpose should trump acontextual meaning.

coverage of the rule is premised on the primacy of purpose, on the fact that even though the statue-vehicle may fall within the formulated rule, it falls outside of the rule's justification. But that justification, preserving peace and quiet in the park, is itself the instantiation of a deeper purpose, say, maximizing the enjoyment of residents of the town in which the park is located. This leads to the possibility that even the rule's justification should be defeasible in the service of *its* justification. Suppose further, for example, that a resident of the town, having just won six gold medals in the most recent Olympic Games, is returning to the town to be honored in a celebration. Suppose as well that she is to be accompanied by an extremely popular President of the United States, a President who because of a childhood disease is unable to walk. A motorcade is planned, and the park is selected as the only feasible location for the motorcade. Is the motorcade to be permitted?

In this case there appears to be no tension between the formulated rule and its most immediate justification. The presence of the vehicles making up the motorcade will, under these circumstances, lessen rather than increase the degree of peace and quiet in the park. Thus, both formulation and first-level justification lead to exclusion of the motorcade from the park. At the next level, however, this can be seen to be a case in which a reduction in peace and quiet will increase rather than decrease the enjoyment of the town's residents. Thus, this is a case in which the first-level justification, maximizing peace and quiet, is over-inclusive with respect to *its* justification, maximizing the pleasure of the town residents, because in this case the probabilistic generalization that more peace and quiet means more enjoyment does not hold. The question is then the same as that arising where the 'No vehicles in the park' formulation conflicted with the first-level (peace and quiet) justification, but at one remove. Here we again ask whether the generalization constituting the first-level justification is defeasible when it does not serve *its* background justification, the maximization of enjoyment. If the first-level justification is defeasible in the same way in which the formulation is defeasible, then the peace and quiet factor should yield in this case to the maximum enjoyment factor. If the first-level justification is entrenched rather than defeasible, however, the reduction of peace and quiet caused by the motorcade provides a reason for excluding the motorcade despite the fact that in this case more peace and quiet will not serve the deeper justification of maximizing enjoyment.

If this latter alternative, treating the formulation as defeasible but the first-level justification as entrenched, were to be chosen, the consequence would be that the first-level justification had the status of an entrenched generalization—a *rule*—with respect to its generating justification. And we can imagine that the same issue might arise at even deeper levels of justification, until we could go no further. Thus, if at every level the instantiation were taken *not* to be entrenched with respect its background justification, the decision procedure would reject any decision in which application of an instantiation departed from the decision that would be reached were that instantiation's justification to be applied directly. As a result, a decision procedure treating all instantiations as defeasible in the service of their next level justifications turns out to be extensionally equivalent to a decision procedure in which ultimate justifications are applied directly to each case. Extensional equivalence is therefore avoided only when, and to the extent that, at one or more levels of justification the instantiation of a justification is treated as entrenched *vis-à-vis* that very justification,

Thus, we can recast the idea of a rule into a *relationship*. A rule exists (for some agent or in some decision-making environment) insofar as an instantiation of a justification is treated (by that agent or by the decision-makers in that decision-making environment) as entrenched, having the power to provide a reason for decision even when that instantiation does not serve its generating justification. The form of decision-making that we can call rule-based, therefore, exists insofar as instantiations resist efforts to penetrate them in the service of their justifications. Because justifications and their instantiations exist at multiple levels within the normative universe, then so too can we say that rules have the potential for existing at multiple levels within that same normative universe.[33]

---

[33] Because rule-based decision-making makes sense only in the context of a relationship between an instantiation and its justification, the idea is inapplicable to a priori prescriptions. When justification runs out, then a form of decision-making that is coherent only if there is a justification lying behind a prescription runs out as well. Whatever might be said, therefore, about the source, effect, and contours of ultimate moral rules is not something that I aim to address in this book. 'Justification' is thus a technical and stipulative term, and for my purposes rules can have morally unjustified justifications.

5
DECISION-MAKING BY ENTRENCHED GENERALIZATION

5.1 *A Distinction With a Difference*

We have now distinguished two types of decision-making, the distinction being a function of the way in which prescriptive generalizations directed to any decision-maker are, ordinarily, under- and over-inclusive instantiations of deeper justifications. Under one sort of decision-making, these instantiations are intrinsically unweighty guides to the application of their background justifications, and so provide no normative pressure in cases in which the results they indicate diverge from the results indicated by direct application of those background justifications. But under another sort of decision-making these instantiations are treated as entrenched, such that the instantiation provides normative pressure *qua* instantiation even in those cases in which application of that instantiation frustrates the justification (or justifications) lying behind it.

We can now label the two forms of decision-making. Because one treats what look like rules in form only as weightless rules of thumb (a term I will subject to closer scrutiny in the concluding section of this chapter), not allowing them to interfere with the fullest consideration of all relevant (according to the applicable justification or array of justifications) features of the event calling for a decision, I will refer to it as *particularistic*.[1] Particularistic decision-making focuses on the particular situation, case, or act, and thereby

---

[1] The procedure I designate as 'particularistic' is quite close to Joseph Raz's idea of acting 'on the balance of reasons', *Practical Reason and Norms*, 36, and could be called *act-based*, for it is structurally (although not axiologically) identical to act-utilitarianism. What I call 'particularism' is consistent with 'act-X', where X is any theory, array of theories, justification, or array of justifications. I prefer to avoid the term 'act-based', however, because it locates the decision procedure more exclusively within ethical consequentialism than is necessary for this enterprise, and because there are differences between the distinction I draw and some often drawn between act- and rule-utilitarianism.

comprehends everything about the particular decision-prompting event that is relevant to the decision to be made. By contrast, the second type of decision-making, excluding from consideration some properties of the particular event that a particularistic decision procedure would recognize, is the one I refer to as *rule-based*. Rule-based decision-making fails to be particularistic just because some otherwise relevant features of the decision-prompting event are actually or potentially ignored by the under- and over-inclusive generalization constituting the factual predicate of any rule.[3]

In practice, even a particularistic decision-making procedure employs prescriptive generalizations, which under such a procedure have the appearance of rules even though treated only as transparent guides. Thus, both species of decision-making, the particularistic and the rule-based, project the generalizations of the past onto the realities of that past's future. The two diverge, however, when a decision-maker applying yesterday's generalizations to today is faced with a recalcitrant experience—a situation in which application of the generalization to the current decision appears to frustrate rather than serve the justification lying behind the generalization. In such cases, particularistic decision-making adapts the generalization to the needs of the moment, treating the prior generalization as entitled to no intrinsic weight in the calculus of decision. Rule-based decision-making, however, rejects the continuous revisability of generalizations, and consequently imbues them with force even in those cases in which that force appears misplaced.

Once we see that decision according to rule is decision according to entrenched generalization (or instantiation), we are able to understand in a quite different way David Lyons's argument that utilitarian generalization, as well as one form of rule-utilitarianism, is extensionally equivalent to act-utilitarianism.[2] With respect to utilitarian generalization, Lyons arrives at this conclusion by taking the central point of normative generalization to be captured in a question like 'What would happen if everyone did the same?'.[3] He then focuses on the idea of 'the same', and concludes, correctly, that any action is susceptible to an immense number of logically correct but extensionally divergent descriptions (see above, Chapter 2, Sections 1 and 2). As a result, we cannot determine which actions are 'the same' by atheoretical inspection, for two actions might be

---

[2] David Lyons, *Forms and Limits of Utilitarianism*, *passim*.

[3] Formulations such as this are an established part of the literature. See, e.g., A. K. Stout, 'But Suppose Everyone Did the Same'.

the same or different depending on which of their properties was taken to constitute their description.[4] In order to determine the description of an action for purposes of locating the universe of similar actions, therefore, we need a theory to determine the *relevant* description of that action. Such a theory, according to Lyons, can be supplied (within utilitarianism) only by the principle of utility itself. That principle tells us which features of any act are morally relevant, and the resultant description of that act will include all those features that are morally relevant and none that are not. The principle of utility thus generates a *complete relevant description* of the act at issue, and other acts are 'the same' as that act only insofar as they have the same complete relevant description. It turns out, however, that the decision indicated by considering the utility of the class of all the same completely and relevantly described acts will necessarily be identical to the decision indicated by considering only the one act. Lyons concludes, therefore, that act-utilitarianism and utilitarian generalization, by indicating the same decision in every case, are extensionally equivalent.[5]

Lyons's critics have largely accepted the requirement that the act from which the generalizer will generalize must be completely described in all relevant respects. They have then sought to demonstrate that even under this condition the proof of extensional equivalence fails.[6] This dispute is tangential to the analysis of rules as entrenched generalizations, however, for what matters here is the requirement of complete description that both Lyons and his critics are equally willing to embrace.

Even if Lyons is correct in concluding that an act-based decision-making procedure is extensionally equivalent to one based on generalizations from fully described acts, that conclusion does not

---

[4] 'I flip the switch, turn on the light, and illuminate the room. Unbeknownst to me, I also alert a prowler to the fact that I am home. Here I need not have done four things, but only one, of which four descriptions have been given', Donald Davidson, 'Actions, Reasons, and Causes', 4.

[5] This precis hardly does justice to Lyons's elegant and intricate proof, but rehearsing Lyons's argument in greater detail would serve no purpose here.

[6] Most of these challenges have focused on the interrelationship among multiple agents, the consequence of which is that the complete description of a category of acts performed by a class of agents is different from the complete description of one act performed by one agent. See, e.g. Donald Regan, *Utilitarianism and Cooperation*, 95–103; Gertrude Ezorsky, Book Review; Holly Goldman, 'David Lyons on Utilitarian Generalization'; Paul Horwich, 'On Calculating the Utility of Acts'; Gregory Kavka, 'Extensional Equivalence and Utilitarian Generalization'; Harry Silverstein, 'Simple and General Utilitarianism'; J. Howard Sobel, 'Utilitarianism: Simple and General'.

entail extensional equivalence between an act-based procedure and one in which the generalizations from an act are deliberately incomplete. Consider the ambiguity of 'the same' in 'What would happen if everyone did the same?' In one sense, the one Lyons appears to adopt, the word 'same' is descriptive, used to refer to an identity that is logically and temporally prior to the act of identification. Often when we say that two particulars are 'the same', we mean, in some perhaps naïve way, that they just *are* the same. In another sense, however, the word 'same' is *ascriptive* rather than descriptive, used to mark a decision to treat as similar even those particulars that are, at least in part, descriptively divergent. In this second sense, the identification of two particulars as 'the same' is itself the act of determining that two particulars, different in some respects, will nevertheless be treated as if those differences did not exist. And in this ascriptive sense of 'same', 'What would happen if everyone did the same?' need not mean that the expanded universe of relevant acts must be identical, even within a given relevance-determining theory. Rather, the ascription of sameness might serve other purposes, and the identification of other acts as 'the same' could be consistent with either 'What would happen if everyone did *something that they perceived to be* the same?', or 'What would happen if everyone performed acts included within the same entrenched linguistic and conceptual category as the act you propose to perform?' Both of these questions prompt a generalization from a particular act, but in neither case does the generalization proceed from what Lyons identifies as a complete description. This does not show that these forms of generalization are intrinsically fallacious. What it does show is that there are forms of generalization other than generalization from complete description. Generalizations, as we have seen, commonly involve the suppression of actually or potentially relevant features of some particular, thus proceeding from something less than the complete description that Lyons takes to be axiomatic. When in Chapters 2 and 3 we examined incomplete generalization as an implement of communicative facility, we glimpsed some of the reasons for engaging in incomplete generalization. And in Chapter 7, when we explore the various reasons for having rules, we will see further grounds for treating generalization from an incomplete description as desirable. Here, however, the point is only that a strategy of generalization proceeding from a complete description of the precipitating act is only one of two approaches to generalization, and the other, generalizing from a less than complete description of the precipitating act, is not plausibly extensionally equivalent to a decision procedure focusing only on the precipitating act itself.

Lyons reaches the same conclusion about extensional equivalence with respect to one form of rule-utilitarianism, one which instructs agents to act in accordance with those rules the universal compliance with which would maximize utility. Such a rule is, according to Lyons's definition, of unlimited specificity, and he again demonstrates that an agent acting in accordance with such ideal rules of unlimited specificity will always perform the same act as will an agent who applies utilitarian principles directly to every act. Let us once again accept the correctness of Lyons's proof, and consequently let us assume that act-utilitarianism will produce the same results as decision according to utility-based rules of unlimited specificity.[7] Nor is there any reason to restrict these assumptions to questions within utilitarianism. Generalizing Lyons' proof to all varieties of rule-based decision-making, let us accept that a decision procedure directly applying ultimate justifications will necessarily produce the same results as a decision procedure applying rules of unlimited specificity which are in turn based on those same ultimate justifications.[8]

This conclusion, however, says little about the decisional import of entrenched generalizations of limited specificity. Extensional equivalence, and the consequent congruence of act-based and rule-based decision procedures, follows precisely because a conception of a rule allowing unlimited specificity, just like a conception of generalization presupposing a complete description, goes a long way towards eliminating by definition the possibility of any difference. Moreover, Lyons does not incorporate into his definition of a rule the exclusion of continuous malleability. Instead, his account of rules is largely static, viewing them through the perspective of an agent considering simultaneously what rule to adopt and what action to take. By not taking into account dynamic considerations, at the very least the temporal gap between making a rule and

---

[7] I accept this conclusion because nothing is lost by doing so. If an act-based decision procedure is not extensionally equivalent to one based on rules of unlimited specificity, then act-based and rule-based decision procedures are different, which is all I seek to show here. Thus, accepting Lyons's conclusion, despite the (in my view successful) challenges to it, entails no costs but helps understand the nature of rule-based decision-making.

[8] See also Richard Brandt, 'Toward a Credible Form of Utilitarianism', 119–23, discussing a 'specious' form of rule-utilitarianism.

applying it in a particular situation, Lyons in effect allows his rules to be crafted at the moment of application, and to be crafted in light of the application now confronting the decision-maker. Yet this crafting at the moment of decision, which amounts to the same thing as continuous malleability, excludes what we often think to be a central feature of ruleness—the way in which something from the past controls the present. If we can make a rule whatever we *now* want it to be, then it ceases to incorporate the very component that distinguishes rules from unconstrained decisions. Rules are necessarily *sticky*, resisting current efforts to mould them to the needs of the instant. By excluding this stickiness at the definitional stage, Lyons finds himself comparing two different characterizations of the same form of act-based decision-making, instead of comparing necessarily sticky rules with decision-making that does not rely on rules.[9]

In addition to eliminating by definition the temporal gap between rules and their application, Lyons dampens the difference between rule-based and act-based decision-making with the assistance of the stipulation that rules can be of unlimited specificity and still be rules. He allows, and indeed requires, his rules to be maximally relevantly specified.[10] This conception of a rule, however, just like its parallel conception of generalization, once again excludes as an alternative to act-utilitarianism a form of decision-making in which rules of limited specificity, rules themselves designed to advance utilitarian premises, are applied directly and opaquely to particular cases.[11] By showing that decision-making according to rules of unlimited specificity is extensionally equivalent to decision-making by justification alone, Lyons has in the process advanced our understanding of what a rule is. His demonstration that continuously

---

[9] See Larry Alexander, 'Pursuing the Good—Indirectly', 322.

[10] On relevant specification, see further Marcus Singer, *Generalization in Ethics*, *passim*; Jonathan Harrison, 'Utilitarianism, Universalisation, and Our Duty to be Just', 116–20.

[11] Lyons does acknowledge that one form of rule-utilitarianism is not extensionally equivalent to act-utilitarianism. This non-equivalent rule-utilitarianism selects rules on the basis of their potential *acceptance* rather than on the basis of the results they would produce under hypothetical conditions of *total compliance*. With respect to this version of rule-utilitarianism, however, Lyons argues that its desirability can be explained only by recourse to such non-utilitarian values as justice and fairness. But as others have noted, see A. D. Woozley, Book Review, 184, it is far from clear that the principle of utility cannot itself provide grounds for the adoption of intentionally oversimplified rules. This is especially true once we distinguish the question of what an agent should do from the question of what rules should be institutionalized and taught. On this distinction, see esp. R. M. Hare, *Moral Thinking*, *passim*.

malleable rules of unlimited specificity produce the same results as would be reached were there no rules at all alerts us to the possibility that continuously malleable rules of unlimited specificity may be rules only in form and not in effect. Lyons has helped us to see, therefore, that exclusion of these features of continuous malleability and unlimited specificity is necessary to the definition of the concept of a rule, or at least necessary to any definition that preserves the distinction between two extensionally divergent forms of decision-making. For once we compare act-decision-making with decision-making according to generalizations neither maximally specific nor continuously malleable, in other words once we compare particularistic decision-making with decision-making based on entrenched generalizations, we see, as I sought to show in Chapter 4, that the two are in no way extensionally equivalent.[12]

We should not, however, make too much of the role of limited specificity in distinguishing rule-based from particularistic decision-making. Although entrenching a generalization of limited specificity is a sufficient condition for the existence of a rule, limited specificity can be seen not to be a necessary condition. Suppose there existed a rule of great specificity, crafted in such a way as to incorporate within the rule every conceivable relevant distinction and qualification. Such a rule would, from the perspective of whatever background justification or justifications informed the creation of the rule and its qualifications, correctly decide every case. This rule could hardly be of limited specificity, for by definition every relevant specification has been incorporated within it. Yet even such a maximally precise rule remains vulnerable to the phenomenon of open texture. It might still turn out that some new and heretofore unexpected event arose, such that now the application of the highly specific rule generated a result inconsistent with the specific rule's background justification. In that case the question would arise whether that rule could be then modified *at the moment of application*. If the rule can be so modified, then the form of decision-making remains extensionally equivalent to decision-making according to the justifications alone. But if the rule cannot be modified in order to deal with the previously unanticipated case, then in that case

---

[12] Hare recognizes the role played by limited specificity, and offers a theory immune from Lyons' challenge. Hare, *Moral Thinking*, 35–43; id. 'Principles', *passim*. Limited specificity is also presupposed in Richard Brandt's version of rule-utilitarianism, and it too survives Lyons untouched. Brandt, 'Toward a Credible Form of Utilitarianism', 164–72. See also Kent Greenawalt, *Conflicts of Law and Morality*, 97; Robert Merrihew Adams, 'Motive Utilitarianism', 480.

there is a divergence in outcome between the result generated by the rule and that generated by the background justification. Hence, the malleable and non-malleable decision-making modes would not be extensionally equivalent, despite the fact that the original rule was maximally specific.

Thus, the absence of continuous malleability, rather than the presence of limited specificity, is the feature that is both a necessary and a sufficient condition for the existence of rule-based decision-making. Limited malleability, even more than limited specificity, is consequently central to explaining the difference between rule-based and particularistic decision-making. For any given two-level (justification and instantiation) relationship, rule-based decision-making exists only insofar as the instantiation resists continuous modification in the service of its generating justification.[13] If the fact of the instantiation offers no resistance, then decision according to the instantiation and decision according to the justification alone are extensionally equivalent. Decision according to rule, therefore, is distinct precisely because, and consequently when, instantiations

---

[13] As I explore in Chap. 6, this resistance need not be absolute. Still, if there is *no* resistance, then no instances will occur in which rule-generated results differ from justification-generated ones. For rule-based decision-making to be other than a different name for particularistic decision-making, the rules employed in the former must pre-exist any particular application of them, and must supply some resistance in that application. As a result, maintaining the distinction between rule-based and particularistic decision-making requires resisting the temptation to think of rules as incomplete prior to their specific application. Steven Burton, *An Introduction to Law and Legal Reasoning, passim*; Daniel Farber and Philip Frickey, 'Practical Reason and the First Amendment', *passim*. This claim of incompleteness, often couched as an interpretation of Aristotlelian practical reason, is curious. Inasmuch as any rule's factual predicate will subsume some specific cases, just as 'dog' subsumes Angus and 'book' subsumes this one, then no rule is necessarily incomplete. Thus, a rule is complete for those cases in which some putative specific application is subsumed under the general rule. See Richard Susskind, *Expert Systems in Law, passim*. (I do not take the word 'subsume' to entail any greater degree of logical derivation than the perhaps looser notion of an 'extension'). Some of these specific applications, however, will prompt the rule-applier to question the rule. If the rule is questioned by modifying it *after* this application, the permissibility of questioning and then modifying the rule for the *next* case is not analytically inconsistent with the rule's exercising a constraint in *this* case. But if the rule's previously assumed applicability to this case is called into question by rejecting that subsumed application in this case, the rule turns out to be continuously modifiable and thus decisionally irrelevant. Unless for some number of at least potential cases the weight of the rule *qua* rule is sufficient to carry the day even in the face of a contrary belief about how this case ought to be decided, the rule is superfluous. If a decision-maker's belief about the particular trumps the force of the rule in every case of conflict between the two, then the rule exists only as a rule-of-thumb, the effect of which I explore further in Chaps. 5.7 and 8.5.

are treated as themselves grounds for decision, rather than as merely defeasible indicators of the results likely to be reached by direct application of their background justifications.

As I explained in Chapter 4.5, rules might exist, to reiterate a heuristically simplified linear regress model of decision-making, at various levels in a hierarchy of justifications and instantiations. Some decision-making environment, for example, might contain prescriptive generalizations at four different levels, such that the decision-making environment consisted of: (*a*) a single ultimate justification; and (*b*) an array of second-order justifications that were instantiations of the ultimate justification; and (*c*) a further array of third-order justifications that were instantiations of the second-order justifications; and (*d*) a still further array of fourth-order instantiations (perhaps canonically inscribed) of the third-order justifications. In this decision-making environment, it could be the case that the fourth-order instantiations were transparent with respect to the third-order justifications, exerting no normative pressure when the results they indicated diverged from the results indicated by the third-order justifications. Were that so, then the relationship between the third and fourth levels would be rule-free. Yet it could still be that in the same decision-making environment the third-order justifications *did* exert normative pressure as instantiations of the second-order justifications, and that the second-order justifications *did* exert normative pressure as instantiations of the ultimate justification, such that at each of these levels the lower level offered resistance to direct application of the higher level on those occasions in which that direct application would have generated a different result than that generated by application of the instantiation. Were that the case, rule-based decision-making *would* exist within the decision-making environment, but just not with respect to the most specific instantiations in that system. The system, taken as a whole, would not be rule-free, for at least at some level within the environment certain otherwise desirable results would be impeded by the stickiness of lower-order instantiations.[14]

---

[14] My remarks track the perspectives of those who have commented on the role of 'dispositions' in utilitarian decision-making. See, e.g. Mill's discussion of the relation of justice to utility in Chap. 5 of *Utilitarianism*, and also Robert Merrihew Adams, 'Motive Utilitarianism', *passim*; Philip Pettit and Geoffrey Brennan, 'Restrictive Consequentialism', *passim*. My conclusions are similarly consistent with perspectives stressing the different levels of moral thinking, with intermediate principles operating in rule-like fashion. See Hare, *Moral Thinking*, *passim*; Michael Bayles, 'Mid-Level Principles and Justification', *passim*. I also take Hart to be making a similar

5.2 *The Structure of Extensional Divergence*

Rule-based decision-making is thus to be distinguished from particularistic or 'all things considered' decision-making. When the question of rules arises as part of an internal debate in the utilitarian tradition, the notion of 'all things considered' is not problematic, for the theory of value of whatever version of utilitarianism is at issue determines what is to be considered when the mandate is to consider 'everything'. The distinction between the rule-based and the particularistic, however, is not restricted to alternative forms of utilitarian decision-making. *Any* single justification, or any overarching theory or framework of justification (no matter how complex), will select an array of facts as relevant to decision-making pursuant to that justification or theory of justification, and will conversely treat the remaining features of the world as decisionally irrelevant.

Rule-based decision-making, therefore, is a form of decision-making arising *within* some theory of justification and existing only relative to it.[15] Consequently, within a theory of justification, the fact of extensional divergence entails that for some number of cases the result indicated by direct application of the theory will differ from the result indicated by a rule operating *on* that theory. A rule may operate on a theory of justification in one of two ways: The constraints of rules existing within a theory of justification may apply their force by excluding from decision-making pursuant to that theory factors that the theory would otherwise have deemed relevant, or by including within decision-making pursuant to the theory factors that it would otherwise have deemed irrelevant.

observation when, commenting on his debates with Fuller, he recognized that the meaning of a legal rule might not be solely a function of its verbal formulation, but also of its agreed upon purpose. Hart, *Essays in Jurisprudence and Philosophy*, 7–8, 106.

[15] I will use 'theory of justification' to encompass both specific justifications, such as pleasing the patrons in a restaurant or preventing unsafe driving, and all-embracing systems of justification, including but not limited to utilitarianism.

It is worthwhile repeating, however, that my analysis of rule-based decision-making presupposes some justification lying behind a rule. Consequently, my account is about a set of problems not directly touching categorical and ultimate rules of a Kantian variety, although it is certainly the case that such ultimate rules may themselves constitute the justifications lying behind lower-order rules instrumental to them. In this respect these lower-order instrumental rules may be under- or over-inclusive *vis-à-vis* higher order ultimate and non-consequential rules, but as to the ultimate and non-consequential rules themselves nothing I say here is very pertinent. When justification runs out then so too does the possibility of under- or over-inclusiveness.

We thus see rules as essentially frustrating, exercising their influence by getting in the way. They impede access to those facts that would otherwise, under a given theory of justification, be relevant to making the decision, and they interpose facts that would otherwise be irrelevant. Consequently, the effect of rules is either to truncate or to bloat the array of decision-guiding facts, and to do so in a way that is likely to appear artificial. A rule establishing a speed limit of 55 miles per hour, in order to serve the justification of reducing unsafe driving, presumptively eliminates from consideration those facts that would otherwise be relevant in the determination of unsafeness. The dryness of the road, for example, is relevant to determining safety but irrelevant determining speed. Similarly, the rule prohibiting smoking prior to toasting the Queen is presumably based on the justification of refraining from interfering with the dining enjoyment of others. Many factors might be relevant to determining whether a particular act of smoking served that justi-fication (Had everyone finished eating? Were there non-smokers at the table?), but the rule precludes consideration of those factors, substituting instead an exclusive focus on the occurrence of the toast.

In these examples rules make irrelevant some facts that would otherwise be relevant, but there are as many cases in which the opposite occurs, with rules making otherwise irrelevant facts relevant. In the toasting case, for example, the justification of maximizing the dining enjoyment of those at the table might not itself select as relevant to that justification the occurrence of a toast to the Queen, but the rule makes relevant that otherwise irrelevant fact. Similarly, the justification of ensuring safe driving would not appear to make relevant the existence of a sign on which certain numbers appear, but the rule makes relevant the otherwise irrelevant fact that a sign limiting speed to 55 miles per hour stands at a certain location.

The facts I have just been discussing are 'raw' facts, usefully distinguished from facts not about the physical structure of the world, but about the existence of some rule or principle. In decision-making environments involving multiple prescriptions, this latter variety of fact is of great importance. Rules manipulate this array of multiple prescriptions, and the ability of rules to truncate or inflate the otherwise relevant array of facts is equally at work when the facts eliminated or added are facts about the applicability of some rule. A 'Keep Off the Grass' rule renders irrelevant the Golden Rule in a walking-on-the-grass situation, foreclosing the addressee

of the 'Keep Off the Grass' rule from considering whether walking
on the grass under these circumstances is an activity that would be
precluded by the Golden Rule. Even if the 'Keep Off the Grass' rule
were the instantiation only of the Golden Rule, access to the
justifying rule would still be foreclosed by the instantiating rule.
And although 'two wrongs do not make a right' is a commonly
accepted principle, Anglo-American legal systems have rules that
in some circumstances have the effect of making a 'two wrongs do
not make a right' argument immaterial.[16]

As with raw facts, the phenomenon of exclusion of otherwise
relevant rules also has its inclusionary analogue, with some rules
making relevant other rules or principles that would but for the first
rule have been irrelevant. The 'obey the Constitution' rule, as
addressed to an American public official, makes relevant for that
official some rules, such as the rule requiring that certain government actions be preceded by notice to any affected parties and a
hearing on their objections, that that official might not otherwise
have considered relevant in determining what to do.[17]

With respect both to raw facts and to facts relating to the
existence of other rules, rules foreclose consideration of the otherwise material, and at times compel consideration of the otherwise
immaterial. In doing so they get in the way, and it is just this ability
to get in the way that produces the extensional divergence between
rule-based and particularistic decision-making.

5.3 *Raz and Exclusionary Reasons*

Although there are interesting differences between raw facts and
facts about the existence of other rules, both can be reasons for
action. Accordingly, rules can be seen to act with respect to otherwise applicable reasons for decision, a conclusion parallel to that
reached by Joseph Raz.[18] Yet if we look carefully at Raz's analysis,
we can see the way in which it remains in important ways incomplete.

Raz argues that in addition to primary or first-order reasons for

---

[16] One of these rules is the principle of *in pari delicto*, precluding recovery in some
cases in which a plaintiff is just as much a wrongdoer as the defendant. And, within
the system of equity jurisprudence, the principle of *unclean hands* serves much the
same purpose.

[17] I refer here to the requirement of 'procedural due process', a body of rules
derived by the courts from the requirement in the Fifth and Fourteenth Amendment
amendments that states and the federal government not deprive citizens 'of life,
liberty, or property, without due process of law'.

[18] Raz, *Practical Reason and Norms*, 15–84; id. *The Authority of Law*, 3–33.

action, our decisional apparatus commonly includes second-order reasons that furnish reasons to act for a first-order reason or to refrain from acting for a first-order reason.[19] Among second-order reasons are those Raz calls 'exclusionary reasons', reasons excluding first-order reasons by providing reasons to refrain from acting for those first-order reasons. To Raz a mandatory rule is the combination of a first-order reason to perform some act and an exclusionary reason excluding conflicting first-order reasons. Exclusionary reasons thus mandate for those who accept them that certain otherwise applicable reasons will be excluded from the decision-making process.

Raz's account of rules as including exclusionary reasons is largely consistent with the conclusions I have just reached. The primary inconsistency appears to be in the way in which Raz takes exclusionary reasons as incapable of override, claiming that an exclusionary reason 'always prevails' in cases of conflict with a first-order reason. Although Raz acknowledges that any number of cancelling conditions or scope-affecting considerations may eliminate direct conflict between the exclusionary reason and the first-order reason, he still maintains that an uncancelled exclusionary reason will always prevail within its ambit.

This account of the peremptory force of exclusionary reasons is at odds with my account of the way in which rules can be overridden even within their uncancelled scope by recourse to the very kinds of facts the consideration of which the rule appears to exclude. Take Raz's example of Jill, who adopts as a rule for herself that she will always spend her holidays in France, thereby excluding the possibility of acting on the reason that hotels in some other part of the world are offering particularly good deals this year.[20] All well and good, but now suppose that Jill learns that a hotel in the Austrian Alps, as part of a special promotion, is offering rooms at ten dollars per night, dramatically lower than the one hundred dollars per night Jill expects to spend in France. Under my account Jill could see this as such an obviously good deal that the exclusion of considering such factors could be overridden, even though were she to learn of a special promotion at seventy or eighty dollars per night the difference between this and what she expects to pay would not be so dramatic

[19] Raz's distinction between first-order and second-order reasons for action bears an interesting relationship (but not an identity, Raz, *Practical Reason and Norms*, 146–8) to Hart's notion of primary and secondary rules, Hart, *The Concept of Law*, 77–96, for Hart's secondary rules are defined by the way in which they determine the force, scope, operation, and existence of primary rules.

[20] Raz, 'Facing Up: A Reply', 1156–7.

as to lead her to pierce the pre-emptive exclusion of determining every year on the balance of reasons (including but not limited to price) where to spend her holiday.

By contrast, Raz appears committed to one of two views, either of which seem poorly to reflect the actual nature of exclusionary reasoning. He could continue to insist that an exclusion must 'always prevail', so that in this case Jill, by going to Austria, has simply repealed the rule. But that seems wrong, for Jill could maintain the rule, and refuse to recalculate in the closer cases, while still being open to override in the especially dramatic case. Just as one who exceeds the speed limit in order to rush an injured person to the hospital has not rejected the rule, and may very well follow it in cases of slighter but still present reasons to disregard it, so too might Jill not be rejecting the rule although acting in this case on the basis of a particularly dramatic reason not to follow the rule.

Alternatively, Raz could maintain that what looks like an override is really just outside of the scope of the exclusion. The exclusion would only be an exclusion of, say, considering low hotel prices down to fifty dollars a night, but not an exclusion of considering the price of hotels below that figure. Under this view, we mistakenly perceive an override only because our understanding of the content of the rule is too coarse. Once we see finer differences between what is within and what is outside the rule, we see that what often looks like an override is simply an instance of behavior not within the scope of the rule (or within an exception to the rule). Again, however, this account seems a poor picture of the nature of actual decision-making. Although any override can always be reformulated as outside the scope of the overridden norm, we commonly employ broader but non-absolute norms rather than narrow and intricate norms with all of the overriding possibilities already built in as caveats, qualifications, and exceptions. Again, we think the obligation to rush a critically injured person to the hospital as overriding the obligation to obey the speed limit rather than as an exception to it. Similarly, when we exclude certain factors from consideration we exclude at the wholesale level, using broad and crude exclusions but leaving open the possibility of override by particularly exigent but perhaps now unforeseen factors.

If I am correct in thinking that Jill's willingness to consider certain excluded factors when and only when they are particularly compelling is a more faithful account of the realities of decision-making, then Raz seems mistaken in failing to recognize the distinction between the idea of exclusion and the weight of the exclusionary force. Because Raz does appear to acknowledge the logical distinction between the two, it becomes clear that the difference between us on this issue turns on a question that is ultimately an empirical and psychological one. If an exclusionary reason is capable of override by a particularly compelling manifestation of the very factors that the exclusion excludes, then it must be necessary for the agent to look at the excluded first-order reason to determine whether this is one of the occasions on which the force of the exclusionary reason is overridden. But it might then seem to Raz that if the agent must look at the first-order reason, and must determine if it is to control in this case, then it has not been excluded at all. My account, however, does not see this as a psychologically impossible situation, supposing instead that there may be a difference between a careful look at a first-order reason and merely a perfunctory glimpse at it. Insofar as it is possible for an exclusionary reason to tell an agent to look just quickly, if possible, at the excluded first-order reason to see if this is one of the cases in which the exclusion of that factor should be disregarded, it changes the decision-making procedure from one in which the agent is expected to look at every first-order reason with equivalent care. Jill might, on my account, look casually at price in the normal case, relying on the force of the rule to look no harder at the effect of a somewhat low price on her final decision. But if that casual look reveals a dramatically low price, then and only then would the factor be considered as possibly overriding the rule. The rule would still have effect, for under this picture some number of cheap but not extremely cheap deals, cheap enough to tip the balance of reasons were there no rule, would still be excluded from consideration by the rule. A rule capable of override in this way, therefore, is not without consequence, even though that consequence is manifested only in some but not in all cases within the scope of the exclusion.[21]

Even apart from the question of override, Raz's account of rules as exclusionary reasons remains incomplete in several important respects. First, there is no reason to suppose that the second-order reasons must be *ex*clusionary, for, as we have seen, they can be *in*clusionary as well. Second-order reasons can act on the array of first-order reasons not only by diminishing that array, but also by supplementing it. It may seem as if second-order reasons can only

[21] Implicit in all of this is an account of presumptive decision-making, an account that is at the heart of the discussion of *presumptive positivism* I take up in Chap. 8.6.

subtract from and not add to the full array of reasons that would otherwise be part of the balance of reasons, but rules can also direct an agent to consider those things an agent would or should otherwise have ignored, such as non-utilitarian considerations for an otherwise utilitarian agent. Why and when rules *should* do this is something else again, but it seems plain, if we are only concerned with examining what rules *can* do, that we should not ignore their inclusionary capacities.[22]

Raz's conception of an exclusionary reason is also incomplete insofar as it does not address the issue of the generality of exclusionary reasons. His account is consistent with the existence of both general and particular exclusionary reasons. When a person (with authority) says to another, 'Don't listen to him', referring to some third person, this particularized command appears to fit Raz's conception of an exclusionary reason, for the command excludes the otherwise relevant words uttered by the third person from the reasons for acting considered by the addressee of the command. Still, the command is situation-specific, and appears to lack the dimension of generality we have been taking as central to understanding rule-based decision-making. Noting the way in which the particularized command is an exclusionary second-order reason and lacking in generality does not mean that rules are not exclusionary reasons. It just means that the reverse does not necessarily follow. Although all rules are exclusionary (or inclusionary) second-order reasons, not all exclusionary or inclusionary second-order reasons are rules. 'Don't listen to him' and 'Never listen to the advice of fools' are exclusionary second-order reasons, but only the latter contains the

---

[22] Raz briefly acknowledges the possibility of positive second-order reasons in *The Authority of Law*, 17 and 'Reasons for Action, Decisions and Norms, 132, accepting that there can be second-order reasons that provide reasons for acting for a reason. Still, very little in the remainder of Raz's work is devoted to the kinds of second-order reasons that would provide an agent with reasons for acting on a first-order reason that that agent would otherwise have considered irrelevant. The assymetry in Raz's focus on exclusionary and not inclusionary reasons appear to be a function of Raz's dependence thesis (Raz, *The Morality of Freedom*, 47–53), according to which the set of potential reasons is limited to those that 'already independently apply to the subjects of the directives'. If the array of reasons is so limited at the outset, as in the ethical framework within which the dependence thesis functions, then it follows that a second-order reason can only decrease the size of the so-limited array. But if the dependence thesis is not germane, as it is not in many other areas of decision-making, then there are no grounds for taking an agent's pre-rule array of reasons as constituting the largest array of reasons that that agent might potentially employ.

dimension of generality we have now seen to be a necessary condition for the existence of a rule.

Unless we draw the distinction between particular and general exclusionary reasons we will be unable to focus on an important question about the status of an exclusionary reason. The issue of entrenchment does not arise with respect to particulars, but only in the case of under- or over-inclusive generalizations. Only when we have general but not particular exclusionary reasons, therefore, is the issue posed as to whether to treat those reasons as entrenched. Suppose some exclusionary second-order reason excludes some number of first-order reasons based on the difficulty of making certain kinds of calculations under certain sorts of time-constrained conditions. A situation might arise, however, in which the exclusionary reason would by its terms be applicable, but in which the justification that generated that exclusionary reason would be inapplicable—in *this* case, perhaps, less time is necessary to make the calculation than is necessary for others of its type. Here nothing in Raz's conception of a rule as an exclusionary reason answers the question that is preoccupying us here: Will the rule, the general exclusionary reason, provide a reason to act in accordance with the mandate of the rule *even when the justification lying behind the rule is inapplicable*? To put it differently, will exclusionary reasons of general application be taken to exclude when the justifications for exclusion do not obtain? Raz's notion of a rule as an exclusionary reason helps us to understand what rules might do, but still stops short of addressing this question. Rules, consequently, must be seen not only as partly composed of second-order exclusionary or inclusionary reasons of general rather than particular scope, but also as second-order reasons whose generality is entrenched even in those circumstances in which the justification lying behind the second-order reason is inapplicable.

5.4 *Two Types of Justification*

The switch at the end of the previous section to a concern with the reason for having a rule leads to consideration of an important complication of everything that I have said to this point. Heretofore I have distinguished the result indicated by a rule from the result indicated by the justification lying behind it. That distinction, however, which suggests that particularistic or justification-based decision-making has no use for rules, is too simple. In order to recognize the way in which some decision-makers look both to the value of rules and to the particulars of the immediate case, it is necessary to draw a further distinction between two types of justification. One, which I call a *substantive justification*, establishes the background rationales or goals behind the rule. Thus the justifications I have been considering up to now, such as minimizing traffic accidents, pleasing the patrons in a restaurant, and ensuring peace and quiet in the park, are all substantive justifications. By contrast, another type of justification, which I call a *rule-generating justification*, provides the rationale for specifying the substantive justification *in the form of a rule*. Rules do not emerge from nowhere, but are created as an alternative to a direct and uninstantiated statement of the rule's substantive justification in prescriptive form, a form of decision-making that leaves the justification to do all of its own normative work. But often this alternative is not selected, and the substantive justification is instantiated in the form of a rule. That decision to instantiate the substantive justification must itself be justified, however, and this latter justification, the justification for having a *rule*, is what I call the rule-generating justification.

The distinction between substantive and rule-generating justifications exposes what appears to be a gap in my analysis. The thesis of extensional divergence between rule-based and particularistic decision-making has been based on the seemingly odd assumption that only substantive and not rule-generating justifications lie behind a rule. Thus it is now time to relax the assumption and recognize the existence of rule-generating justifications. What happens, therefore, if we think of the particularistic decision-maker as one who considers the reasons for having a rule in making the decision whether to apply the rule or its substantive justifications? And if particularistic decision-making can take the value of rules into account, is there any case to be made for decision-making in any other way?

If we acknowledge the existence of rule-generating justifications as part of the array of justifications lying behind a rule, a decision-maker consulting the justifications behind a rule finds both substantive justifications and the justifications for specifying those justifications in the form of a rule. Consequently a decision-maker deciding on the basis of this full array of justifications would be entitled in some cases to conclude that obedience to the rule itself was required even though the rule indicated a different result from that indicated by the rule's substantive justifications taken alone. The conclusion that the rule ought to be followed even though its substantive justifications would have indicated a contrary result need not be the outcome in every case. Sometimes the decision-maker might determine that the substantive justifications outweighed the rule-generating justifications when in some case the two pointed in opposite directions. When the justifications for having a rule weigh less in the balance of reasons than the substantive justifications as applied in the circumstances, the decision indicated by consulting all of the rule's justifications would be consistent with the substantive justifications, but inconsistent with the rule itself.

It now appears that the claim of extensional divergence is in danger of collapse. Under this decision procedure, application of the rule's full array of justifications not only seems highly sensible, but also appears to produce results consistent with the rule in every case in which following the rule is justified under the circumstances. The outcome indicated by direct application of *all* the justifications will thus match the outcome produced by the rule in every case except those in which the reason for having a rule at all is insufficient to overwhelm the force of the rule's substantive justifications.[23]

In order to consider this decision procedure, we need to make less abstract the idea of a rule-generating justification. Rules are commonly seen to serve the goals of certainty, reliance, and predictability (see below, Chapter 7.2). Assuming that the substantive justification for a speed limit is maintaining safety on the highways, for example, the justification for 'Speed Limit 55' rather than 'No Unsafe Driving' is that it is thought beneficial to give drivers notice of what they may do without incurring sanctions. The justification for having a rule is recognition that direct application of the substantive justification of safety would engender excess uncertainty on the part of those whose conduct is to be regulated. Now suppose on some occasion driving five miles per hour in excess of the speed limit established by the rule is as safe (and maybe even safer) under certain conditions as driving at or below the speed limit. Although direct application of the substantive justification behind the rule produces in this case a different result (no violation) from that produced by applying the rule (violation), this might not be the case when we take into account the rule-generating justification of lessening addressee

---

[23] This decision procedure also appears to call into question Raz's distinction between first-order and second-order reasons, for now the rule is like any other first-order reason to be weighed against all other first-order reasons. See Chaim Gans, 'Mandatory Rules and Exclusionary Reasons', *passim*; Michael Moore, 'Authority, Law, and Razian Reasons', *passim*.

uncertainty. When that is taken into account, it may turn out preferable on the balance of reasons to find a violation here, for failure to do so might so lessen the extent of predictability for future cases that this loss exceeds the gain from reaching the correct justification-based substantive result on this one occasion. If drivers must now continuously calculate whether theirs is a case in which the substantive justifications for not driving at an excessive speed are applicable, some people will drive in excess of the safe speed, concluding erroneously that the speed at which they are driving, although greater than that established by the rule, is not greater than the safe speed determined by direct application of the rule's substantive justification. And others will sometimes drive too slowly, worrying needlessly that they cannot drive with impunity at even the posted speed.[24]

Taking all of this into account, therefore, the particularistic decision-maker aware of the value of rules (e.g. the police officer deciding whether to stop the driver, the police officer deciding whether to let the driver off with a warning, or the judge deciding whether an offence has been committed) can now answer the question, 'Will the justification for the rule be served by applying it in this case?', by considering the effect on future conduct of deciding according to the substantive justification rather than according to the rule. Under some circumstances the result of this expanded consideration would still match the result reached upon consideration of the rule's substantive justifications alone. It might be the case, for example, that the likelihood of other people finding out about this softening of the rule was negligible, and thus the benefits of predictability would persist even were the rule not stringently applied in this case. Or perhaps predictability would indeed be diminished, yet in the particular case the disparity between rule and substantive justification was so great that the consequences of diminished predictability were outweighed by the values supporting the substantive justification. Under other circumstances, however, the inclusion of rule-generating justifications would have the effect of eliminating the space between rule and justification, for the rule's full array of justifications, now including the justification for having a rule at all, would indicate the same result as that indicated by the

---

[24] The issue is not only uncertainty in the sense of doubt, but also in the sense of encouraging a greater degree of challenge to the rule than might otherwise take place. 'The knowledge of a rule broken is the knowledge of it being breakable', E. H. Gombrich, 'The Logic of Vanity Fair', 934.

rule itself, even though the rule's substantive justifications alone would have indicated a different result.

This decision procedure appears to recognize the formal values of having rules while at the same time taking into account all relevant factors in every particular case. It is thus different both from rule-based and particularistic decision-making, and might therefore be labelled *rule-sensitive particularism*. This form of decision-making treats rules as rules of thumb in the sense of being transparent to their substantive justifications, but allows their very existence and effect *as* rules of thumb to become a factor in determining whether rules should be set aside when the results they indicate diverge from the results indicated by direct application of their substantive justifications.[25] And if we now substitute rule-sensitive particularism for the seemingly less plausible pure particularism, it appears that we emerge with a decision-making procedure that takes account of the virtues of rules without at the same time elevating those rules into an absurd position of formal importance purely for formality's sake. It may thus seem that rule-sensitive particularism, although logically different from both a pure particularism in which the virtues of rules may not be considered in the individual case and a pure rule-based model in which the value of having rules is taken to be immune from evaluation in the individual case, is so clearly superior to the alternatives that these alternatives are of no practical interest.

I want to argue that part of the apparent superiority of rule-sensitive particularism is illusory, and that there is indeed something to be said for a stronger rule-based model of decision-making in which the virtues of having rules are settled at the level of rule-making and not open for re-evaluation at the level of rule-application. Unfortunately it is difficult to make this argument without interfering with the order of the analysis, for the argument requires anticipating the discussion in Chapter 7 of the various reasons for preferring rule-based decision-making. More specifically, only when we see

---

[25] This is the form of decision-making attributed to Bentham in Gerald Postema, *Bentham and the Common Law Tradition*, 410, 446–8. It is also the form of decision-making that both Chaim Gans and Michael Moore use to criticize Raz's account of rules as second-order reasons, for under this approach the justifications for ruleness are no longer identifiable by any first-order/second-order distinction, but are instead embedded within the array of first-order reasons that a decision-maker would consult. Gans, 'Mandatory Rules and Exclusionary Reasons'; Moore, 'Law, Authority, and Razian Reasons'. Similar themes are explored in M. J. Detmold, *The Unity of Law and Morality*.

that there are grounds *other than predictability* for having rules can we see that there is much to be said for rule-based decision-making even as compared to rule-sensitive particularism. So although full development of the argument must be delayed, it is useful here to provide a bit of a preview, if only to convince the reader that taking seriously the analysis of rule-based decision-making remains worthwhile.

If the virtues of rules are seen to reside largely in the fostering of predictability, reliability, and certainty, then rule-sensitive particularism appears to take account of these virtues without committing the sin of rule-worship. That conclusion does not follow, however, if what is to be said for rules is something quite different. If instead we see rules not so much as implements for achieving predictability but as devices for the allocation of power, then it is far from clear that granting the power to a rule-applier to determine whether following the rule is on the balance of reasons desirable on this occasion is necessarily desirable. When we see rules as devices whose virtues reside primarily in decision-maker disability (and I so maintain in Chapter 7), then the difference between rule-sensitive particularism and rule-based decision-making becomes a chasm.[26] Thus if the designer of a decision-making environment is guided by a concern that certain decision-makers not make certain kinds of decisions, it appears psychologically counterintuitive (although not logically inconceivable) to authorize decision-makers to determine in each case whether this is the kind of decision with respect to which they should not be trusted. If we do not trust a decision-maker to determine x, then we can hardly trust that decision-maker to determine that this is a case in which the reasons for disabling that decision-maker from determining x either do not apply or are outweighed. Nor is the issue solely one of trust or distrust. If rules function in the service of a division of responsibility among agents or institutions, if they serve jurisdiction-apportioning roles, then rule-based decision-making can patrol the boundaries between jurisdictions in a way that no other decision-making procedure can. To have an agent operating in one jurisdiction determine if this is a

---

[26] As I explain first in Chap. 6.5 and then develop in Chapters 7 and 10, the plausibility of rule-based decision-making also increases if the standpoint from which it is evaluated is changed. From the perspective of the agent deciding what to do, anything more rule-bound than rule-sensitive particularism is difficult (although I think not impossible) to defend. But from the perspective of some society or environment deciding what institutions to establish, and whom to empower to do what, stronger commitments to rules become considerably more appealing.

case in which she should invade the decision-making jurisdiction of another is in substantial tension with the very idea of jurisdictional separation.

I will say no more now about this variety of justification, for a lengthy exploration of various rule-generating justifications would interefere with a train of argument now designed first to distinguish decisional modes, rather than providing grounds for preferring one to another. Still, once we see the possibility of justifying pure rule-based decision-making, we can see as well why a distinction of fundamental importance exists between rule-sensitive particularism and rule-based decision-making. Where rule-sensitive particularism is the governing decisional mode, nothing is removed from a particular decision-maker's agenda. Everything about this event, and about the effect of this decision on other decisions, is open for consideration by a particular decision-maker. As a result of this willingness to comprehend every relevant feature of the decision-prompting event, a form of decision-making resembling what I have called rule-sensitive particularism has traditionally been thought to be consistent with an act-utilitarian decision-making procedure.[27] In the same vein, it is understandable why Gerald Postema can maintain that something like rule-sensitive particularism is the proper way to reconcile Bentham's insistence on rules with Bentham's act-utilitarianism.[28] Postema has properly recognized that as long as the virtues of having rules can be considered as part of the relevant circumstances of each act, taking the extent to which those virtues will be served or frustrated by one decision or another *in this case* is fully consistent with an act-utilitarian outlook.[29]

[27] See Lyons, *Forms and Limits of Utilitarianism*, 119–20; Regan, *Utilitarianism and Cooperation*, 147, 169–72; J. J. C. Smart, 'Extreme and Restricted Utilitarianism', 346–8.

[28] Postema, *Bentham and the Common Law Tradition*, 445–9.

[29] Although Postema succeeds in thus reconciling Bentham's act-utilitarianism with his attraction for rules on the grounds of order and predictability, Postema has not succeeded in reconciling Bentham's act-orientation with his pervasive distrust of judges. If judges are truly to be distrusted, and if rules are one of the implements of this distrust, it is anomalous for judges to be the guardians of this distrust. As a result, someone with Bentham's distrust of judges might very well have chosen rule-based decision-making as the mode most appropriate for adjudication, although this would be inconsistent with those judges acting in an act-utilitarian mode. This inconsistency might say one of two things about Bentham's act-utilitarianism. It might be that Bentham was not really an act-utilitarian after all, at least in terms of what he thought to be the appropriate *judicial* posture, the self-understanding that judges should bring to their role. Or it might be that act-utilitarianism, even if correct as a theory of individual decision-making, is defective as a theory of institutional design. On this distinction, R. Wasserstrom, *The Judicial Decision*, is particularly relevant.

Thus, we are back where we were at the beginning of this section, although with a greater awareness of how we got there. The excursus into and evaluation of rule-sensitive particularism provides greater confidence in both the conceptual possibility and the normative plausibility of a decisional mode in which decision-makers treat the result indicated by a rule as itself a reason for action, even when that result diverges from the result that would have been indicated by direct application of the justifications lying behind the rule, and even when that result diverges from the result that would have been reached, within a given substantive theory of decision, by direct application of all relevant considerations recognized within that substantive theory of decision. This strong sense of rule-based decision-making, therefore, requires not only that rules be taken at least partially to impede recourse to the justifications behind the rule, but also that evaluating the strength of the rule-generating justifications as they apply to the instant case not be left solely to the decision-maker.

5.5 *The Suboptimality of Rules*

The emerging picture depicts rules as necessarily *suboptimal*. Rules may sometimes or frequently be good things to have, but a system committed to rule-based decision-making attains the benefits brought by rules only by relinquishing its aspirations for ideal decision-making.

What is it to say that rules are suboptimal? In many cases, indeed in most cases, the result indicated by applying a rule will be the same as the result indicated by directly applying the rule's background justifications, and even the same as the result indicated by directly applying the entire substantive theory of decision governing the decisional environment. But we have now seen that there will be some cases in which the result indicated by the rule will be inferior to the result indicated by direct application of its justification. Yet these instances will not be accompanied by any offsetting instances in the opposite direction. Although there will be occasions on which the rule-indicated result will be inferior to the justification-indicated result, there will be *no* occasions on which the rule-indicated result will be *superior* to the justification-indicated result.

Note that this is not an empirical claim but a logical one. Suppose our normative universe consisted exclusively of one ultimate justification and some number of rules designed to further that justification. What would it mean to say that a given result was best?

The only standard for measurement would be the one ultimate justification, and thus the result indicated by that justification would by definition be the best for any particular case. Consequently, any rule-indicated result diverging from the justification-indicated result would *eo ipso* be an inferior result.

Albeit with a more complex calculus, the same conclusion would emerge even within a multi-valued normative structure. If, for example, there were one ultimate justification, it would constitute the standard of evaluation for any mid-level justification,[30] and thus no mid-level justification could generate a result superior to the best result that would have been generated without it. Consequently, the injection of mid-level justifications does not change the conclusion reached in the previous paragraph—that it is logically impossible for a rule to generate a result for a particular case superior to the result that would have been generated in the absence of rules, but that it is indeed quite possible for rules to generate results in particular cases that are inferior to those generated without them.[31]

The consequences of suboptimality will not, as I have stressed, be suffered in most cases. But these consequences will be suffered in some, and thus suboptimality will be a burden in the aggregate if not in every individual case. If over a run of cases falling under a rule most results will be the same but no better than the results that would have been generated absent the rule, but some of the results will be worse than the results generated absent the rule, the aggregate results will fall short of an aggregate optimum defined in terms of the accumulation of best results in each case. Thus, for a run of cases, rule-governed adjudication will be suboptimal, failing to achieve the ideal of reaching the best result on every occasion.[32]

We know, of course, that the optimal decision *procedure* may not be the one aimed at producing the best result for each case. A decision procedure that aims to optimize in every case may be self-

---

[30] On mid-level or intermediate justifications, see above, Chaps. 4.5 and 5.1.

[31] The same conclusion would obtain even in a normative structure with multiple ultimate or irreducible values, for it would still be impossible for any rule within that intricate system to generate a result better than that that would be generated by the optimal application of the ultimate values to the particular case.

[32] 'We thus have a formal characterization of a variety of well-known phrases such as "habits", "rules of thumb", "routines", "administrative procedures", "traditions", "customs", "norms", and so forth. Each one refers to some kind of limitation on agents' flexibility to make different decisions or to use information. In contrast, a fully optimizing agent should be charged with only a single maxim: do whatever is the very best without any restriction to use any information to make any potentially beneficial decision', Ronald Heiner, 'Imperfect Decision and the Law', 236.

defeating, producing worse results in the aggregate than a decision procedure with more modest ambitions. In this sense, the theoretically optimal decision procedure may very well be suboptimal. This is where rules come in, for, as we shall explore in greater depth below (see Chapter 7.6), rules may at times represent second-best solutions, optimal in reality even though suboptimal from the perspective of an unattainable (in practice) ideal. To put it differently, rule-based decision-making can be seen to be intrinsically and logically conservative (in the non-political sense of that word), abjuring the possibility of complete optimization in an attempt to avoid disaster. When, if ever, this may be appropriate will be taken up in Chapter 7. For now all we wish to do is distinguish decision-making modes, and in pursuit of that task it is important only to identify the inevitable conservatism, the unavoidable lowering of sights, of a decision procedure premised on entrenching the generalizations of the past.

5.6 *Ruleness and Behavior*

I have referred on occasion to 'ruleness', hoping in the process to make the point that both entrenchment and the effect of rules on agents are matters of degree. This becomes more apparent when we consider rules as operating against the background of the reasons for action that would otherwise determine the behavior of some agent. We know now that rules get in the way in the sense of impeding a decision-maker from doing what that decision-maker would otherwise, all things considered, have done. Yet not all rules appear to operate in this manner. Consider some number of rules that, at least formally, govern our daily behavior. Under those rules, I am prohibited by laws against indecent exposure from appearing unclothed in public, by the rules of etiquette from eating spinach soufflé with my fingers, and by the Bible and civil law from murdering my neighbor. In like fashion I may neither molest children, nor worship an idol, nor set houses on fire, nor eat the flesh of another human being.

What all of these prohibitions have in common, at least for me, is that none of these 'prohibited' activities are ones that I have ever seriously contemplated performing. The existence of these rules, therefore, seems to have no effect whatsoever on my behavior. In this respect they are different from many of the rules of road, the requirement that I pay income tax, and the rule prohibiting me from lifting a soup bowl to my lips. *These* rules make a difference. They channel my behavior away from what it would otherwise have been, making me do things I would otherwise not do, and avoid activities in which I would otherwise have indulged.

Rules that have no effect on my behavior, such as those prohibiting cannibalism and indecent exposure, for me might as well not exist. If we were engaging in a Kantian evaluation of the moral worth of an act, we might want to inquire into what an agent would have done had that agent had different preferences, for only those actions performed for the right reasons are to count as having moral worth. But for much of everyday decision-making, rules that are congruent with non-rule-based preferences seem superfluous. Not only is it that those rules for me might as well not exist, but it is also possible that for me they *do* not exist, for, as we shall see in Chapter 6, the existence of a rule is in an important way agent-specific. True, I am a formal addressee of those rules that track my preferences, but their effect on me is entirely hypothetical. *If* I were contemplating going out unclothed or publicly eating the uncooked liver of a recently deceased human being, then I would encounter rules prohibiting what I otherwise wanted to do. But at this time these rules have no more effect on my behavior than do rules with respect to which I am not a formal addressee, such as rules applicable only to residents of Kansas, or rules contained exclusively in the Koran.[33]

None of this is to deny that many of the acts I would now not think of performing are acts that became unthinkable for me by a process of socialization that is itself substantially determined by regulative rules. I have no way of knowing whether my aversion to killing (or eating) my fellow human beings is partly a product of a network of rules, in a way that my aversion to anchovies plainly is not. Rules have undoubtedly assisted in the process by which certain activities are not ones I would otherwise consider even in the absence of a currently applicable rule.

Still, without denying the way in which rules contribute to the development of rule-independent preferences, we can still mark the

---

[33] With respect to Kansas but not the Koran, it is important to distinguish authority from geographic jurisdiction. Although I am neither a resident nor a domiciliary of Kansas, some of its laws have an authority over me I acknowledge, such as those laws that would regulate my behavior when travelling in Kansas or doing business with a Kansas company. Conversely, those who subscribe to the teachings of Islam recognize the authority of the Koran and those who do not so subscribe do not recognize the authority, but the distinction is independent of place. Thus, the coverage of a rule is only contingently related to political notions of geographic jurisdiction. See R. Lea Brilmayer, *Justifying International Acts*.

interesting distinction between rules that seem to affect, at a particular moment, otherwise eligible behavior for some agent, and rules that have no effect on that agent's behavior at that time. Because rules cover a multiplicity of instances, this distinction between currently decision-altering and currently superfluous rules can be expressed in terms of the proportion of all results generated by a rule that would have been different for a particular agent or class of agents in the absence of a rule.[34] Ruleness is a useful term to identify this dimension, to note the way in which some rules do a great deal, while others do almost nothing at all. Ruleness will be greatest where rules commend the highest proportion of extensionally divergent results for a given agent or class of agents. Conversely, the property of ruleness will diminish insofar as a rule does not indicate, for an agent or a class of agents, actions different from those the agent or agents would have performed in the absence of the rule.

Thus, it is a mistake to equate the dimension of ruleness with the dimension of specificity.[35] Some highly specific normative generalizations may not diverge substantially from their background justifications, in which case the process of specification (instantiation) adds little. Similarly, some equally specific normative generalizations may be virtually congruent with the rule-independent preferences of the class of agents to whom those normative generalizations are directed. Although it is important to recognize the way in which such rules may make a difference for some agents within the class of their addressees, it is equally important to recognize the difference of degree between rules that for an agent or class of agents make little difference, and rules that are far more normatively intrusive.

5.7 *Rules of Thumb Revisited*

At one extreme of the dimension of ruleness is the rule of thumb, the rule that does nothing at all. Rules of thumb, according to the

---

[34] I have found suggestive the discussion of 'incommensurability' in Jaako Hintikka, 'On the Incommensurability of Theories'.

[35] The mistake to which I refer is common in the legal literature, which regularly distinguishes precise rules from vague *standards* such as 'reasonable' or 'necessary under the circumstances'. But once we see that a specific rule requiring a police officer to carry a weapon in a dangerous neighborhood may be far less behavior-altering than a vague standard requiring that same officer to 'be more concerned about the victim than the perpetrator', we recognize that the impact of rules on the behavior of decision-makers is more than can be captured in a dimension of specificity and vagueness.

traditional conception I have followed up to this point, usefully identify the decision most likely to result from direct application of a justification or set of justifications, but do nothing more. A rule of thumb exerts no independent normative pressure, and if the result indicated by a rule of thumb differs from the result that would be reached by direct application of justifications that *do* exert normative pressure, then the rule of thumb falls by the wayside, contributing nothing to the decisional calculus. Rules of thumb, quite simply, do not make a difference.

Or do they? Are rules of thumb truly as normatively impotent as the traditional conception supposes? A closer look at rules of thumb gives us cause to question this long-standing view.

That traditional normative theory takes the impotence of rules of thumb as beyond question seems clear. Only rarely do we see a reference to rules of thumb that is not preceded by an emphatic 'mere', as if it were thought important to emphasize the distinction between 'mere rules of thumb' and real rules, those with the power to supply reasons for action *qua* rules.[36] Hare's pronouncements on the subject are typical: 'The term "rules of thumb" . . . should be avoided as thoroughly misleading. Some philosophers use it in a quite different way from engineers, gunners, navigators and the

---

[36] See, for example, J. O. Urmson, 'The Interpretation of the Moral Philosophy of J. S. Mill', 36: '[F]or Mill moral rules are not merely rules of thumb which aid the unreflective man in making up his mind, but [are] an essential part of moral reasoning.'; J. J. C. Smart, 'Extreme and Restricted Utilitarianism', 344: '[G]eneral rules . . . are mere rules of thumb which we use only to avoid the necessity of estimating the probable consequences of our actions at every step.'

In taking this conception of rules of thumb as the object of my discussion in this section, I specifically do not address Joseph Raz's quite different and to me unfortunately stipulative use of the term 'rules of thumb' throughout much of his work. Raz uses the term to refer to rules having much more normative weight than do the rules of thumb imagined by Urmson, Smart, Hare, and others, and in fact there is little difference in effect between Raz's rules of thumb and the stronger rules that I contrast *with* rules of thumb. Presumably Raz uses the term to contrast rules that under his service conception of authority are dependent on and serve reasons otherwise accepted by some agent from more ultimate rules of the Kantian variety, but in doing so he injects a confusion about the structure of rule-based decision-making that I choose to resist. Donald Regan's *indicator rules*, 'Reasons, Authority, and the Meaning of 'Obey': Further Thoughts on Raz and Obedience to Law', do have real weight, and are thus closer to what Raz calls rules of thumb and I call rules *simpliciter*, but Regan's indicator rules, unlike Raz's rules of thumb and my rules, always preserve for the agent the possibility of not following them when the agent determines that it would all things considered be best not to follow them on this occasion. Regan's conception of the role of rules, therefore, comes closer to (but is different from) rule-sensitive particularism, and that is a real substantive disagreement, whereas that between me and Raz is, at least on this point, almost wholly about terminology.

like, whose expression it really is, and in whose use a rule of thumb is a mere time- and thought-saving device, the breach of which, unlike the breach of the moral principles we are discussing, excites no compunction.'[37] Although I am about to take issue with Hare's conclusions, his formulation of the issue is correct. Does a rule of thumb, even as used by 'engineers, gunners, navigators, and the like', excite compunction when violated?

Hare's identification of the excitement of compunction as central properly focuses on whether a rule provides a reason for action *qua* rule. Hare appears to agree that a rule lacks normative force *qua* rule when its violation, apart from the violation of the justifications lying behind it, is normatively irrelevant. Where a rule has normative force, its existence as a rule supplies a reason for decision beyond any reason supplied by the rule's underlying justification. Thus, a rule has normative force, even if that force is not absolute, when the fact of a rule's being broken, without more, is sufficient to warrant criticism,[38] sanction, or some other negative consequence. The question, therefore, is whether rules of thumb indeed lack normative force, as Hare's account supposes, or whether some rules of thumb have normative force and thus more affinity with 'real' rules than is commonly understood.

The presence of normative force is not identified by the source of a rule. Although Rawls and others have sought to show that rules having their source as summaries of non-rule-mandated decisions are not themselves mandatory rules,[39] this claim is mistaken. It is true that rules often emerge from a process in which the rule-maker summarizes previous decisions made on non-rule-mandated grounds. Such *ad hoc* decisions are in effect direct applications of some justification or set of justifications, and are thus logically as well as temporally antecedent to the rule. Still, a series of *ad hoc* decisions may fit a pattern not identifiable at the time each of the decisions was made, and Rawls is correct in observing that some rules are constructed by just such a process of *post hoc* organization of *ad hoc* decisions.

Although Rawls and others take this summary conception of rules to define a normatively impotent rule of thumb, such a move

---

[37] Hare, *Moral Thinking*, 37.

[38] My reference to 'criticism' should not be taken too seriously. After all, we may at times wish to praise a rule-breaker. The point is only to identify the act of 'breaking' a rule, an occasion on which something, for better or for worse, has gone amiss.

[39] John Rawls, 'Two Concepts of Rules', 19–24.

confuses the source of a rule with its force. Take, for example, the prescriptive generalization, 'Don't fire until you see the whites of their eyes.' Perhaps Captain Prescott, having previously served as a rifleman, derived this rule as a summary of his own previous battlefield experiences. He may have recollected that when he fired his rifle too soon and was thus in jeopardy, he was unable to discern the whites of the enemy's eyes, and when he waited too long and was again in jeopardy, he had seen the whites of the enemy's eyes for some time. On those occasions when he had fired at just the right time, the shot had coincided with the time when he first saw the whites of the enemy's eyes.

Having made these individual calculations by himself in the past, and having then summarized them in the form of a descriptive rule, Captain Prescott might thereafter find himself in a position of authority. He could then decide to convert what had previously been his own descriptive generalization of his own previous particularistic decisions into an *order* to the soldiers under him, who would be punished for violation of the order (rule). And because Captain Prescott might not have confidence in the *ad hoc* calculations that would be made by his soldiers, or because he might not want them to waste their time even trying to make such *ad hoc* calculations, he could decide to treat all shooting at other than the whites-of-their-eyes moment as a violation of the rule, even if it could be shown that in the particular case this was not the best time at which to shoot. Consequently, the rule, summary in origin, would be fully a rule in effect, carrying with it normative force *qua* generalization even in those cases in which this generalization from past experiences was inapt. Thus, *pace* Rawls, the summary conception of rules does not entail the ability to reconsider the application of the rule in any particular case. Where the rule comes from and what it does are logically separate, and the origin of a rule, except possibly as a contingent empirical observation, offers no assistance in identifying those rules that lack normative force.

Thus, normatively irrelevant rules are not to be identified by their ancestry. Nor are they to be identified by their lack of conclusive force. The whites-of-their-eyes rule is no less a rule if one of the soldiers does not fire at the appointed moment because in doing so he would endanger a 3-year-old child who strayed on to the field of battle. Instead, normatively irrelevant rules are said to be those in which the inapplicability of the justifications behind the rule to this case renders the rule of thumb superfluous. Consistent with the

analysis we have developed, rules of thumb are said to be superfluous, and thus normatively irrelevant, when the applicability of
the justifications lying behind the rule exhausts the applicability of
the rule.

In many cases, however, rules of thumb, even the kind used by
Hare's engineers, gunners, and navigators, appear to have normative
force that is not extinguished by the inapplicability of their generating
justifications. Suppose that the whites-of-their-eyes rule has *ceteris
paribus* status. Riflemen are expected to make their own calculations
with respect to the optimal shooting moment, but should rely on the
whites-of-their-eyes rule when, all things considered, their own
calculations provide no answer. If the whites-of-their-eyes rule has
ceteris paribus status, then a rifleman who having no reason on the
basis of his own calculations to prefer one moment to another still
fires at other than the whites-of-their-eyes moment has *broken* the
rule.

Suppose instead that the whites-of-their-eyes rule has not merely
ceteris paribus status, but is instead formulated in such a way that
riflemen should fire at some moment other than the whites-of-their-
eyes moment if and only if they are *convinced* that the whites-of-
their-eyes moment is not the best moment for firing. Although the
strength of the reason necessary for disregarding the rule has been
increased, the situation is structurally analogous to the last. If the
rifleman, despite not having the level of confidence established by
the rule, adheres to his own justification-based judgement, he has
once again *broken* the rule. And the same analysis would apply if
the rule of thumb were formulated in terms of *certainty* instead of
conviction.

It is thus apparent that at *any* level of confidence, a rule of thumb
raises the confidence level required to justify taking an action other
than that indicated by the rule of thumb. Insofar as any rule,
including the type commonly described as a rule of thumb, has even
ceteris paribus force, it establishes a confidence level necessary for
taking actions inconsistent with the rule. Taking an action other
than that indicated by the rule of thumb when this confidence level
has not been reached can properly be considered a violation of the
rule of thumb.

In a world of uncertainty, decision-makers inevitably take actions
based on imperfect information. Indeed, to the act-utilitarian that is
exactly the point of rules of thumb. But if that is why we have rules
of thumb, we must recognize as well that to serve this function a rule

of thumb will ordinarily be taken to increase the burden of justification for acting inconsistently with the rule of thumb in exactly the way in which the existence of any rule increases the burden of justification for acting inconsistently with the rule. Thus, most rules of thumb are not devoid of normative force. They exert, as generalizations, normative force *qua* generalization by elevating the level of confidence necessary for taking action inconsistent with them, even when there is reason to believe, short of the elevated level of confidence, that the generalization is inapplicable on this occasion.

Not all rules of thumb need fit the model I have just constructed. I have supposed that even a rule of thumb, at the very least where the otherwise available information is inconclusive, exerts prescriptive pressure in a world of uncertainty. This conclusion is not logically compelled. There may be some rules of thumb, having only the status of descriptive generalizations, that exert no pressure even on the levels of confidence applicable to determining what to do. But such rules of thumb will be rare, for if a rule does not even raise the level of confidence necessary to take actions inconsistent with it, it is hard to see any reason for having it at all.[40]

We can now redefine a rule of thumb as a rule that is vulnerable to the inapplicability of its background justifications. A rule of thumb is potentially inapplicable if its justifications are inapplicable. But insofar as rules of thumb raise the level of confidence in inapplicability (or the level of the consequences of inapplicability) above what it would have been in the absence of the rule of thumb, rules of thumb remain structurally similar to rules that are not vulnerable to their own inapplicability but which are vulnerable to defeat or override in

---

[40] There is an intriguing parallel between rules of thumb and the reasoning process that Rawls describes as 'reflective equilibrium', *A Theory of Justice*, 20–2, 48–51. A key component of the process of reflective equilibrium is the obligation to reconsider. A decision-maker using the method of reflective equilibrium will be expected to reconsider particular intuitions in light of theory, and to reconsider theory in light of particular intuitions. Although neither particular intuitions nor theory are therefore ultimately dispositive in the decision of what to do, both influence the decisional process by mandating reconsideration. Similarly, the point I make in the text about the way in which rules of thumb elevate the burden of justification necessary to act inconsistently with them can be recast in terms of reconsideration, and a rule of thumb can be said to exert its prescriptive power by mandating at least reconsideration in those cases in which an agent would act contrary to the rule. If the agent is also perceived to have the authority on some occasions either to disregard or to remake the rule (and note in this connection the analysis of the common law in Chap. 8.2), then the back-and-forth between rule and particular is even closer to the relationship in a reflective process between theory and intuition.

the face of reasons external to what this rule is designed to accomplish.

In cases of override, we are reluctant to say that the rule (or the justification behind it) evaporates when it is overridden by a reason of sufficient exigency. The rule's insufficiency in this case is neither inconsistent with its sufficiency in others, nor with its possessing some ongoing force, or residue, even in the cases in which it is overridden. In some domains this residue triggers remorse, even as we correctly override the strictures of the rule, and in other domains it may trigger compensation. But there is still something left over when a rule is (properly) overridden.

So too, we can now see, when rules of thumb are not followed because of sufficient confidence in the inapplicability of their background justifications. This is not apparent when we are operating in the realm of single-valued moral theories (such as utilitarianism), for if the (say) utilitarian justification for the rule is inapplicable, refusing to follow the rule appears to leave no residue except for those trapped in the rule-worship castigated by many act-utilitarians. But if in some other realm we are dealing with mid-level or intermediate principles, then the values secured by rules (e.g. stability, notice, predictability, allocation of power among decision-makers) may themselves occupy a status equivalent to the status of other mid-level principles (e.g. increasing traffic safety, maximizing income, decreasing hunger). In other words, at the level of mid-level principles or dispositions, rule-generating justifications may be equivalent in importance to those substantive justifications external to this rule that may override this rule. And if this is so, then there ought to be just as much residue when a rule is not followed for reasons of the inapplicability of its own justification as when a rule is not followed because it is overridden by substantive justifications external to this rule. Consequently, if the value of having rules *qua* rules, undoubtedly a non-ultimate value, can itself be justified in terms of even deeper values, then the values served by having rules explain why rules can and frequently do have as much resistance to being rendered inapplicable by the inapplicability of their background justifications as they do to being overridden by reasons external to the rules themselves. Because this resistance appears to exist even with respect to many of the rules now commonly referred to as 'rules of thumb', there is little to distinguish the rule that is vulnerable to the inapplicability of its own justifications from the rule that is vulnerable to overriding by reasons external to that rule. In both cases the presence of the rule *qua* rule ordinarily decreases this vulnerability, and it is in this decrease in vulnerability that we find the way in which rules may provide reasons for action *qua* rules.

6

THE FORCE OF RULES

6.1 *Rules as Reasons*

Rules, we can now see, are neither entities nor properties, my earlier suggestions notwithstanding. Rather, a rule is most usefully understood as a *relationship*, or better yet, a *status*. The status of being a rule is one that may (or may not) be possessed by a general prescription *vis-à-vis* that prescription's background justification or justifications. The instantiation of any justification is a rule just insofar as that instantiation is entrenched, supplying a reason for action *qua* instantiation. When the existence of an instantiation adds normative weight beyond that supplied by its underlying substantive justifications, the instantiation has the status of a rule.[1] But still the way in which rules operate eludes us. What are the consequences of supplying a reason for action? By what means is prescriptive weight added to the process of decision-making? Just how do these phenomena make a difference, and how much difference do they make?

[1] The very idea of a reason for action has of course generated an enormous literature. See, e.g., Steven Darwall, *Impartial Reason*; David A. J. Richards, *A Theory of Reasons for Action*; Joseph Raz (ed.), *Practical Reasoning*; Donald Davidson, 'Actions, Reasons, and Causes'. Although most of what I say in this book is based on the idea of a reason for action, I nevertheless try to avoid taking unnecessary positions with respect to the nature of reasons for action. But insofar as it is not already clear, I should state that I follow Raz, 'Introduction', in being concerned primarily with what he calls 'guiding reasons', and in taking guiding reasons as facts. Thus it is the *fact* of the existence of a certain status or relationship that supplies the reason for action. This is in turn consistent with a generally internalist account of reasons for action, and the concerned reader may wish to assume that my references to reasons for action are consistent with the following definition provided by Darwall in *Impartial Reason*, 81: '*p* is a reason for S to do A if, and only if, *p* is a fact about A awareness of which by S, under conditions of *rational consideration*, would lead S to prefer his doing A to his not doing A, other things being equal.' The existence of a rule R including A within its extension is thus a reason to do A for some agent when that agent is aware of R and is led by her awareness of the existence of R to prefer A to not-A, other things being equal. Most of what I argue in this book is embedded in the previous sentence precisely because nothing in that sentence makes reference to the justification lying behind the rule, and thus the ability of R to provide a reason for A is logically independent of whether J, the justification lying behind R, also provides a reason for A.

With respect to any decision-making agent, a rule exists for that agent (a question different from the question whether some rule exists within a society or a decision-making environment) only when an instantiation provides a reason for action independent of that supplied by the instantiation's background justification. The existence of such a reason for action, however, is not indicated by mere coincidence of behavior. Following a rule requires being *guided* by that rule, for we would hardly describe the Gentile vegetarian as following the rules of the Kashruth. Thus one might be said to *follow* or be guided by a rule when and only when someone performs an act *because* the rule indicates that it be performed.

This account is inaccurate, however, for to be guided by a rule is not necessarily to act, all things considered, in accordance with the rule. Reasons for action need not be absolute, in the sense of incapable of being outweighed or overriden. I am guided by a speed limit of 55 and take that limit as a reason for driving at or below that speed even when other reasons (such as the need to keep an important appointment) guide me so much to do otherwise as to prevail on the balance of reasons. Thus whether I have a reason to ϕ, and whether I should ϕ, all things considered, are two different questions, which on occasion may generate divergent answers. We can stipulate, therefore, in what seems to follow ordinary usage, that to be *guided* by a rule requires only that the agent take the existence of a rule as a not-necessarily-conclusive reason for action, but that to *follow* a rule requires *both* being guided by the rule and acting consistent with (complying with) its indications. Compliance with a rule is therefore different from following a rule precisely because of the way in which only the latter requires guidance by the rule. Conversely, non-compliance with a rule does not presuppose non-guidance, for non-compliance may be the conclusion of a reasoning process in which a guiding reason was outweighed by other guiding reasons.

Non-absolute reasons for action are commonly referred to as *prima facie* reasons, suggesting, by this use of lawyer's terminology, that they might be outweighed or overridden by particularly exigent reasons inclining in the opposite direction.[2] This use is unfortunate, however, for it may create misimpressions about the way in which non-absolute reasons operate. As I previewed in Chapter 1.2, there

---

[2] The locus classicus is W. D. Ross, *The Right and the Good*, 19–47, discussing prima facie obligations.

is no reason we cannot just mark the difference between a reason and an absolute reason is exactly those words, without the distortions and distractions of the term 'prima facie'. What is most troublesome about using 'prima facie' as a description of non-absolute reasons is that it suggests that under some circumstances, that of being opposed to even stronger reasons, the prima facie reason might just go away. But such a characterization is misleading. Reasons, even non-absolute ones, do not evaporate when they are outweighed or overriden, any more than the security guard evaporates when she is overcome by the bank robber. It is just that the reason, like the guard, is sufficient in certain circumstances, but insufficient in others. But reasons and security guards supply *resistance* even when they are insufficient, and in each case the presence of resistance requires more force to overcome it than would otherwise have been necessary.

Moreover, the term 'prima facie' has a tendency to suggest a reason of some considerable strength.[3] In its primary legal usage, 'prima facie' represents the amount of evidence necessary in some contexts to establish the plaintiff's (or the prosecution's) case. If the plaintiff has presented evidence sufficient to establish a prima facie case, and the defendant neither overcomes any of that evidence nor successfully maintains an affirmative defense, then the plaintiff may prevail, or at least may resist a motion for a directed verdict in the defendant's favor. Yet when we speak of reasons, such a high degree of effectiveness seems reflective of only a subset of the universe of reasons. There may be moderately weak reasons which do not because of their weakness lose their status as reasons entirely. I can have a reason to act even when that reason is no more than a *ceteris paribus* reason, by which I mean that it is so weak as to determine the outcome *only* if all else is equal. Such a reason would still have an effect in those cases in which other things were equal, and thus should count as a reason, although the reason's ability to do so may not be captured by the term 'prima facie'.

The reasons I have just described, having so little weight that they matter only in the *ceteris paribus* case, mark one extreme of a spectrum of normative force. If a reason does not determine the

---

[3] The term is used in this way, to designate a rule of 'intermediary strength', in Edna Ullmann-Margalit and Avishai Margalit, 'Analyticity by Way of Presumption', 439, and Edna Ullman-Margalit, 'On Presumption', 152. Ullman-Margalit and Margalit do not, however, commit the common error of refusing to recognize the decision-guiding force of rules having weaker than intermediary strength.

result even when there are no other applicable reasons or when the other applicable reasons are so evenly opposed as to provide no reason for decision one way rather than another, then it is simply not a reason at all. At the opposite extreme, an *absolute* reason is as powerful as a reason can be. Because such a reason is by definition infinitely stringent and cannot be overridden, the very applicability of an absolute reason is conclusive or action-determinative.

The degree of normative force for any rule commonly lies between these extremes, most rules having enough power to determine an outcome even if all else is not equal, yet falling short of absoluteness. Ronald Dworkin maintains to the contrary that it is definitional of a rule that it be conclusive if applicable,[4] but this picture appears unfaithful to everyday experience. When I drive in excess of a precise speed limit in order to rush an injured child to the hospital, or when the observant Jew eats pork in order to avoid starvation, the force of the applicable rule has been overridden by more exigent considerations. Surely these are rules, if anything is, and just as surely rules are routinely overridden in circumstances comparable to those just mentioned. In these and countless other instances, the reason for action supplied by an applicable rule is not in the particular circumstances sufficient to resist the reasons for action supplied by other considerations, some of which may but need not be other rules.

Examples like these tempt us to describe the overriding factors as *exceptions* (or qualifications), and in so doing to note, following Hart, that a rule with an 'unless' clause is still a rule.[5] A rule providing that 'Driving in excess of 55 miles per hour is prohibited unless the driver is taking an injured child to the hospital' is simply not broken by someone who drives at 75 precisely for that purpose. If the observant Jew were bound by a rule prohibiting eating pork unless the eater were starving, then eating pork to avoid starvation would no more be a violation of that rule than it is stealing for someone to remove goods from a store after having paid for them. And although each of these rules contains only a single qualification, a rule would still be a rule even if its list of qualifications were considerably longer.

Yet to identify the way in which rules and exceptions are compatible is to miss the point. The primary issue, one to which I have

---

[4] Ronald Dworkin, *Taking Rights Seriously*, 22–8, 78–80. For more extensive discussion on this point, see above, Chap. 1.6.

[5] H. L. A. Hart, *The Concept of Law*, 136.

alluded earlier (see above, Chapter 5.1), is whether *additional* exceptions may be added at the moment of application, additional exceptions that then apply even to the case that generated the impetus for the exception. Suppose we now have a rule providing that, 'Driving in excess of 55 miles per hour is prohibited, unless (*a*) the driver is taking an injured child to the hospital; or (*b*) the driver is a police officer in the line of duty; or (*c*) the driver is a member of the military in the service of his or her country; or . . . *n*.' And suppose then that some occasion arises, call it *n+1*, in which all things considered it appears justifiable to permit a driver to drive at greater than 55, but that this case does not fall within any of the existing enumerated 'unlesses'. If in such a situation it is permissible to add an exception *at that time*, and if the newly added exception applies to the case at hand, then the rule turns out to be the logical equivalent of one that reads, 'Driving in excess of 55 miles per hour is prohibited unless all things considered it is proper to drive at greater than that speed', and, as demonstrated above in Chapter 5.1, *this* rule is extensionally equivalent to 'Driving in excess of the speed that is proper all things considered is prohibited.'[6] Thus the issue is not whether rules may have exceptions and still be rules, for of course they may. It is whether rules may be subject to exceptions added at the moment of application in light of the full range of otherwise applicable factors and still be rules, and the answer to that question is 'no'.[7]

[6] The conclusion of extensional equivalence assumes that the existence of grounds (all things considered) for adding an exception is a sufficient condition for adding that exception. If (see above, Chap. 5.7) on the other hand the existence of a rule raises the threshhold of justification, such that the grounds for supplanting the rule would have to be stronger than they would have had to be to dictate an outcome absent the rule, then the rule has supplied a reason in itself and the conclusion of extensional equivalence does not hold. Similarly, as Raz has argued (*The Authority of Law*, 114–15), continuously revisable rules do not collapse if the set of allowable justifications for revision is smaller than the set of justifications used in making the rules in the first instance.

[7] The point is reinforced by Quine's observation, adapted from Richards, that '[A] painter with a limited palette can achieve more precise representations by thinning and combining his colors than a mosaic worker can achieve with his limited variety of tiles, and the skillful superimposing of vaguenesses has similar advantages over the fitting together of precise technical terms.' Willard v. O. Quine, *Word and Object*, 127. Quine's point, in its greatest breadth, is that current precision is inconsistent with future flexibility, and that, conversely, we buy future flexibility only at the cost of some sacrifice in short term detail. My argument in the text, consistent with Quine's insight, is essentially that the only way simultaneously to have the maximal amount of both current precision and future flexibility is with mirrors.

There is some tension between the statement in the text and the claims of those who have identified it as a feature of *legal* reasoning that previously unrecognized

Rules thus have a dimension of weight, or a degree of resistance to being overcome, that can also be expressed in terms of a rule not being completely *defeasible*. But we must take care to distinguish two phenomena. When a rule is not applicable in those cases in which the justification *for that rule* is inapplicable, the rule becomes inapplicable by virtue of an *internal failure*. And as I have argued at length throughout this book, a rule that is inapplicable in every case of internal failure is in an important way not a rule at all. A rule is vulnerable to internal failure, therefore, when a rule is inapplicable for grounds relating only to the applicability of the justifications behind the rule itself. By comparison, rules with some resistance to internal failure, rules thus having the status I take to be a necessary condition for the existence of a mandatory rule, might still be

exceptions may permissibly be added at the moment of application. See, for example, S. C. Coval and J. C. Smith, *Law and its Presuppositions*, chs. IV–VI; J. W. Harris, *Law and Legal Science*, 5; W. Twining and D. Miers, *How To Do Things With Rules*, 216–17; A. M. Honoré, 'Real Laws', 109. Other statements to this effect are collected in Richard E. Susskind, *Expert Systems in Law*, 194–8. We can identify four possible interpretations of these claims. First, most are claims about judicial decision-making within the *common law*, a method of legal decision-making defined by the non-canonicity and continuous revisability of its rule-formulations. In this sense the claims about revisability may be descriptively correct, but if so merely shift the question to that of the status as rule-based of common law decision-making, a question I take up in Chap. 8.2. Secondly, and not unrelated to the first, the claims about revisability may understate the effect of presumptions and non-absolute rules, failing to distinguish two forms of exception-creating power. Under one form, the decision-maker has the authority to create an exception, and apply it to the case at hand, on every occasion in which the correct result, all things considered, requires the creation of that exception. Alternatively, however, the existence of the rule, while not precluding creation of the exception for this case, might still have the effect of allowing the exception to be created if and only if applying the rule to this case would constitute, all things considered, an error of particularly great magnitude. This alternative, consistent with the concept of *presumptive positivism* I set out in Chap. 8.7, retains some space for cases that would be decided contrary to the rule were there no rule, but which because of the existence of the rule will be decided in accordance with the rule. Thus, the claims about revisability that I am questioning may be using language that sounds like a description of the first alternative when in fact what those claims mean (or ought to mean) to describe is the second. Thirdly, assertions of an exception-creating power may confuse making a decision with respect to a borderline case with the creation of an exception in a case that was previously a core, or clear, or 'easy' case. This is a common confusion, often leading people to describe the legal system as more rule-based than it in fact is. I will return to this issue in much of both Chapters 8 and 9. Finally, these claims may have embedded in them quite strong presuppositions about judicial power, conflating what a rule *is* with what a judge ought to *do*. These presuppositions may be normatively appealing and empirically accurate, but it is important to distinguish them from arguments about the nature of rules. In any event, these presuppositions about judicial power are still worth bringing to the surface for closer inspection. In this regard, see below, Chap. 7.6.

subject to being overridden by particularly exigent factors external both to the rule and *its* justification. When rules are inapplicable (or, more accurately, non-controlling) on the basis of such factors not themselves a function of what this rule itself is designed to accomplish, we can say that such rules are *externally defeasible*, subject to being defeated or rendered non-controlling by factors external to the rule itself.[8]

Much of this book is devoted to the subject of internal failure, and to the proposition that rule-based decision-making and complete vulnerability to internal failure are incompatible. But for a rule to be a reason for action it must also, as we have just seen, have some degree of resistance to external defeasibility. A reason with no resistance to any other reason is no reason at all. Yet where does this resistance come from? Nothing *in* 'Speed Limit 55' or 'Thou shalt not kill' or 'No dogs allowed' specifies the weight those rules shall have in the face of competing considerations. But of course nothing in those rules specifies that they shall have any weight at all. The issue of weight, therefore, is tied up with the very issue of a rule's initial *applicability*, and it is to those issues that I now turn.

6.2 *The Roots of Normative Force*

It is a post-Wittgensteinian commonplace that rules do not determine their own application. This is true not only of non-reducible rules of language and mathematics with which Wittgenstein was primarily concerned, but also of rules that may be written *in* language, and whose ability to guide relies *on* the rules of language that Wittgenstein attempted to explain.

Any rule presents the threshold question of its applicability. Does this rule apply to this situation, to me, and to the decision that I must now make? If we look at the rule itself, what looks like an answer will be there before us. Rules necessarily specify the scope of their application since the designation of scope is part of the factual predicate of the rule. This designation of scope may not appear on the face of the rule, but if not will be either implicit or incorporated

---

[8] The distinction between internal failure and external defeasibility collapses in any single-valued justificatory system. A system of unmediated (by dispositions or mid-level principles) utilitarianism, for example, pursuant to which maximizing utility is the only guide, cannot draw the distinction between the justification behind this rule and some other reason, a distinction that supports the distinction between internal failure and external defeat.

by reference to some other rule within the same array of rules.[9] Thus a 'No Dogs Allowed' sign on a restaurant is not a universal prohibition of dogs in society, but only of dogs *in the restaurant*, with the 'in the restaurant' clause being implicit in the location of the sign (as well as in our understanding of the jurisdiction of the restaurant's proprietors, but that is getting ahead of things). Similarly, the rules of law necessarily specify the people and places to whom their requirements attach, as when an income tax provision applies only to residents and those earning money within the geographic boundaries of the taxing authority, and not to complete strangers to the jurisdiction. The tax laws of France, where I do not live and do not earn money, do not apply to me.

Designation in the rule—whether explicit, implicit, or arising from the operation of some secondary jurisdictional rule—is thus a necessary condition for the applicability of a rule. That such designation is a necessary condition for applicability, however, does not make it a sufficient condition, and at this point figuring out the issue of applicability becomes more treacherous. If the tax laws of France were specifically amended so that they *did* explicitly purport to extend their requirements to foreign residents who earned no money in France, I would still not (assuming I stayed out of France) take them as reasons for paying taxes to France. As a non-Catholic I do not perceive myself to have broken a rule by failing to attend mass, and would take that position even were the requirement of attendance to be worded so as to apply to Catholic and non-Catholic alike.[10] And consider the effect of altering the sign on the restaurant so that it read, without referring to any other rule, 'No Dogs Allowed in Any Restaurant in This City'.

Such examples show that the mere assertion of applicability is insufficient to make it so. But what is missing? Preliminarily we must distinguish applicability from *validity*, for a rule that by its terms appears applicable may still be an invalid rule and therefore inapplicable. Validity, itself a function of other rules, is thus a necessary condition for applicability. The regulations of the Interstate Commerce Commission are applicable throughout the United

[9] This is why the question, 'What is one rule?', is often complex, and one reason why the enterprise of *individuating* rules is important. See Jeremy Bentham, *Of Laws in General*; H. L. A. Hart, *Essays on Bentham*, 211–19; Raz, *The Concept of a Legal System*, 50–77, 140–7, 170–5.

[10] 'According to classical Judaism, *all* persons, and not only Jews, are under a Noachite commandment not to worship idols; such behavior is ultimately punishable by death', Sanford Levinson, 'Who is a Jew(ish Justice)?', 2369.

States not merely because those regulations say they are, but because an Act of Congress grants national regulatory authority to the Commission. Similarly, that Act of Congress is applicable throughout the United States not because it says so, but because the Constitution of the United States grants national regulatory authority over interstate commerce to Congress.

Rules are therefore ordinarily situated within hierarchical rule systems which establish, among other things, the *internal* validity of rules within those systems. We have learned from Hart's discussion of *rules of recognition*[11] and from Hans Kelsen's hierarchical analysis of norms[12] that a rule is valid just in case there is a rule within the rule system making it so. But for a rule to be valid within some rule system does not say anything about the validity of the system itself. The validity of the regulations of the Interstate Commerce Commission pursuant to a chain of validity going back to the Constitution of the United States does not establish the validity (and thus the applicability for which it is a necessary condition) of a document called the 'Constitution of the United States' *in* the United States. Why is it that the Constitution of the United States regulates the behavior of Americans in a way that the German Basic Law does not? And why is the 'Constitution of the United States' applicable *to* the United States when a document I might draft tomorrow, looking for all the world *like* a constitution for the United States, is not? Even if all the internally specified conditions of my newly written Constitution's validity and applicability were satisfied, that would not be sufficient for it to supplant the 'Constitution of the United States' as the constitution of the United States, and that is because, as elucidated by Kelsen in his discussion of the *grundnorm* and by Hart in describing the ultimate rule of recognition, the validity of a system is not a question of validity at all, but of the social fact that a certain system is treated as the law of some community by that community.[13]

To make even an external statement about validity, however, says only a little about applicability. A rule of French law specifying that I am to pay French income taxes might be both facially applicable to me and a valid rule of French law, but it does not

[11] Hart, *The Concept of Law*, 92–107, 245–7. Validity is of course not a sufficient condition for applicability, for many perfectly valid laws do not apply to me.
[12] Hans Kelsen, *Pure Theory of Law, passim.*
[13] To say that the validity of a legal system is not a question of validity is slightly misleading. Although the concept of validity is rule-based, it is not meaningless to ask whether a legal system as a whole is valid under some larger moral rule system.

follow from either of these that I will *treat* the existence of that rule as a reason for action.[14] This is the issue that Hart discusses in terms of *internalization*,[15] and we could say that an agent has an internal point of view with respect to a rule when that agent treats a rule's *existence* as relevant to the question of what to do. This makes sense if 'existence' refers to a rule's location (and validity) within a society or decision-making environment, but agents might internalize rules that do not have such a social existence, as when I make a rule for myself that I will exercise four times a week, and they might refuse to internalize rules that do, as when I treat some rule of etiquette with which I disagree as not even supplying the slightest reason for action. Moreover, even with respect to the acceptance by a society of some rule system, we are still left to contemplate why and how each of the component decision-makers of that decision-making environment internalizes the rule. It is thus circular to rely on the idea of existence as an account of what it is to internalize a rule, for as we have seen a rule exists for an agent only to the extent that that agent does treat it as a reason for action. It is thus necessary to avoid the question-begging idea of existence and say instead that an agent internalizes a rule when an agent treats a prescriptive generalization as entrenched, taking the fact of a decision's falling within the extension of that prescriptive generalization as a reason for making that decision a certain way. When an agent does so, the rule exists for that agent. Consequently, a rule is for some agent applicable to some situation when the situation is within the extension of some rule the fact of whose existence (whether social or individual) the agent treats as a reason for action.

This formulation of internalization is weaker than one possible reading of Hart's notion of *acceptance*. The word 'accept' is ambiguous, potentially encompassing not only something close to logical presupposition, but also some form of agreement with or normative commitment to that presupposition. Insofar as 'accept' suggests the latter, it seems ill-chosen, for there is no reason to

---

[14] It should be apparent that I take reasons for action to be subjective rather than objective in the sense of the distinction drawn by Thomas Nagel in *The Possibility of Altruism*. Whatever the merits of an objectivist account of moral reasons, pursuant to which only reasons that apply to all persons are legitimate reasons for action, such an account is implausible in explaining the universe of reasons, moral and otherwise. In part because of this, and in part because I take the subjective account of even moral reasons to be compelling (see the discussion of the asymmetry of authority in Chap. 6.5), I adhere to a subjective or agent-relative understanding of what it is for some fact to be a reason for action.

[15] Hart, *The Concept of Law*, 54–60, 86–8, 99–101.

suppose that one who internalizes a rule must agree with its content.[16] Indeed, internalizing a rule *qua* rule supposes that it is the rule's status as rule that is internalized, rather than the rule's underlying justifications, and thus internalization of a rule is meaningful only if the reason for action produced by the fact of internalization persists even when the agent *disagrees* with the content of the rule. Now it is clear that 'disagrees' is too strong a word to characterize what is going on when an agent is guided by a rule whose indication on this occasion is other than that which the agent would wish all things considered to do, but I put it this way only to emphasize that insofar as 'accept' connotes agreement, it is a mistaken characterization of what it is to treat a rule as a reason for action. And insofar as 'accept' does not connote agreement with the content of the rule, then the idea of acceptance adds nothing to what we say when we simply see internalization as an agent taking the existence of a prescriptive generalization as a reason for action.

Now, however, we are led to consider why an agent *should* (or does) take the existence of a rule as a reason for action? Why would an agent ever take the existence of an instantiation as entrenched with respect to its background justification, and thereby treat the fact of some act falling within the extension of that instantiation as a reason for acting in accordance with the instantiation even when the indications of its background justification appear to point in the opposite direction?

Commonly the answers to this question begin (and sometimes end) with consideration of questions of personal morality, with the focus being entirely on what the independent moral agent *ought* to do. But if we are concentrating on questions of institutional design (including but not limited to questions of institutional design from a moral perspective), then it may make sense to start not with ideal 'oughts', but with the seemingly more prudential role of sanctions and rewards. For if reasons include the prudential as well as the

---

[16] See D. Neil MacCormick, *H. L. A. Hart*, 33–40. There is a difference between my conclusions and those of both MacCormick and Raz (*The Concept of a Legal System*), who stress what Raz calls a 'detached normative statement'. It is true that Hart's notion of acceptance has no explanation for what takes place when the Gentile says, 'You shouldn't eat that!' to the observant Jew about to eat pork. But even an agent who internalizes a rule to guide his own behavior need not agree with its content. If the agent agreed with the content, it would be hard to say that the agent had internalized the *rule*, or that the rule *guided* the agent's behavior. That is why, as both Hart and Raz say, the notion of a rule is content-independent.

moral, then agents have (at least) prudential reasons for following rules if doing so brings rewards and failing to do so incurs punishment.[17] Thus even though my hypothetical rule of French law purporting to make me pay French taxes is to me and is in fact a morally outrageous rule, and thus although I might perceive myself to have no (good moral) reason to treat it as a reason for action, it is possible that if the amount of tax is small enough, and the likelihood of sanctions large enough (I might desire to travel frequently to France for holidays), then I might still have (prudential) reasons for treating the morally unjustified rule as a reason for action.

If we look therefore at prudential reasons for action, and at the connection between sanctions and such reasons, we can see that the role of sanctions is likely to be particularly large with respect to rules. The value of a rule *qua* rule, when separated from any apparent value to its addressee for what the rule requires in this case, is likely to appear so slight that it will be difficult for many agents, but for the fear of sanctions (including criticism) or the hope of rewards (including praise), to recognize it. Consequently, if some social system with the ability to do so penalizes agents for taking actions inconsistent with a set of rules even when the justifications behind those rules would be ill-served by doing so, then the agents subject to those sanctions will have prudential reasons for taking those rules *qua* rules to be reasons for action. If for example judges were routinely censured when they did not follow rules, even on those occasions when it would be best all things considered not to follow them, then judges wishing to avoid censure would have good cause to take rules as reasons for action. Moreover, if judges who were most faithful to the rules were the ones most likely to be elevated to higher positions, then the hope of this reward might for

---

[17] A focus on rewards and punishment as incentives implicates an entire account of coercion, a task I can hardly take on here. Thus I ignore, *inter alia*, empirical questions about the effectiveness of one or another form of coercion, and questions of moral theory about the circumstances under which an agent should take the morally correct action at some personal cost. Few of us would (or should) sacrifice our lives or our fortunes to keep a promise to meet for lunch, and conversely it is simply wrong to avoid saving a drowning person to avoid the expense of having one's clothes cleaned. But this is not to say that there are not difficult questions involved when the balance between the moral and the prudential is closer, nor that one cannot inquire fruitfully into the moral status of prudential reasons for action. I leave these inquiries for others, but, as the discussion here and in the final section of this chapter makes clear, I do focus on the morality of justified coercion, a topic different from that of identification of unjustified coercion. See Alan Wertheimer, *Coercion*, xi.

many judges provide the incentive for taking rules to be reasons for action.[18]

However prudentially important punishment and reward may be for most decision-makers, and however important it is to recognize that sanctions are an essential part of an account of the reasons for internalizing rules if we are adopting the standpoint either of the maker of rules or the designer of a decision-making environment (see below, Section 4), we cannot of course assume that such incentives exhaust the reasons for an agent to treat the presence of a seemingly applicable rule as a reason for action. Other agents might have reasons, still prudential but other than the avoidance of punishment or the search for reward, for making decisions simply according to the indications of some rule. Some might see rules as serving an important role in decisional simplification. I will return to this theme at the conclusion of this book, but it is worthwhile mentioning now that few of us can deploy our rational faculties fully with respect to every decision we make. Consequently we take certain families of decisions to be less important, and are satisfied simply to follow the rules without inquiring whether they accurately serve their background justifications in this instance.[19] Although a decision-maker using rules for this purpose might on some occasion fall into awareness that the rule on this occasion was inapt, and then might (or might not) set aside the indications of the rule, the rule *qua* rule would still provide a reason for action insofar as it dissuaded the decision-maker from looking behind it at all, or at least very seriously (recall the discussion of the 'glimpse' in Chapter 5.3), or insofar as it elevated the degree of assurance the decision-maker needed in order to decide contrary to the indications of the rule (recall the discussion of rules of thumb in Chapter 5.7).

Even the agent willing to take seriously a certain range of decisions, and as a result willing to try to make the best decision she

[18] Conversely, it may be the central point of Legal Realism (see below, Chap. 8.5) that legal systems exist in which faithfulness to rules on the part of judges is not rewarded and departure from rules in the service of individualized justice is not punished (in the broadest sense of punishment). Accordingly, there is little reason in such systems for judges to internalize rules *qua* rules.

[19] As Dostoevsky's Grand Inquisitor reminds us, it is by no means self-evident that an increase in the breadth of choices available to an agent produces a commensurate increase in the happiness of that agent. From that perspective we might be able to understand why it could be rational for an agent to adopt a decision procedure reducing the choices available even with the knowledge that such a reduction in choice would produce a larger than otherwise possible number of suboptimal decisions.

can on a particular occasion, may have prudential epistemic reasons for doubting her own decision-making capacities compared to those of the rule-maker. Again such a decision-maker might (or might not) reconsider that epistemic deference in particular cases when convinced her own judgement was correct, but for the same reasons as just mentioned it may be that the way in which the decision-maker considers this possibility is itself influenced by rules, and once again the consequence would be that the rule provided a reason for action by virtue of the decision-maker's distrust of her own capacities with respect to some family of decisions.

In addition to these and other prudential considerations, some agents might be guided by moral considerations, and here the questions of why agents should follow rules *qua* rules relates very closely to questions about the legitimacy of authority or about the obligation to obey the law, where such questions are defined in terms of an obligation to obey some directive independent of its content. The obligation to follow a rule is part of any such inquiry, for obeying a rule when its background justification would counsel disobedience is to treat the rule as having content-independent authority. Thus from the agent's point of view, the arguments for taking a rule to be a reason for action might stem from agreement with and willingness to co-operate in the system from which the rule emanates. By simplifying the decision process and by making certain results salient even if suboptimal, rules may assist in the solution of Prisoner's Dilemma or co-ordination problems, or assist in other dimensions of co-operative enterprises, and thus an agent with a reason to participate in and assist in the effectiveness of some co-operative enterprise would have a reason for following rules emanating from that enterprise.[20]

[20] On these issues, see, for example, John Finnis, *Natural Law and Natural Rights*; Friedrich Kratochwil, *Rules, Norms, and Decisions*; Raz, *The Morality of Freedom*; Philip Soper, *A Theory of Law*; Ullman-Margalit, *The Emergence of Norms*; Finnis, 'Law as Co-ordination'; id. 'The Authority of Law in the Predicament of Contemporary Social Theory'; Gerald Postema, 'Coordination and Convention at the Foundations of Law'; Raz, 'The Obligation to Obey: Revision and Tradition'; Donald Regan, 'Authority and Value: Reflections on Raz's *Morality of Freedom*'; id. 'Law's Halo'; Noel Reynolds, 'Law as Convention'. I do not mean to suggest more agreement than exists among those who have written in this tradition. First, there are those who are sceptical of the ability of the co-ordination perspective to provide a reason for following authority. See, for example, Leslie Green, 'Law, Co-Ordination and the Common Good'. And such perspectives fit within a tradition of denying that there is any obligation, even prima facie, to obey the law *qua* law. See A. John Simmons, *Moral Principles and Political Obligation*; M. B. E. Smith, 'Is There a Prima Facie Obligation to Obey the Law?' Even among those who recognize

The agent trying to do the right thing might also take rules as reasons for action on the basis of considerations that are simultaneously moral and epistemic. That is, if an agent doubts that she is best situated to know what to do, these doubts about her own knowledge of the good as it applies in this case might lead her to defer to rules set forth by some rule-maker she believes is likely to have superior moral knowledge and judgement.[21]

I will say no more here about the various reasons why an agent would take a rule to be a reason for action, but I will return to these ideas, more from the perspective of the agent as designer of a decision-making environment, in Chapter 7. For now it is sufficient to note that regardless of *why* an agent might treat the existence of a rule as a reason for action, it remains the case that the process of taking a rule to be applicable depends not only on the rule's own designation of applicability, even presupposing internal validity, but of something external to that rule and to the rule-system of which it is a part. To say that a rule exists for any agent is thus to say that that agent treats the rule, for non-rule-based reasons of the kind just sketched, as supplying a reason for action. And to say that a rule exists within some decisional environment is similarly to say that the decision-makers in that environment, again for ultimately non-rule-based reasons, treat the rule as relevant to the decisions they are called upon to make.

6.3 *Internalization and Weight*

Although the decision of any agent or set of agents to internalize a rule is thus a function of something outside the rule itself, this 'something' may operate not only to determine whether a rule is applicable, whether I as a non-Catholic am bound by those rules of Catholicism purporting by their terms to bind me, but also to determine certain characteristics of the rule itself. The process by which rules are internalized need not be limited to determining that

the ability co-ordination concerns to generate reasons to follow rules or authorities, some, such as Finnis, take this as sufficient to establish an obligation to obey the law, while others, such as Regan and Raz, reject these implications. Although I return to these themes in Chapter 7, little in this book requires that I resolve these controversies.

[21] Such considerations are at the heart of Raz's 'service' conception of authority. Raz, *The Morality of Freedom*. The ideas set forth by Regan in 'Law's Halo' and 'Authority and Value' are also epistemic and service-oriented, although Raz and Regan disagree about whether an agent who relies on an authority solely for epistemic reasons is 'obeying' in any interesting sense. See Regan, 'Reasons, Authority, and the Meaning of "Obey" '.

certain rules should always or never be treated as reasons for action. Internalization might instead involve the adding of content to some written or otherwise socially existent rule such that written rule R is internalized by some or many agents as R'.

Most commonly, such supplementation in the course of internalization will involve determining what weight some rule or array of rules will have in the calculus of decision.[22] In the opening section of this chapter I explored the question of weight, considering the varying weights that rules might have. But where does this weight come from? What distinguishes an absolute 'No Dogs Allowed' rule from a 'No Dogs Allowed' rule that is merely presumptive? Occasionally the weight of a rule is specified in the rule-formulation itself. Some rule might say 'Driving in excess of 55 miles per hour is prohibited except in cases of emergency', where the very term 'emergency' suggests a rule of great weight but not in its own terms absolute. 'Driving in excess of 55 miles per hour is prohibited except in cases of emergency' is very different from 'Driving in excess of 55 miles per hour is prohibited except when the balance of reasons would indicate driving at a different speed', for the former creates a class of cases in which the balance of reasons would indicate driving at a speed greater than 55, but as to which the standard of 'emergency' is still not met.

Such specification of weight could still be explicit even if it did not appear in the same *rule fragment* as the primary prohibition.[23] Some part of the traffic code other than the designation of speed limits might make all of the rules in the code overridable in the event of emergency, or an overridability provision (or any other weight-determining standard) might be a component of another rule existing within the given decisional environment. More interestingly, such weight-determining standards, applicable to all or part of some

---

[22] Note that the process of internalization need not itself be anything other than a particular act at a particular time. Internalization may be situation specific rather than rule-based, or it may be an instance of a more general rule of internalization, such that the internalized rule is treated as applicable because it is a member of a larger class of rules that are to be treated as applicable. Thus, the process of internalization need not be rule-based in my sense of rule. To speak of 'rules about rules', following Hart, overstates the case, for outside the structure of a legal system there are interesting cases of 'acts about rules'.

[23] I use the term 'rule fragment' to denote one of the problems of individuating rules, problems explored by Bentham in *Of Laws in General* and by Raz in *The Concept of a Legal System*. What looks like a rule in some system of rules may not be a complete rule without incorporating seemingly distinct jurisdictional or similar rules found elsewhere within the rule system.

decision-making environment, might not be canonically articulated at all. Were all the relevant rule-appliers within a decision-making environment to treat the rules within that environment as over-ridable, then those rules *would* be overridable, even though the rules as canonically inscribed incorporated no provisions for over-ride.[24]

Where the weight-determining standard does not appear in canoni-cal form, however, it is less likely to be uniform throughout a decision-making environment. *I* might choose to treat the speed limit rule as conclusive even though I know that others will not, and even though I know that the enforcing authorities will treat it as overridable as well. Internalization—determining whether, the extent to which, and the way in which a rule provides a reason for action—is located initially and primarily within individual decision-makers. Patterns of internalization across numerous decision-makers may of course develop, or be inculcated by education, or be enforced by sanctions. But the way in which and the extent to which, if at all, rules become a part of a decisional process is ultimately determined by the decision-maker alone. The necessary implication of this is that a general prescription like 'No Dogs Allowed' or 'Honor Thy Father and Thy Mother' or 'Speed Limit 55' could be taken by its addressees and its enforcers to be either a mandatory rule or a truly unweighty rule of thumb, with nothing in the canonical form of the prescription dictating one of these options rather than the other. Something *about* a rule and not the rule itself determines not only what weight the rule will have, but whether it is even a rule at all.

6.4 *The Asymmetry of Authority*

By focusing on an agent's reasons for internalizing a rule, and by stressing the (non-exclusive) role of sanctions within the array of such reasons, I mean to redirect philosophical treatment of the problem of authority. Existing analyses of authority start, correctly,

---

[24] Similarly, it is conceptually open to all or most of the decision-makers in some environment to treat canonical prescriptive generalizations as largely transparent rules of thumb rather than as mandatory rules, and it is quite possible that American appellate judges, at least as compared to judges in many other countries, have done just that, the result being that the same set of words might have dramatically different effect, and thus be dramatically different rules, depending on the decision-making environment in which they were applied and enforced. On the British/American comparison in this regard, see Patrick Atiyah and Robert Summers, *Form and Substance in Anglo-American Law*, *passim*; Dworkin, 'Political Judges and the Rule of Law', in *A Matter of Principle*, 9–32.

from the premise that authority is, in the terminology of Hart and Raz, content-independent. Authority exists when and only when the source of a directive provides a reason for the addressee to follow it independent of the content of that directive.[25]

Because authority is content-independent, its presence makes a difference only when the subject of the authority disagrees with the content of an authoritative directive. Though an authoritative directive may give a subject an additional reason to do what she would otherwise have done, authority exerts its true decisional bite when the subject would not otherwise have conformed to the content of the directive. Thus when the directive is a rule, the problem of authority arises when the subject is convinced that the rule indicates an incorrect result on this occasion, and perhaps even a result that the rule-maker herself would not have reached were she here making the decision. From the standpoint of the subject, therefore, the authority of the rule appears least rational when the subject is asked, solely because of the existence of the rule, to perform an act the subject is convinced ought not to be performed, or not to perform an act the subject is convinced ought to be performed.

Although any *defence* of authority will be a defence of the rationality of compliance on at least some such occasions, I want now to assume the soundness of the arguments *against* authority.[26] I therefore want to assume that it would be an irrational rule-worship for a subject to follow a rule when, *all* things considered (including epistemic, co-ordination, and Prisoner's Dilemma reasons for following the rule) the subject is convinced that the rule should not be followed in *this* case. I make this assumption in part because the arguments may indeed be sound, but mainly because it is the most rigorous assumption for what it is to follow. If authority is asymmetric, if the lack of a (good moral) reason for obeying authority does not entail the lack of a (good moral) reason for imposing it, then, *a fortiori*, the practice of imposing authority, and

---

[25] I use 'directive' rather than 'rule' because, as shall presently become clear, it is important to begin the immediate argument with the particular and only thereafter move to the general.

[26] In varying degrees of stringency, and with varying qualifications, some of the works in this tradition include Richard Flathman, *Political Obligation*; Simmons, *Moral Principles and Political Obligations*; Robert Paul Wolff, *In Defense of Anarchism*; Regan, 'Law's Halo'; id. 'Reasons, Authority, and the Meaning of "Obey" '; Smith, 'Is There a Prima Facie Obligation to Obey the Law?'; Richard Wasserstrom, 'The Obligation to Obey the Law'.

of enforcing compliance with rules *qua* rules, can be seen as sometimes justified both if the argument against obedience is valid and if it is not.

According to the argument against authority, the rational subject is justified in refusing to follow an allegedly authoritative directive when the subject is convinced, all things considered, that it would be best not to follow the directive. Donald Regan argues, for example, that there is no good reason for an agent to stop at a red light in the middle of the desert when she can see and is thus convinced that there are no cars for a mile in any direction, assuming that this isolated and unknown to others act of non-compliance does not weaken the agent's resolve to comply with those laws the compliance with which would have good consequences. It may be, Regan argues, that the very existence of the directive *indicates* to the agent the possibility of an intrinsic reason for compliance (perhaps the light is there because drivers at that location are likely to misperceive the absence of traffic), but this reason is only epistemic, capable of dropping out when there is sufficient cause to believe its epistemic indications inapt on this occasion.

But now let us look at the question from the standpoint not of the subject but of the imposer of authority (or the designer of some decision-making environment). Suppose the imposer of authority is just as convinced that the subject is mistaken in believing she is not mistaken as the subject is convinced that she is correct. In that case it would appear that the rational imposer of authority ought to try to prevent non-compliance just as strenuously as the subject would try not to comply.

Suppose a parent tells her child that he should go to bed tonight at 9 p.m. The child, desiring to stay up until 10 p.m. for the purpose of helping a friend with his homework, concludes that, all things considered, it is morally preferable to disobey. But if the parent is equally convinced that helping the friend is not nearly as beneficial to the friend as the child thinks, and that disobeying on this occasion is more causally connected with future and less-justified cases of non-compliance than the child supposes, then the parent might conclude that, all things considered, the child should go to bed at 9 p.m. in this case. Here we can say that, from the child's perspective, non-compliance is justified if the child is convinced that, taking everything (including the superior knowledge and experience of the parent) into account, it would be preferable not to comply, and we can without any inconsistency also say that, from the parent's perspective, requiring compliance is preferable if the parent is convinced that, taking everything into account, compliance on the part of the child is the optimal outcome. If under these circumstances compliance by the child (as seen by the child) is indefensible except as blind obedience, then so too is tolerating non-compliance by the parent (as seen by the parent) indefensible except as equally blind acquiescence. Given that the question of authority arises in an interesting way only when there is disagreement between authority and subject, the rational authority is led to attempt to require obedience just as the rational subject is led to disobey.

This asymmetry between the irrationality of obedience from the subject's perspective and the rationality of requiring it from the authority's is equally at work in the case of rules as it is with particular commands. Because rules are necessarily made in advance of their application, a subject of a rule at the time of its application by that subject will consider the possibility that this instance lies in the area of under- or over-inclusion, and that consequently (remember, we are assuming the validity of the argument against authority) this is a case in which the rule should not be followed. From the perspective of the authority-rejecting subject, therefore, particular applications are either ones in which the rule's justification is applicable and the rule should thus be followed, or in which the rule's justification is inapplicable and the rule should thus be ignored.

In every case of rule application, however, we can imagine (and we will see why we should in a moment) the possibility that the rule-maker (the authority), were she present, would herself have a view about whether this application did or did not reflect her justifications in setting forth the rule. Consequently, four different possibilities are available: (a) The subject will believe that in this case the rule should be followed, and the authority, if present, would agree. (b) The subject will believe that in this case the rule should not be followed, and the authority, if present, would agree. (c) The subject will believe that in this case the rule should not be followed, and the authority, if present, would disagree. (d) The subject will believe that in this case the rule should be followed, and the authority, if present, would disagree.

At the time of making the rule, the authority can eliminate from consideration the first two possibilities, for both involve congruence in judgement. Where that is the case the issue of authority does not arise.[27] But the authority also sees down the road the possibility of disagreement represented by the third and fourth categories. Suppose the authority predicts that the incidence of the third will be greater than that of the fourth, that from the perspective of the authority there will be more cases of mistaken non-following than of mistaken following. If this is so, then the actual occurrence of a case of mistaken non-following will represent the future manifestation of the case of the particular directive—a case of disagreement in which the rational subject disobeys and the rational authority takes steps to keep her from doing so.

The process of rule-making can be seen as the prior anticipation of just these kinds of situations. The rule-maker adds sanctions for violating the rule (and thus furnishes prudential reasons for following the rule) even under circumstances in which the subject perceives it to be best, all things considered, to violate it, and even when it *is* best, all things considered, to violate it, for otherwise there would be little reason for the subject to obey in those cases in which the subject believes, *erroneously*, that this is a case in which violation is justified.

Obviously there is a price to be paid for such diminution in subject error, a price in terms of the suboptimality resulting from discouraging subjects from disobeying rules when, speaking optimally, it would be best if the subjects disobeyed. But if the authority predicts that the cases of erroneous disobedience will outweigh (in number, or, more precisely, in expected consequences) the cases of justified obedience, then the rule-maker will wish to stifle disobedience *simpliciter*. In other words, even accepting that it is irrational rule-worship to follow rules when it is best, all things considered, not to follow them, it is still rational for the authority, in advance, to encourage (by sanctions or otherwise) the very rule-worship she would avoid were she the subject. Rule-worship, however irrational from the standpoint of the subject, is something the rational authority may seek to inculcate.[28]

To put the matter somewhat differently, the question of authority arises only when there is disagreement between authority and subject. If when there is such disagreement the subject makes the

[27] Actually it does, for, as we saw in distinguishing being guided by a rule from following it, congruence in outcome does not presuppose congruence in the reasons generating that outcome. But for the sake of simplicity I have eliminated that complication here, and nothing turns on it.

[28] On the strategic inculcation of suboptimal rule-worship, see R. M. Hare, *Moral Thinking*; Larry Alexander, 'Law and Exclusionary Reasons'.

decision she thinks best all things considered, then in those cases the authority should also make the decision *she* thinks best all things considered. But if we are talking about rules, the question for the authority arises prior to any particular occasion of disagreement, and arises from the expectation by the authority that in the future there will be cases in which the subject will *mistakenly* attempt to substitute her judgement for that of the authority. Predicting such occurrences, the authority makes in advance the best all things considered decision not by creating a procedure in which the subject will be free to make mistakes, but instead by creating a procedure in which the subject will be dissuaded from exercising that subject's best (but expected to be mistaken) judgement.

If authority is asymmetric in this way, then the rule-maker's task is often one of inducing a rule-applier or rule-subject to relinquish her best judgement. This might be done either with punishment or reward, and the positive or negative sanctions can be applied in one of two ways. First, the rule-subject could be punished in any case of rule-violation, including those violations that appear *ex post* to have been for the best. But, however effective this approach might be in discouraging the imposition of expected-to-be-mistaken judgement, it may be difficult to carry out in practice insofar as many potential punishers may find it difficult to punish an act that can now be seen to be correct all things considered. Alternatively, therefore, punishment, but punishment of special severity, might be imposed only in cases in which a rule-violation was *ex post* not best all things considered. This form of extreme negative sanction (and all of what I say applies, *mutatis mutandis*, to rewards), in effect a surcharge for exercising judgement, will likely produce in the rational punishment-avoiding subject the necessity of a high degree of certitude before contravening the indications of the rule, and thus in some number of cases subjects will not violate the rule when *they* think it is probably but not certainly best to do so. This alternative, avoiding some of the weakness of the will problems stemming from the difficulty of punishing the agent who has behaved correctly all things considered, might be more precisely tailored to produce in the subject the desirable degree of distrust of her own judgement.

Sanctions are not the only way for a rational imposer of authority to induce hesitation in those whose well-intentioned contraventions of rules are expected to be more often mistaken than wise. A different process, education in the broadest sense, could inculcate rule-following values. This process is partly education in the formal sense, but is also a function of whom a society glorifies and whom it scorns, who is promoted and who is passed over. I will say no more about this here, but it should now be clear that rules will at times be reasons for action for reasons that are, from the agent's perspective, prudential, but which prudential reasons are based in turn on not-necessarily-prudential reasons for having and enforcing rules from the perspective of either the rule-maker or the designer of some decision-making environment. The question of why to have rules is thus different from the question of why to follow them, or even why to take them seriously, and this is the subject of the following chapter.

7

THE REASONS FOR RULES

7.1 *The Argument From Fairness*

The preceding chapters have, I hope, painted a clear picture of rule-based decision-making. Yet that picture is hardly an attractive one. The decisional force of a rule has been seen to reside in the entrenchment of an instantiation of a background justification. Where there is entrenchment, agents decide (or have a reason for deciding) in accordance with the indications of the instantiation even when doing so produces results divergent from and inferior to those that would be produced by direct application of the background justification. Rule-based decision-making thereby entails an inevitable under- and over-inclusiveness, and accepting a regime of rules necessitates tolerating some number of wrong results— results other than those that would have been reached by the direct and correct application of the substantive justifications undergirding the rule. If rules therefore get in the way, if they doom the decision-making of today to the categories of yesterday, and if they mandate the unattainability of excellence in decision-making, then what is to be said for them?

Rules are often promoted as an element of fairness. According to a common account, decision-making according to rules of necessarily general application is at least part of what fairness, and justice, are all about. Indeed, the association of the idea of justice with the generality of rules seems captured by the simple stricture, 'Treat like cases alike.' To fail to treat similar cases similarly, it is said, is arbitrary, and consequently unfair and unjust. We achieve fairness by decision-making geared towards consistency across a range of decisions, with rules as the instruments of that end. Because rules are general and consequently impersonal, so the argument goes, rule-based decision-making becomes a way for decisions to turn on *what* you are (or what you did) and not on *who* you are. Rules stand as obstacles to particularization, and hence the acontextuality of rule-based decision-making is under this account a virtue. The argument from fairness as an argument for rule-based decision-making, therefore, appears to emanate from an even larger normative principle of consistency.[1] It is not without interest that the Golden Rule is just that—a rule; and Kantian themes about universalizability similarly call to mind the generality associated with rules.[2]

Although the generality of rules may at first appear to be an instrument of sameness and therefore of consistency, it turns out upon closer inspection that neither the principle of consistency nor the argument from fairness have the ability to generate a self-sufficient argument for rule-based decsion-making. We know now that the essence of rule-based decision-making lies in the way that rules, as generalizations, suppress differences that in the circumstances of application *are then relevant*. If 'No Dogs Allowed' is justified by the goal of minimizing annoying disturbances, entrenching the generalization 'dogs' suppresses a likely relevant distinction between seeing eye and other dogs. When a 55 miles per hour speed limit seeks to promote safety by sanctioning all who exceed that speed, it suppresses an otherwise relevant difference between a wet road and a dry one. Rules have bite when they ignore differences that are then relevant, consequently treating as alike some cases that are not alike at all. Moreover, rules at times draw distinctions that are in the circumstances irrelevant, so that rules also at times treat differently cases that are actually alike.[3]

When we entrench a generalization, therefore, we do not further the aim of treating like cases alike and unalike cases differently. On the contrary, it is *particularism* that recognizes relevant unalikeness, drawing all the distinctions some substantive justification indicates ought to be drawn. And it is particularistic rather than rule-based decision-making that recognizes all relevant similarities, thereby

---

[1] Consistency can have both a spatial and a temporal dimension. Often we express the spatial dimension in terms of 'equality', and the temporal in terms of 'precedent', yet both equality and precedent, by mandating a similarity of treatment of potentially dissimilar cases, and by mandating the neglect of potentially relevant differences, can be seen as but variations on the basic theme of a rule as an entrenched normative generalization.

[2] On universalizability, see, e.g., R. M. Hare, *Freedom and Reason, passim*. Similar themes are captured in the Rawlsian veil of ignorance (John Rawls, *A Theory of Justice*, 136–42), which, premised on ignorance, is rule-like in its heuristic suppression of real differences.

[3] The entrenchment of distinctions is especially apparent when values change over time. A rule-based approach would recognize more distinctions between, say, men and women than would a particularistic decision procedure able to adapt more smoothly to the rejection of the substantive basis for some number of previously drawn distinctions.

ensuring that substantively similar cases will in fact be treated similarly.

The claim that the generality of rules serves to treat like cases alike is thus seen to be hollow. When rule-based decision-making prevails, what increases is the incidence of cases in which relevantly different cases are treated similarly, and not the incidence of cases in which like cases are treated alike. As we shall see, there are sometimes good reasons for treating different cases alike and like cases differently, and rules can play a large role in serving those reasons. But if cases are actually alike under a substantive theory of decision, we do not need rules to treat them similarly. And if cases are unalike under a substantive theory of decision, then not only do we not need rules to treat them as unalike, but the existence of rules may prevent us from doing so.

Thus there is nothing essentially *just* about rule-based decision-making.[4] There is no reason to believe, and much reason to disbelieve, that rule-based decision-making is intrinsically more just than decision-making in which rules do not block a decision-maker, especially a just decision-maker, from considering every factor that would assist her in reaching the best decision. Insofar as factors screened from consideration by a rule might in a particular case turn out to be those necessary to reach a just result, rules stand in the way of justice in those cases and impede optimal justice in the long term. We equate Solomon's wisdom with justice not because Solomon followed rules in resolving custody of the baby, but because he came up with exactly the right solution for that case. Frequently the goals of justice are served not by the rule-followers, but by those whose abilities at particularized decision-making transcend the inherent limitations of rules. If we are searching for arguments to support rule-based decision-making, therefore, we will have to search elsewhere than in the moral force of consistency, fairness, or justice.

7.2 *The Argument From Reliance*

Arguments for rule-based decision-making have traditionally focused on the ability of rules to foster the interrelated virtues of reliance, predictability, and certainty. According to such arguments, decision-makers who follow rules even when other results appear preferable enable those affected to predict in advance what the decisions are likely to be. Consequently, those affected by the

---

[4] For other arguments seeking to distinguish rule-following from justice, see Duncan Kennedy, 'Legal Formality', *passim*, and Judith Shklar, *Legalism, passim*.

decisions of others can plan their activities more successfully under a regime of rules than under more particularistic decision-making. Though no one word fully captures these virtues, 'certainty' has stronger connotations than are necessary for the point to hold, and 'predictability' has value only insofar as it facilitates reliance. As a result I will refer to this argument as the *argument from reliance*.

Understanding the force of the argument requires distinguishing two types of decision-maker. One is the rule-enforcer, empowered (see below, Chapter 8.1) to punish those who break rules and bestow rewards on those who follow them. The other is the primary addressee of a rule, also a decision-maker in the sense of deciding if a rule is applicable and then deciding whether to follow it if it is. Although those who enforce rules and those to whom they are addressed are both decision-makers, the virtues of reliance are premised on the existence of potential action by someone other than the relier, and the argument from reliance thus presupposes a commonality of understanding between the relying addressees and the enforcers on whose actions reliance is placed.

Reliance is possible just because someone affected by a rule-enforcing decision can predict the outcome of that decision prior to its making. Rules can foster reliance, therefore, only insofar as a number of interrelated conditions are satisfied. First, the relying addressees must be able to identify certain particulars as instances of a given category. If the rule is 'No dogs allowed', then addressees must be able to identify *this* dog as a dog. When there is a comparatively stable understanding that this particular is a such-and-such, and as a such-and-such is a member of the category specified in the rule, less potentially variable judgement clouds an addressee's determination that this rule applies to this particular.[5]

In order for the addressee's assessment to translate into a prediction of a rule-enforcing decision, it must also be that rule-enforcers will apprehend those particulars as being members of the same category apprehended by the addressees, and will be seen as so apprehending by the addressees. That is, addressees of the rule will perceive Angus as a dog, rule-enforcers will perceive Angus as a dog, and addressees will know that rule-enforcers will perceive Angus as a dog.

---

[5] This point is but an application of the argument in Chap. 4.1 that the very idea of a rule presupposes the ability to recognize the extensions of words, phrases, sentences, and other items of language.

Reliance thus requires that a rule encompass a category whose membership, at least with respect to some number of cases, is substantially non-controversially shared among the addressees of the rule and those who enforce it. In addition, the goals of reliance can be served only when rule-enforcers enforce a rule according to its terms, or at least according to other rules whose content is known to the addressees of the primary rule. Only if the consequences specified in the consequent of a rule are as accessible as the coverage specified in the factual predicate can the rule produce predictability as to its enforcement.

Rules are not the only device by which people predict and thus rely on the actions of others. Consequently the ability of rules to foster more predictability and more justified reliance than would otherwise have been present turns on the simplifying properties of rule-based decision-making, on the way in which the commonality of classification and outcome that make reliance possible are more likely present with fewer possible outcomes and fewer and larger classificatory categories. Rules assist reliance by providing this simplification, and also by providing a public categorial designation, such that the likelihood of divergent categorization by enforcer and addressee diminishes when both are looking at the same rule. What is a harmless pet to me may be a smelly nuisance to you, but we can still both agree that it is a dog.

Rules thus have their greatest marginal advantage when addressees and enforcers have (or can be predicted to have) different outlooks on decisions while still sharing a common language. When addressees and enforcers employ more or less the same pre-rule categorial apparatus, and have more or less the same normative views about how the items in certain categories should be treated, rules become less important, merely reinforcing the pre-rule ability of agents to predict how other quite similar agents will behave. When the other agents are not similar, however, but still as speakers of a common language attach a similar array of extensions to the same terms, rules employing that common language can increase the ability of addressees to predict the enforcement decisions of otherwise dissimilarly situated enforcers.

Although rules can thus increase the ability to rely on the decisions of others, the value of reliance is neither transcendent nor free from conflict with other values. Still, the ability to rely appears plainly, *ceteris paribus*, desirable. Part of this is the psychological value of repose. I simply feel better knowing that the letter carrier will come at the same time every day, that faculty meetings will not be scheduled on short notice, and that April brings the opening of the baseball season. And although some of what accrues to me from this knowledge is tangible and plainly consequential—I can do things I could not otherwise have done if I do not have to worry about mandatory meetings called on short notice—much is simply a function of the psychological limits of uncertainty. This obviously varies among individuals, for some have much greater tolerance for uncertainty than others. Still for most of us one component of psychological well-being is having at least some idea of what tomorrow will look like, and continuously confronting the abyss of uncertainty is something few of us can manage.

More commonly, however, the value of reliance is tangible. When I know what is going to happen, I can plan accordingly and thereby do things I could not otherwise have done. Thus the ability to predict the sanction-imposing decisions of others opens up otherwise less available options for action. If the penalty for speeding is severe and if I am risk-averse, I will likely drive faster under a regime of 'Speed Limit 55' than if I am required simply to 'Drive Safely'.[6] Predictability of legal enforcement of contracts, wills, trusts, and other legal instruments is often the only thing that makes the transaction possible.

Although the ability to predict and then rely on the decisions of others has undeniable value when viewed in isolation, decision-making environments can offer predictability only by diminishing their capacity to adapt to a changing future. Since following a rule may produce a suboptimal decision in some particular case, the question of the comparative value of rule-based reliance is the question of the extent to which a decision-making environment is willing to tolerate suboptimal results in order that those affected by the decisions in that environment will be able to plan certain aspects of their lives.

When so reformulated, it becomes clear that the force of the argument from reliance will vary across decision-making environments. More specifically, and even apart from any inter-personal or inter-institutional variance in the value of reliance, the costs

---

[6] Others may have a different reaction, and would drive more quickly under a 'Drive Safely' regime than under a 'Speed Limit 55' regime. This disparity does not defeat the point in the text, but only illustrates the way in which rule-based decision-making is inherently conservative, and thus more appealing to risk-averse agents, or risk-averse decision-making environments, or decision-making environments that have determined to be risk-averse about certain subjects.

of suboptimality cannot be expected to be constant. First, the *frequency* of those suboptimal results will vary from environment to environment. To evaluate the cost to be paid in order to attain the benefits of predictability, it is necessary to gauge how often the entrenchment of generalizations would prevent making optimal decisions on the basis of those case-specific facts that would be dispositive in the cases in which they arose. This is just another way of saying that the cost of predictability is measured in terms of the potential relevance of facts suppressed (or irrelevance of facts highlighted) by the factual predicate of the prevailing rule. Plainly this is a difficult assessment, for it depends on the ability to forecast a future array of decision-prompting events. Yet even putting aside the ever-present difficulty of predicting the future, the degree of expected factual variance will not be constant across decision-making environments, simply because some parts of the world are more regular than others. Where the world is regular, however, the necessity of rules to harness that regularity will be minimal. Only when factual variance is large are rules likely to be needed in order to ensure predictability, but those are the very cases in which the costs of ensuring predictability will be greatest. The marginal gains in reliance that come from imposing rules on a decision-making environment will thus be greatest where gross rather than fine factual predicates are employed to suppress what would otherwise be a wide range of decisionally relevant factual variance. The frequency of suboptimal decisions, therefore, will be highest in those cases in which the predictability advantages of rule-based decision-making are likely to be largest.

The price of fostering predictability is a function not only of the frequency of suboptimal decisions, but also of their *consequences*. The issue is one of expected costs, the frequency of suboptimal decisions times their magnitude, where the magnitude of a cost is the degree to which a suboptimal decision falls short of the decision that would have been made were all relevant facts taken into account to reach the best decision under the circumstances. Again it is impossible to generalize across decisional domains about the magnitude of these costs. When Justice Louis Brandeis of the Supreme Court of the United States noted, in the context of the related topic of precedential constraint,[7] that 'in most matters it is more important that the applicable rule of law be settled than that it

---

[7] I discuss the relationship between rules and precedent at some length in Chap. 8.4, and also in Frederick Schauer, 'Precedent', *passim*.

be settled right',[8] he reminded us that the argument from reliance is premised on the virtues of reliance for its own sake, independent of the correctness of the decision on which reliance is placed. But the other side of the issue is that sometimes it is more important that things be settled correctly than that they be settled for the sake of settlement. To take an extreme example, if the sentence of death were imposed in accordance with accessible rules strictly applied, people (including those contemplating committing capital crimes) could predict with some confidence which acts would generate the death penalty. That predictability, however, would come only at the risk of putting to death some people who would live if their particular acts were scrutinized in the full richness of relevant detail. On the other hand, many rules involving the formalities of contracts, wills, trusts, and real estate transactions are premised on the assumption that the costs of a mistaken decision are comparatively minor, at least when compared to the enormous virtues of predictability, without which few contracts, wills, trusts, or real estate transactions would ever be consummated.

Thus, the relative benefit of predictability, and therefore the relative force of the argument from reliance, is irreducibly a question of comparing costs and benefits. The psychological and tangible value of justified reliance for the expected array of reliers must be weighed against the expected costs of suboptimal decisions for those affected by them. Because the product of this calculation will vary with the nature of the decision-making domain, the identity of the decision-makers, the type of decisions expected to be made, and the interests of those affected by the decisions,[9] it is no surprise that the force of the argument from reliance is in the final analysis highly context-dependent.

In saying that the soundness of the argument from reliance is context-dependent I do not mean that it varies from case to case. That is so, but it is meaningless to say that we can redesign a decision-making environment for every decision. The very idea of a decision-making environment presupposes a design transcending the individual decision. Thus context-dependence means only that

---

[8] *Burnet* v. *Coronado Oil & Gas Co.*, 285 US 393, 406 (1932) (Brandeis, J., dissenting). To the same effect is *Sheldon* v. *Goodrich*, 8 Ves. 481, 497, 32 Eng. Rep. 441, 447 (1803) ('better that the law should be certain than that every judge should speculate on improvements').

[9] Nor do I suggest that the issue is determinable in any precise or mathematical way. The expected value formulation is designed to express a relationship rather than call for a numerical calculation.

the virtues of reliance come at the price of disempowering some array of decision-makers, and that the consequences of disempowerment are a function of the type of decisions those decision-makers do and do not make. We know that situations arise in which putting this particular into that category and producing the result specified for that category seems to the rule-applier to be wrong—something about this particular warrants different treatment. *This* vehicle is merely a statue, emits no fumes, makes no noise, and endangers no lives; it ought to be treated differently from those whose characteristics mesh with the justifications lying behind the 'No vehicles in the park' rule. Accepting the argument from reliance, however, requires that the difference be ignored, for to acknowledge this difference is also to create the power, the *jurisdiction*, to determine whether this vehicle or that vehicle actually serves the justification behind the rule. It is the jurisdiction to determine that only some vehicles fit the justification behind the rule that undermines the confidence that *all* vehicles will be prohibited, and that consequently undermines the ability of the addressee of the rule to predict that *this* vehicle will be prohibited. No longer is it the case that anything that is a *vehicle*, an arguably stable and accessible category, is excluded from the park. Instead, the category of particulars excluded from the park is now the category of *vehicles whose prohibition will serve the justifications of the 'No vehicles in the park' rule*, a category less stable, less mutually and consistently accessible to rule-enforcer and addressee, and thus less able to serve the goals promoted by the argument from reliance.

The key to understanding the relation of rules to reliance is consequently the concept of decisional jurisdiction.[10] The issue is not merely whether prohibition of the statue/vehicle serves the purpose of the 'No vehicles in the park' rule. It is also, and more importantly, whether giving some decision-maker the jurisdiction to ascertain the rule's purpose (as well as the jurisdiction to determine whether some particular fits that purpose) injects a possibility of variance greater than that involved in giving that decision-maker the jurisdiction solely to determine whether some particular is or is not a vehicle. To repeat, this is not to say that increasing the possibility of variance is, all things considered, a bad thing. Increasing the

---

[10] On jurisdiction in this sense, the classic is John Rawls, 'Two Concepts of Rules'. Also exploring the same idea are Charles Fried, 'Two Concepts of Interests: Reflections on the Supreme Court's Balancing Test'; Schauer, 'Slippery Slopes'; id., 'Formalism'.

possibility of variance is the only way to increase sensitivity to the complexity of a changing world. But that virtue is in irremovable tension with the countervailing virtues of reliance, and an increase in sensitivity can thus come only by a commensurate decrease in the ability on the part of addressees to predict and thus to rely on what rule-enforcers are likely to decide.

The jurisdictional question has a double aspect. The increase in variance that comes with a grant of jurisdiction is at times a consequence of the range of equally correct decisions that might be made in the exercise of that jurisdiction. If there is neither an authoritative statement of nor widespread agreement about the purpose behind the 'No vehicles in the park' rule, the grant of jurisdiction to determine that purpose would allow a decision-maker to decide whether it was to preserve quiet, lessen air pollution, or prevent accidents. Given the stipulated absence of either an authoritative statement of the purpose (which might then itself *be* the rule) or some general agreement about what the purpose is (which might then also be the rule), each of the three proffered purposes would be equally correct, for each could quite plausibly explain and thus justify the rule itself.[11] As a result a recurring concern is with the extent to which some determinations may have a wider degree of *permissible variance* than others, where that wider range consequently decreases the ability of those affected by and thus relying on a decision to predict what it will be.

In addition to increasing the range of correct (or at least not incorrect) decisions, certain grants of jurisdiction increase the likelihood of *erroneous* determinations. Compare 'No vehicles in the park' with 'The park is closed to vehicles whose greatest horizontal perimeter dimension, when added to their greatest vertical perimeter dimension, exceeds the lesser of (*a*) sixty-eight feet, six inches, and (*b*) the greatest horizontal perimeter dimension, added to the greatest vertical perimeter dimension, of the average of the largest passenger automobile manufactured in the United States by the three largest automobile manufacturers in the preceding year'. This second rule has no more inherent variance than the

---

[11] This assumes that the rule does not incorporate a *historical* test of purpose. Were it the case that a rule's purpose was, within some decision-making environment, taken to be coextensive with the specific intentions of those who wrote it, there *might* be a smaller array of potential purposes for any rule, although epistemological problems of locating the original purpose, as well of problems involving multiple authors (such as exist within a legislature), might still produce some disagreement. I explore these issues further in Chap. 9.4.

'No vehicles in the park' rule, and indeed has less, insofar as has a smaller range of fringe cases around a non-controversial core.[12] Nevertheless, it seems plain that the second increases the likelihood of *computational error* on the part of an expected array of decision-makers, and when the likelihood of decision-maker error is increased, the ability of a rational addressee to predict those decisions is decreased commensurately.

From the perspective of the argument from reliance, the cases of computational error and permissible variance are equivalent. The ability to rely is logically distinct from the soundness of the decision on which reliance is placed, and thus the argument from reliance is separate from arguments going to the quality or correctness of the decisions made. But increasing the likelihood of decision-maker error, computational or otherwise, is disfunctional not only because it diminishes the possibility of reliance. Though consistency in error serves the value of reliance every bit as much as consistency in correct decision-making, errors are usually harmful in themselves apart from the way in which they make it more difficult to rely on those who commit them. The argument from reliance stresses values that are associated with consistency for consistency's sake, but reveals as well the limitations of that perspective. In addition to increasing the predictability of decision-making, rules may at times increase the quality of decision-making by diminishing the quantity of errors. I will turn to those arguments in Section 4 below, but first we must examine another argument for rules that, like the argument from reliance, purports to identify virtues independent of the quality of the decisions reached.

7.3 *The Argument From Efficiency*

When a rule is but a (pure) rule of thumb with no decisional weight *qua* rule, or when there are simply no rules to consult, the conscientious decision-maker looks at each decision-prompting event in as much relevant detail as the event offers. But when a decision-maker decides according to rules and therefore relies on decisions made by others, she is partially freed from the responsibility of scrutinizing every substantively relevant feature of the event. It is true that in the final analysis the decision to treat a rule *as* such is for the decision-maker, and thus every decision presents the

---

[12] On core and fringe applications of rules, a subject I take up at length in Chap. 9, see H. L. A. Hart, *The Concept of Law*, 119–50; id., 'Positivism and the Separation of Law and Morals', 607–12.

choice whether to follow even a plainly applicable rule.[13] Still, individual decision-makers use rules to allocate their own decision-making resources and systems employ sanctions to induce their decision-makers to leave certain decisions to others; for when a decision-maker follows a rule she no longer examines every facet of the decision-prompting event with the same degree of care she would have employed had there been no rules. In this way rules allocate the limited decisional resources of individual decision-makers, focusing their concentration on the presence or absence of some facts and allowing them to 'relax' with respect to others. At times a rule removes so many factors from consideration that a decision-maker may relax almost completely, making decisions that require virtually no effort whatsoever. Sometimes this frees decision-makers to do other things, and within the larger decision-making environment may eliminate duplication of effort. The result of this, it is often argued, is greater efficiency in decision-making, a goal generating the *argument from efficiency* as an argument for rule-based decision-making.

Manifestations of the efficiency of reliance on rules are all around us, but we may fail to recognize them precisely because of the role that rules play. It is just because reliance on rules eliminates the necessity of making some kinds of investigations and calculations that often we do not consider the kinds of investigations and calculations that would otherwise have been required.[14] Our lives proceed more efficiently because by relying on posted speed limits we spend less time calculating how fast to drive, in the same way that the observant Jew is relieved by the rules of Kashruth from having to train herself as a biologist just to know which foods to eat and which to avoid. And in cultures in which a particular style of

---

[13] See Kennedy, 'Legal Formality', 380–91. Kennedy's point, consistent with the argument in Chap. 6, is that decision-makers such as judges must necessarily make their own decisions whether to treat the rules written in lawbooks as the ones they will employ in reaching a decision. This question, ultimately the question of examining the *self-understanding* of judges and other decision-makers, seems also to undergird much of the enterprise in Ronald Dworkin, *Law's Empire*.

[14] As Alfred North Whitehead wrote, 'It is a profoundly erroneous truism, repeated by copy-books and by eminent people when they are making speeches, that we should cultivate the habit of thinking what we are doing. The precise opposite is the case. Civilization advances by extending the number of important operations which we can perform without thinking about them', *An Introduction to Mathematics*, 61. (I am grateful to Neil Cohen for bringing this quotation to my attention.) See also Stephen Holmes, 'Gag Rules, or the Politics of Omission'.

dress is mandatory (e.g. grey flannel suits for business; gowns at high table; no white shoes before Memorial Day), a common argument for those rules is precisely that they eliminate the calculations, the anguish, and the expenditures that would otherwise be necessary, thereby freeing time, money, and mental space for more worthwhile endeavors.

Similar considerations apply to more formal decision-making environments. When judges in courts of law are channelled by relatively precise rules into deciding cases on the basis of a comparatively small number of easily identified factors (Was the defendant driving faster than 55 miles per hour?; Did the plaintiff become ill after consuming a product manufactured by the defendant?), the entire proceeding is streamlined, requiring less time and evidence than would have been necessary under a more rule-free procedure in which a wider range of factors was open for consideration (Was the defendant driving safely? Was the plaintiff's illness caused by the defendant's negligence?). A rule-based system is consequently able to process more cases, operate with less expenditure of human resources, and, insofar as rule-based simplicity fosters greater predictability as well, keep a larger number of events from being formally adjudicated at all. The greatest streamlining, after all, comes when a defendant, charged with driving at 63 miles per hour on a clear dry day with little traffic, nevertheless still simply sends in the fine rather than arguing that she should not be punished because she was not driving unsafely.

As with the argument from reliance, I am taking care to treat efficiency as a value independent of the value of simplified procedures in diminishing the number of decision-maker errors. This is not because reducing decision-maker error is unimportant. Quite the contrary, it is often the most important argument for rule-based decision-making, and one I discuss at length in the following section. But I postpone that discussion precisely because it is important to isolate the way in which efficiency might be fostered by rules despite the lack of any special fear of decision-maker error. Even if a decision-maker freed to look for unsafe driving rather than driving in excess of a certain speed would always make the right determination, even if a judge would always correctly identify negligence, and even if an observant Jew would always correctly determine which foods were unclean, a rule-based system would still result in less time and less effort by these decision-makers, freeing their resources for other tasks.

Like the argument from reliance, it is hard to fault the argument from efficiency as an abstract proposition, for the efficiency fostered by rule-based decision-making would seem to benefit any decision-making environment. But that kind of efficiency could, as Richard Wasserstrom has noted, also be served by a procedure that made decisions 'by the toss of a coin or the cast of a die'.[15] Wasserstrom's extreme case highlights a concern similar to one that arose in the context of the argument from reliance. Efficiency stems from and thus comes at the price of precluding decision-makers from investigating factors that might, for the particular case, have been dispositive. Rule-based decision-making thus achieves its efficiency by increasing the likelihood of a wrong result in any particular case, and over time increasing the incidence of such wrong results.

Assessing the costs and benefits of rule-generated efficiency will again vary among decision-making environments. At times rules will promote efficiency by eliminating duplication of effort, withdrawing from reconsideration by the rule-applier issues that have already been considered by the rule-maker. This is hardly cost-free, however, for the rule-applier would otherwise have had the opportunity to consider in particular context an issue that the rule-maker could consider only in more abstract categorial form. Yet as long as in most cases the result of the particular analysis will be the same as that of the abstract, duplicating the process will in that majority of cases amount to a duplication of effort, much as there is duplication of effort when the second bank teller repeats the calculations of the first in order to identify the one in a thousand mistake. And as with the case of recalculation, the benefits of particularistic decision-making will turn on whether the occasional error discovered and corrected is worth the time expended on a process most of which is merely duplicative.

Alternatively, efficiency may be manifested simply in the desire to make the greatest number of decisions in the shortest period of time, so that time and resources are released for other tasks. Decisional resources can be as scarce as others and like others might be allocated at times to tolerate speed and quantity with attendant errors, and at other times to search for accuracy by sacrificing speed and quantity. When simplifying rules are the basis for decision, investigation of factors screened off from consideration by the rules is rendered unnecessary, producing the benefits familiar in any

[15] Richard Wasserstrom, *The Judicial Decision*, 73.

environment where the same comparatively simple task is performed repetitively.

Generalizing in any interesting way about the costs and benefits of rule-based efficiency is even more difficult than with respect to reliance, for the value of efficiency is itself dependent on the otherwise available uses for the saved decisional resources. Where there are valuable alternative uses for those resources, the argument from efficiency is more attractive, often sufficient to warrant tolerating some number of suboptimal results. But where decisional resources are not scarce,[16] or where there are few attractive alternatives for the use of those resources, then it is less likely that the benefits of efficiency will outweigh the costs necessarily involved in any decision-making procedure that disables itself from seeking the optimal resolution on every decisional occasion.

7.4 *Two Types of Error*

Thus far I have focused on but one type of error—the error that is the consequence of the inevitable grossness of rules. By truncating the array of facts to be considered, rules commit a decision-making process to some number of errors, an error being defined as a result other than that indicated by direct particularistic application of a background justification or theory of justification. These errors are not a function of mistakes that decision-makers may make, but instead are generated by decision-makers faithfully and accurately following the rules. The errors are produced not by decision-makers but by life, for life, unlike the factual predicate of a rule, is probabilistic and not universal, variable and not fixed, fluid and not entrenched. As the complexity of experience clashes with the simplicity of a rule, errors are produced even when rules are applied conscientiously.

Although these errors are defined in contrast to an optimal application of the justifications lying behind a rule, the reference to 'optimal application' signals another type of error, the avoidance of which provides a strong argument for rule-based decision-making. When decision-makers not shackled by rules are thus empowered to inquire into every factor that could lead to the best decision for a

---

[16] Moreover, it may be that decision-making is best viewed not as a resource to be expended, but as a skill to be honed. If that is so, and if like golf or a foreign language decision-making improves with practice, then any process that reduces the occasions of decision-making may also reduce the quality of decision-making, even apart from the necessary proportion of suboptimal results generated by rule-based decision-making.

particular case, they simply might not make that best decision. Freed to look at everything, decision-makers often use that freedom unwisely, employing the factors that *could* produce the best result to produce instead something inferior to it. Unlike the errors that are an inevitable consequence of even a correct application of oversimplifying rules, the errors we must now address are those that arise from an incorrect application of a theoretically optimizing particularistic decision-making procedure.

When free to take all relevant factors into account, decision-makers can err in numerous ways. In Section 2 above I referred to computational error, but that is merely one member of the larger class of failures of understanding. There are only so many factors that people can be expected to take into account, and the more that are part of the decision-making process, the greater the likelihood of confusion, miscalculation, or misunderstanding as numerous factors are evaluated and weighed.[17] Moreover, it is often the case that specialized training or education makes some people better able than the rest of us to evaluate certain factors. When those without that training or education are nevertheless put in positions in which they are required to take those factors into account, errors in application are to be expected. Consider the typical police officer trying to evaluate in a particular case the full array of constitutional doctrines pertaining to search, seizure, interrogation, and confession; or the typical construction worker attempting to calculate the torsional stress that a particular steel beam can bear under certain architectural and atmospheric conditions. In these and countless other situations, we sense that particularistic decision-making will produce not more sensitivity to the nuances that separate one instance from another, but rather simply more error.

Although some errors are the product of simple lack of understanding, others are less benign. Often we fear that some class of decision-makers, whether through unconscious bias or conscious ill-will, cannot be trusted to take certain types of factors into account. An instructive example is the United States Supreme

---

[17] On the relationship of rules to the limitations of human capacity to comprehend complexity, see Hare, 'Principles'; Gregory Trianosky, 'Rule Utilitarianism and the Slippery Slope'. Similar perspectives can be found in the economic and decision theory literature. See James G. March and Herbert A. Simon, *Organizations*; Simon, *Models of Man*; March, 'Bounded Rationality, Ambiguity, and the Engineering of Choice'. Also of relevance are Charles E. Lindblom's *The Intelligence of Democracy* and 'The Science of Muddling Through'.

Court's decision in *Palmore* v. *Sidoti*.[18] The case involved a custody dispute between divorced parents, both of whom were white but one of whom had subsequent to the divorce married a black man. The question presented was whether the reality of prejudice, manifested in potential discrimination against the child of an interracial couple, was relevant in determining which custody arrangement was 'in the best interests of the child'.

The Supreme Court's decision that the fact of an interracial marriage could *not* be considered is a typical example of the fear of error through bias. Although there may be cases, perhaps including this one, in which a conscientious and sensitive decision-maker would make the optimal decision by taking this factor into account, there are likely even more cases in which a decision-maker, empowered to consider the racial identity of any of the participants, will be guided by racial hostility and so make the wrong decision. Thus when rules are designed to constrain police officers as they interrogate suspects, the constraining rules reflect not only the worry that various procedural and constitutional complexities are beyond the understanding of those without legal training, but also the fear that the nature of the police officer's role will cause certain factors to be undervalued. Whether the cause be bias or the less invidious difference of perspective that is a consequence of role differentiation, we suspect that police officers will under-assess the decisional import of those factors aimed specifically at the protection of suspects and defendants. We simply do not expect the police officer to value defendant's rights as much as they would be valued by an ideal decision-maker, any more than in a sporting event we would expect referees appointed by the home team to make as few errors as a less partisan official.

The design of a decision-making environment must thus take into account not only the possibility of errors of under- and over-inclusion emanating out of a faithful application of rules in the face of an unpredictable reality, but also the errors likely to be made by less than Solomonic decision-makers when, released from rules, they are empowered to apply background justifications directly to the cases they have to decide. When fear of this latter type of error predominates, rules are employed to lessen decision-maker error by limiting the ability of decision-makers to take into account a full range of potentially difficult and complex considerations. Rules

[18] 466 US 429 (1984).

sometimes simplify decision-making by excluding from the calculus of decision specific factors likely to be misapplied by some class of decision-makers, substituting cruder but less likely to be abused factors. At other times rules are used less discriminately, serving as the instruments of wholesale decision-making simplification in an effort to minimize decision-maker error. In either case the result is similar. Instead of allowing decision-makers to scrutinize a large, complex, and variable array of factors, rules substitute decision based on a smaller number of easily identified, easily applied, and easily externally checked factors. When decision-makers follow such rules, their opportunity to stray is reduced, and thus the proportion of decision-maker errors is smaller than had the decision-makers more freedom to attempt to make what they perceived to be the best decision, all things considered, for the case at hand.

The two types of error are interrelated, for the attempt to decrease the incidence of errors of under- and over-inclusion will likely increase the probability of decision-maker mistakes, and conversely an attempt to decrease decision-maker mistakes by limiting discretion will entail building into the process a higher likelihood of errors of under- and over-inclusion. Consequently the design of any decision-making procedure involves an assessment of the comparative frequency and consequences of the different errors. Where decision-makers are likely to be trusted, and where the array of decisions they are expected to make will contain a high proportion of comparatively unique decision-prompting events with serious consequences if they are decided erroneously, we might expect the rule-based mode to be rejected, or at least its stringency tempered. But where there is reason to distrust a set of decision-makers with certain kinds of determinations, and where the array of decisions to be made seems comparatively predictable, errors of rule-based under- or over-inclusion are likely to be less prevalent than decision-maker errors, and consequently the argument for rules will be stronger.

Rule-based decision-making is thus an application of the theory of the second-best. When we design real decision-making institutions for real decision-makers, the optimal decision *procedure* for an aggregate of decisions is sometimes one that abjures the search for the optimal in the individual case. With some frequency, decision-making institutions designed to make the best decisions in each particular case produce an incidence of errors higher than that which would have resulted from decision procedures with more modest ambitions.

Decision-making institutions usually involve multiple decision-makers, so that the design of decision-making procedures imposes one decision-making mode on a multiplicity of decision-makers, not all of whom have the same perspective or abilities. When we choose rules, and thus when we choose the option of the second-best, we focus on the worst of any array of decision-makers, for we worry more about decision-maker error than about the errors that are built into the rules themselves. Consequently, the choice of rule-based decision-making ordinarily entails disabling wise and sensitive decision-makers from making the best decisions in order to disable incompetent or simply wicked decision-makers from making wrong decisions. Conversely, a decision procedure that avoids or diminishes the constraints of rules empowers the best decision-makers to make the best decisions, and accepts as a consequence that the same procedure also empowers less than the best decision-makers to make some number of less than the best decisions. A 'best case' perspective is necessarily averse to rules, for rule-based decision-making cannot produce the best result in every case. But a 'worst case' perspective is likely to embrace rules, recognizing that guarding against the worst case may in some circumstances be the best we can do.

A worst case or second-best perspective on decision-making can both reflect and generate a particular evaluative attitude towards decision-makers. Though we usually laud the Solomons whose ability to make the right decision in the right place transcends the constraints of rules, we sometimes condemn even more those whose violation of accepted rules does not turn out as well. When the level of condemnation for erring as a result of evading an applicable rule is greater than the level of condemnation for erring as a result of following some rule, the disparity reflects a contingent presupposition that the problem of careless non-compliance is thought greater than the problem of careless compliance. When such an attitude prevails, those who make mistakes by following rules are treated better than those who make mistakes of equivalent magnitude by breaking rules. Defending one's errors by reference to rules is often a successful strategy, in part because when one makes an error by following a rule, at least part of the responsibility can be attributed to (or blamed on) the rule-maker, whereas the rule-breaker has no such easily available blame-sharing option. To the extent that errors committed in the pursuit of rules occasion less individual blame than errors committed in violation of rules, following rules may be the strategy of choice for the risk-averse *individual*, as well as being the strategy of choice in the design of a risk-averse decision-making environment.

At other times or in other settings (consider the lesson of the Nuremburg trials) the fears of careless compliance exceed those of careless non-compliance. When that is so, punishment or criticism of those who make mistakes by following rules is greater than for those who make equivalent mistakes by substituting their own judgement. Here the costs of the errors built into rules are thought to be potentially greater than the costs of allowing decision-makers to use their best judgement, a determination reflected in the extent to which reliance on rules is accepted as a justification for making a decision that turned out to be mistaken.

Once we recognize that there are two types of error, and that rule-based decision-making attempts to minimize the incidence of decision-maker error even at the cost of increasing the incidence of rule-based error, it appears that a frequently persuasive argument for rule-based decision-making is what we can now label the *argument from risk-aversion*. We understand that any decision-making procedure will make errors. When rule-based decision-making is in place, the most noteworthy error is the failure on some number of occasions to make the best or optimal decision in the particular case. But when particularistic decision-making prevails, the most noteworthy errors will be those in which misguided decision-makers— whether biased, ignorant, incompetent, or simply confused—will make decidedly non-optimal decisions. In attempting to design a decision-making procedure, we assess as best we can the expected frequency and consequences of these two types of errors. When the result of that assessment is a preference for rules, there is implicit in this preference a judgement that the errors that might be made by misguided decision-makers are more serious or more likely than the rule-based errors that come from a built-in failure to reach the very best decision in every case.[19] Rule-based decision-making thus

---

[19] The analysis I offer in the text could be presented as well in statistical terms, designating one of the varieties of error as the Type I error and the other as the Type II error. Pursuing that theme would involve an argumentative style somewhat different from that I employ throughout this book, so I will be satisfied with the observation that I see many decisions for rule-based decision-making as presupposing a decision procedure in which decision-maker errors are, by stipulation or by prediction, treated as the Type I (more serious) error. See Margaret Jane Radin, 'Risk-of-Error

relinquishes aspirations for complete optimization in order to guard against significant decision-maker errors, and in doing so reflects the necessarily risk-averse aspect of rule-based decision-making.

7.5 *The Argument from Stability*

Although the arguments from reliance, efficiency, and risk aversion each retain an irreducible core of plausibility, they also coalesce in interesting ways. The argument from reliance presupposes some mutually accessible consistency of understanding between rule-enforcer and addressee, the argument from efficiency takes ease of decision-making to be a good in itself, and the argument from risk-aversion takes decision-maker errors to be more serious than the errors that are built into rules unable to adapt to a changing reality. Thus, the virtues fostered by reliance, efficiency, and risk-aversion share a focus on stability for stability's sake. All three arguments take the dampening of variance as a good to be pursued in its own right, and see rules as instruments of that dampening process.

The extent to which rules promote stability is partially a function of the grossness of the factual predicates they incorporate. At one extreme of what is a continuum and not a dichotomy, rules whose factual predicates are broad and crude encompass categories such as 'vehicle' or 'dog' rather than drawing fine distinctions within those categories. At this extreme, large numbers of potentially relevant differences are suppressed, and a frequently distorting uniformity is imposed on the diversity of experience. At the other extreme, rules verge on the particular. They are likely to be numerous and finely tuned, with factual predicates so narrow and so precise that all or almost all relevant variation is permissibly taken into account. When this is the case there will be fewer rule-based errors, for the categories demarcated by the rules will approach the richness of life.

The choice of the appropriate degree of rule-based collapse of otherwise relevant difference is necessarily a function of the purpose a decision-making environment is thought to serve. Some decision-making environments will emphasize today, focusing on the rich-ness and uniqueness of immediate experience. Their sights are set on now, and thus on the importance of getting *this* decision just right. In such environments the decision-makers will ordinarily

Rules and Non-Ideal Justification', *passim*. That designation does not make rule-based decision-making inevitable, but it skews the choice of decision-making procedures in that direction.

have the freedom to explore every possible fact or argument that might bear on making the best decision in *this* instance, for it is precisely the *thisness* of the event that is most vital. At its extreme, such a system might, and arguably should, deny the relevance of mandatory rules entirely. The virtues of stability would bow to the desire to get things right, and in such a framework rules *qua* rules ought to have little if any force. More realistically, perhaps, such a system might still have rules, but the factual predicates of those rules would be small rather than large, thereby decreasing the possibility of variance between the strictures of the rule and the complexity of the particular.

Other decision-making environments, however, focus on yesterday and tomorrow as much as today, emphasizing the recurrent rather than the unique elements of the human condition. Here rules have the greatest role to play, generating a format for decision-making that channels decisions toward consideration of a comparatively limited number of factors likely to be repeated over time. In such an environment, missing the right answer now and then is thought to be less than catastrophic. The occasional suboptimal result is seen as an error worth tolerating, a price to be paid for the advantage that comes from crowding the variety and fluidity of experience into the constraining and therefore stabilizing pattern of decision according to broadly applicable rules.[20]

I talk of stability in a formal rather than a political or psychological sense. The stability promoted by rules may very well turn out to be politically or psychologically destabilizing, for entrenchment of the status quo often creates pressures for radical change that might otherwise be accommodated. Rule-based decision-making prevents change, and may consequently produce personal, social, and political instability. But that instability is a reaction to systemic stability, and thus indicates the importance of distinguishing the two. Thus, when

---

[20] It is worth noting the affinity between rules and 'slippery slope' arguments. Although such arguments are often thought to be fallacious, it is now understood that they can be sound when relying on empirical claims about the tendency of people to assimilate the logically distinguishable. Trudy Glover, 'What's Wrong with Slippery Slope Arguments?', 313–16; Schauer, 'Slippery Slopes', 368–83; Trianosky, 'Rule-Utilitarianism and the Slippery Slope', *passim*; L. A. Whitt, 'Acceptance and the Problem of Slippery-Slope Insensitivity', *passim*. And at the heart of a slippery slope argument is the willingness to tolerate an incorrect result in *this* case in order to minimize the number of incorrect results in future cases. By taking tomorrow to be as important if not more so than today, and by taking today's case as merely one of a larger group, the slippery slope argument is but a variant on an argument from and for rules.

I refer to the *argument from stability*, I refer to the argument that rule-based decision-making narrows the range of potential decisions, and in doing so makes changes from the *status quo*, both for better or for worse, more difficult than would be the case were decision-makers freer to depart from the categories and prescriptions of yesterday. Whether that formal variety of stability is likely to promote or hinder social stability, or for that matter whether it is desirable at all, are quite separate questions.

Those separate questions, however, are ones that are virtually impossible to answer outside of a particular social or political context. Although resolute Burkeans might disagree, we cannot even begin to discuss acontextually whether stability or the entrenchment of the *status quo* is a good thing, and without a universal answer to the question of whether stability is a good thing, we cannot assess whether this argument for rules is persuasive. Stability may be unimpeachable in the abstract—individuals and societies all need at least some fixed moorings. In reality, however, stability comes only by giving up some flexibility to explore the deepest corners of the events now before us. Whether this price is worth paying will vary with the purposes to be served within a given decision-making environment, and we get no closer to perceiving those purposes by understanding the relationship between stability and rules. Noticing the relationship is still valuable, however, for it enables us to see more clearly not only how stability might be achieved, but also the kind of price we must pay to obtain it.

Evaluating the argument from stability also involves considering the desirability of some current state of affairs. Because rule-based decision-making entrenches that state of affairs by entrenching its categories and conceptual apparatus, we cannot divorce the value of entrenchment from the value of what it is that is being entrenched. By entrenching the past against the pressures of the present, and thus also by entrenching the present against the claims of the future, rule-based decision-making is necessarily, logically, and unavoidably conservative, in the non-political sense of that term. As we saw in Chapter 5.5, a non-mistaken rule-constrained decision-maker can never do better than a non-mistaken particularistic decision-maker can do under the same substantive theory of decision, but can often do worse. From the perspective of that substantive theory of decision, therefore, rule-based decision-making in furtherance of that theory is necessarily suboptimal, in the way that any second-best solution is suboptimal, even though it may very well represent the optimal decision procedure.

The advantages of second-best solutions, however, are context–dependent, varying with substantive theories telling us how much better off we could be, as well as how much worse. The second-best virtues of rules will likely be most embraced when there is a largely positive view of the *status quo*, one in which the expected harm of destabilization is greater than the expected benefits from that same destabilization. The argument from stability is thus closely tied to the argument from risk-aversion, for to be risk-averse is to have a view not only about the unknown, but about the known. Implicit in risk-aversion is a (comparatively) positive view about the current state of affairs. Rules, by entrenching that state of affairs, serve the goals of stability for stability's sake, but we cannot consider whether that goal is worth serving without having a substantive conception of where we are, and where we want to be.

7.6 *Rules and the Allocation of Power*

A decision-maker instructed to make decisions according to a set of rules is thereby instructed not to consider certain facts, certain reasons, and certain arguments.[21] We now understand that such instructions to ignore the otherwise relevant are usefully seen as withdrawals of decisional jurisdiction, with any of a number of arguments supporting that withdrawal. All those arguments, however, are premised on a reluctance to have some class of decision-makers take on some category of decisions. At times, as with the arguments from reliance and efficiency, the withdrawal of jurisdiction may be grounded simply in a desire to narrow the range of permissible variance in decision or to avoid the waste of decisional resources. At other times, as seen by the focus on decision-maker error in the argument from risk-aversion, withdrawals of decisional jurisdiction are based on a distrust of decision-makers—on a fear that some types of decision-makers, when empowered to consider certain kinds of facts, reasons, and arguments, will consider them unwisely and thus produce mistaken decisions.

---

[21] I say 'instructed' as a way of encompassing much of what I discussed in Chap. 6. At the very least, 'instructed' includes the process by which a decision-making environment, through a system of rewards and punishment (including praise and criticism), induces the decision-makers within that environment to make decisions by certain methods and not by others.

But even though some arguments focus on decision-maker distrust while others do not, any argument for rule-based decision-making can be seen to view rules as essentially jurisdictional, as devices for determining who should be considering what. Rules therefore operate as tools for the *allocation of power*. A decision-maker not constrained by rules has the power, the authority, the jurisdiction to take everything into account. Conversely, the rule-constrained decision-maker loses at least some of that jurisdiction. And although fear of error in the exercise of that jurisdiction is one frequently valid reason for denial of jurisdiction, it is by no means the only one. In political decision-making, for example, questions of role allocation are often determined by issues of legitimacy. The traditional theory of judicial authority, under which legislatures make the rules and judges apply them, is not based nearly as much on a fear that judges will make errors in the process of engaging in open-ended decision-making as it is based on the assumption that determination of questions of substantive value should be for popularly responsible and responsive institutions such as legislatures, and not for non-majoritarian institutions such as the judiciary.

As I will make clear in the following chapter, I do not subscribe, either descriptively or normatively, to this over-simplified model of the argument that judges should be simple appliers of rules. Still, the argument is important, for it shows us how theories of who should be doing what are analytically distinct from judgements about who is *better* at doing what. Although power (in the 'juris-diction' sense) is frequently allocated on the basis of determinations of comparative competence, it is often allocated for other reasons. Sometimes we allocate decision-making power to an agent or institution because of the substantive basis for recognizing or con-stituting that agent or institution, and we allocate the power knowing that other agents or institutions might still do the job better. Societies routinely entrust to parents the power to make a wide variety of choices about how their children will be raised, trained, and educated, even in the face of evidence that parents may not be the ones most capable of performing the task. That moral decisions of public importance might better be made by the members of the Editorial Board of *Ethics* than by the political process is far from a conclusive argument for giving them that power. Thus, although rules *may* allocate power for epistemic reasons, granting power to those who have the greatest knowledge, rules need not be premised on such epistemic considerations. Nor need they be based on questions of comparative competence or ability, even of a non-epistemic variety. Rather, any of the host of reasons that might lead an individual agent to say 'That's none of my business' could lead, institutionally, to the design of institutions, with rules as the implements of that design, such that some institutions made certain decisions and other institutions said, 'That's none of our business.'

Rules therefore allocate power in two ways. First, in entrenching various categories, rules entrench the *status quo* and allocate power to the past and away from the present, and to the present and away from the future. The allocation of power here is temporal, distributing decision-making jurisdiction among the past, the present, and the future. This intertemporal allocation of power is important not only among different institutions or agents. We can also see rules as intertemporally allocating power within a single institution or agent. Within a multi-member institution, rule-based decision-making decreases the degree of difference that a change in personnel would make, and thus may entrench the long-term power of the institution *qua* institution as against the power of particular members of that institution at any one time. And although this may seem most applicable to appellate courts, the point is more pervasive. Consider a people (or a membership of a club) adopting a constitution, or a legislature entrenching a set of legislative procedures, or a governing body of a sport establishing the rules for that sport, or even two parties entering into a contract. In each of these cases, there is an attempt, frequently successful, to use rules to guard against too frequent or too easy change, in effect entrenching the perspective of one group at one time against the potential power of different individuals at different times.

The same phenomenon may even take place within individuals. Afraid of some future weakness of the will, we often make rules for ourselves. Whether in the form of a New Year's resolution, or a list of things to do, or a vow we make silently, we commonly think that the explicit formulation of a rule, even if addressed only to our future selves, and even if enforced only by those same future selves, is likely to be effective. Often we are wrong, but sometimes we are right, and when we are right the rule can be seen to have had the effect of withdrawing decisional jurisdiction from some future self. And when we worry that self-imposed sanctions are likely to be ineffective, we make public pledges and vows, hoping that externally imposed rewards and punishment, even if only in the form of praise and criticism, will serve as the sanctions by which the future self treats a rule made by its former self as a reason for action.[22]

Secondly, by allocating power to some agents and away from others, rules can also allocate power horizontally, determining who, at a given slice of time, is to determine what. Rules determine which decisions are to be made by the umpire and which are to be made by the rules committee, they determine within a family *who* should determine bedtime and who should decide what to have for dinner, and they specify within a religious tradition *who* should determine the rituals and methods of worship. The 'No Dogs Allowed' sign allocates power to the proprietor and away from the patron, and the 'No vehicles in the park' regulation similarly allocates power away from the park-user and to the rule-makers. And when a court determines that a statue of a vehicle, even though a vehicle, is not to be considered a violation of the 'No vehicles in the park' regulation, then that court allocates power to itself and away from the rule-makers. Although the exclusion of the statue may be absurd, the determination of absurdity is also the assertion of the power to determine what is absurd and what is not. We may frequently wish courts or other rule-enforcers to have that power, but that is by no means a self-evident truth. Consider, for example, the power to determine absurdity in cases not of over-inclusion, but of under-inclusion. If someone were to haul a stationary steam calliope into the park, and then proceed to start it up, complete with noise, fumes, and possibly even some danger to pedestrians, it might seem absurd to exclude vehicles but permit the calliope, as a literal reading of the rule would indicate. Yet there is something that troubles us about granting to a court or to a police officer the power to include within the scope of a regulatory rule something not literally encompassed by its words, no matter how absurd the literal distinction may seem.[23] An agent who follows the rules, therefore, need not be taken to agree either with the content of the rule or with the desirability of applying it on this occasion. When rules are followed, especially in those cases in which the act of rule-following

---

[22] See Thomas Schelling, 'Enforcing Rules on Oneself', *passim*.

[23] This is the point of Justice Holmes's opinion in *McBoyle* v. *United States*, 283 US 25 (1931). Hart criticizes the result ('Positivism and the Separation of Law and Morals', 610–11), but that is based on the conclusion that the word 'vehicle' may be taken to encompass an airplane according to the linguistic conventions in force in 1931. That may or may not be true, but it seems to be Holmes's point that it is not. If Holmes is right, then there is something troubling about expanding the literal reach of a criminal prohibition even when it appears absurd not to.

appears to the rule-follower to be within the area of under- or over-inclusiveness, the rule-follower can be characterized as simply deferring to the decision-making capacities of another. An agent who says, 'This is not my job', is not necessarily abdicating responsibility.[24] One form of taking responsibility consists in taking the responsibility for leaving certain responsibilities to others.[25]

7.7 *Rules, Community and Co-ordination*

As devices for the allocation of power, rules may also serve to allocate power away from individual members of a community and to the community as an institution in its own right. Because rules suppress potentially relevant differences, they can serve to suppress differences among members of a community and thereby function as implements of homogenization. Although it has been argued that rules are primarily the instruments of individualism,[26] and although history provides much evidence for this conclusion, it is still far from implausible that rules often operate in just the opposite way. By blocking consideration of all potentially relevant factors, rules may encourage us to see ourselves as relevantly similar to others, rather than relevantly different. Each of us is a unique collection of particulars, and individualism is centrally about uniqueness. Insofar as a method of thinking or decision-making encourages a focus on this uniqueness, on what makes me different from others, on what *I* want, and on why *my* case is special, that method impedes rather

[24] For a perspective to the contrary, stressing the responsibility-avoiding aspects of rule-following, see Frank Michelman, 'Traces of Self-Government', *passim*.

[25] It is worthwhile noting the important strand of feminist thought associating ruleness with maleness, and associating the avoidance of rules with a particularity and a contextual sensitivity that is the antithesis of maleness. See especially Carol Gilligan, *In a Different Voice*, and see this perspective applied to legal rules in Martha Minow, 'Justice Engendered'. The association of ruleness with maleness, however, is not so clear. Although I do not challenge that contingent psychological association, nor the way in which rules can further empower those already in power, there may, from a feminist perspective, be a darker side to the rejection of rules. The particularist looking at every relevant aspect of immediate experience is unconstrained, immodest, non-deferential, and perhaps even arrogant. 'I'm in charge here' and 'Let me do it, dear' are the attitudes of those who think they understand everything and need not accede to the decision-making abilities of others. When seen this way, it is by no means clear that the avoidance of rules is not simultaneously, and paradoxically, the path both to greater empathy and to greater arrogance. I have no solutions to this paradox. Still, insofar as the *avoidance* of rules can be seen as the embodiment of an excessively self-confident avoidance of constraint, deference, and respect for the decision-making capacities of others, an easy association of ruleness with maleness seems a bit too easy.

[26] Kennedy, 'Form and Substance in Private Law Adjudication', *passim*, and also the works cited in n. 25.

than fosters an outlook that sees the individual agent as in important ways part of a group. By suppressing the focus on the unique and the different, rules may encourage us to see our welfare as inextricably linked with and dependent on that of the group and discourage us from claiming distinctiveness of situation and consequent distinctiveness of treatment.[27]

Rules may thus be central to the functioning of any group enterprise conceived along strongly communitarian lines. But even with respect to communal activities involving egoistic members of an egoistically conceived group, it is possible that rules have a role to play. More particularly, it is important to explore the relevance of rules to some number of problems of collective action, and to see if they facilitate the solution to those problems and thereby increase the welfare of all group members who follow the rules.

If we focus initially on Prisoner's Dilemma problems,[28] in which non-communicating rational egoistic agents with different preference orderings suffer for their rational egoism, it appears that rules might be helpful in making it easier for real-world agents to surmount the theoretical condition of non-communication. By creating the salience of certain solutions, and by simplifying the situation as perceived by the egoistic agents, rules may seem to assist in the solution of the Prisoner's Dilemma. Exactly how rules might pierce the obstacle of non-communication is something I will not pursue, however, for in fact the constraint of non-communication is not what creates the dilemma, and thus the removal of it does not tend towards solution of it. Even if the agents are able to communicate, and consequently come to an agreement, it remains rational for each agent to try to break the agreement. Because of this, Prisoner's Dilemma problems are 'solved' not by the introduction of communication between the players, but rather by sanctions making it difficult or impossible for them to pursue what appears to be their individual best interests.

If we concentrate on constraint rather than communication, however, the role of rules, as conceived in this book, seems quite a bit more obscurely related to the solution of the Prisoner's Dilemma. Enforced co-operation, after all, could come from particularized command as well as by general rule, and nothing about the distinction between particularistic and rule-based decision-making, or for that

[27] My point about rules as vehicles of community is consistent with John Finnis, 'On Reason and Authority in *Law's Empire*', 379–80.

[28] For a survey of various perspectives, see Richmond Campbell and Lanning Sowden (eds.), *Paradoxes of Rationality and Cooperation*.

matter between particularized commands and general orders, is uniquely relevant or helpful to Prisoner's Dilemma issues. It is true that rules as opposed to particularized commands might make it easier for some authority to create the enforced co-operation that is a sufficient condition for the solution of a Prisoner's Dilemma problem, but 'easier' is here nothing more than a reference to all of the arguments that have been discussed earlier in this chapter. Consequently, nothing about the Prisoner's Dilemma makes rules especially apt to its solution by enforced co-operation except to the extent that rules in general might, for reasons of ease of communication or enforcement, make the imposition of authority easier in any situation.

If we remove the external coercion, however, things look somewhat different. Now the issue is what, if anything, might lead uncoerced agents to co-operate and to focus on the solution that is better for all. If, following Axelrod in some respects and Schelling in others,[29] we believe that salience or easy recognizability is a necessary condition for the evolution of co-operative solutions to Prisoner's Dilemma and related paradoxes of collective behavior, then it is precisely the simplifying aspect of rules that furnishes the necessary salience and simplicity.

This, however, is not a role that rules serve uniquely in the context of Prisoner's Dilemma problems, which are defined in terms of egoistic agents seeking to maximize their own welfare. Indeed, if we look instead at agents inclined to co-operate with other similarly inclined agents (whether to serve their own interests or whether to pursue altruistic interests in their own right),[30] it seems even more apparent that the very generality of rules is central. If we are looking first at problems of co-ordination and convention in the strict sense, where the convention develops from the co-ordinating agents rather than being imposed on them,[31] we see those agents recognizing the salience of some rule, or plan, or solution. At this point, nothing about the distinction between the

---

[29] Axelrod's views are presented in 'Effective Choice in the Prisoner's Dilemma'; 'More Effective Choice in the Prisoner's Dilemma'; and 'The Emergence of Co-operation Among Egoists'. Schelling's contributions can be found in *The Strategy of Conflict* and 'Micromotives and Macrobehavior'.

[30] On the distinction in the parenthetical, see David Gauthier, *Morals By Agreement*; Donald Regan, *Utilitarianism and Cooperation*. Also relevant is Michael Slote, *Beyond Optimizing*.

[31] Following David Lewis, *Convention*, 102, I take the lack of external imposition to be definitional of 'convention'.

rule-based and the particularistic is especially relevant, and this may explain why much of the literature on the emergence of norms has little if anything to say about the dimension of particularity and generality.[32]

Once some norm exists, however, once it has already emerged and taken on a status as a convention, then agents seeing the norm's usefulness will likely be faced on future occasions with instances in which the situation before them is one falling within the norm as they have previously understood it, but in which it appears better to modify the norm at that point. If in such circumstances they know that other members of the co-ordinating community have previously understood the norm in the same way, if they know that other members are or will be faced with the same situation as that now presented, and if they suspect but cannot know that those other members will contemplate the same modification, then there will be a risk that some modification will not be made by other agents. This last is the crucial factor. When agents are more confident of the content of the norm than of the likelihood that other agents will modify in the same way that now seems to the first agent to be desirable, it is precisely this gap in confidences that leads the first agent to be justified in a fear that the previously well-functioning norm will become less so in the event of a modification. What this means, therefore, is that the agent inclined towards co-operation will have a reason to resist the urge to make a seemingly desirable modification. And the result of this is the conclusion that co-operation, when taken seriously, will tend towards generality, and will tend towards the entrenchment of general rules even in the face of inclinations to modify them at the moment of application. The ability of the rules of language or the rules of the road to work, therefore, may be largely a result of the willingness of co-operatively inclined participants in the rule-system to resist urges to make the rules better, for they can be less sure that other agents will make the same modification than that other agents now employ the unmodified rule.

When conventions are transformed into 'laid down' rules, the same conclusion still holds. Insofar as those laid down rules also serve purposes of co-ordination and co-operation, then these purposes are likely better served with rules of more rather than less generality, because greater generality will produce the greater

---

[32] See Edna Ullman-Margalit, *The Emergence of Norms*; Regan, *Utilitarianism and Cooperation*; Schelling, *The Strategy of Conflict*.

commonality of understanding that is at the heart of co-ordination. Moreover, the co-ordinating functions will be served better if the incentive process is such that addressees of the rules are discouraged from modifying them even when they think that a modification or a departure would be desirable. As with the other arguments for rules, therefore, this one is not without its costs, since each non-departure or non-modification is a cost if that departure or modification would have produced a better result. But this only repeats an earlier and obvious conclusion—that co-ordination and co-operation take collective action to be an (instrumental or ultimate) independent good, and that to serve that good may involve some sacrifice of others. This too is a form of allocation of power, recognizing that agents who participate in co-operative enterprises must be inclined to (or forced to) allocate power away from themselves and to the collective good.

8

RULES AND LAW

8.1 *Rules and the Rule of Law*

Is there a connection between rule-based decision-making and decision-making within that institution we conventionally refer to as 'law'? What is the place of rules within a 'legal system'? To many people these questions answer themselves. Law just *is* decision according to rules, for rules to them are what distinguish law both from the naked exercise of power and from the unmediated practice of politics.[1] To support this conclusion, those who equate decision according to law with decision according to rules can point to common linguistic usage and the phrase 'the *rule* of law'. What is the rule of law, it can be said, if not the rule of rules?

The phrase 'the rule of law', however, trades on an ambiguity in the meaning of the word 'rule'. In the sense that we have *rulers* who *rule* their subjects, 'rule' bears its closest affinity with 'reign' or 'control', and has only the remotest relationship with a form of decision-making characterized either by generality or by the entrenchment of generalizations. Thus, 'the rule of law' could consistent with ordinary usage refer to any system in which organized authority rather than the exercise of brute physical force was the prevailing practice. And if 'the rule of law' designates only a system of organized authority, then systems could exist under the rule of law but still employ modes of decision-making that were not substantially rule-based. This is not to make either an empirical claim about existing legal systems or a normative one about the desirability within law of one or another form of decision-making. It is only to say that we do not get very far into those questions by examining linguistic usage or even the historical practices that usage might

---

[1] A good example is the dissenting opinion of Supreme Court Justice Antonin Scalia in *Morrison* v. *Olson*, 108 S. Ct. 2597 (1988): 'A government of laws means a government of rules. Today's decision on the basic issue of fragmentation of executive power is ungoverned by rule, and hence ungoverned by law.'

reflect, for to speak of 'the rule of' law is at least linguistically compatible with law not being an affair of rules.[2]

But is such a conception any more than linguistically legitimate? Are we able to make sense out of the idea of a legal system without rules? Can there be law without decision according to rules of sufficient generality such that the power of the state is not deployed, and disputes among citizens not resolved, on something other than strictly an *ad hoc* basis?[3] From one perspective, the answer to this question is 'No', but from another there appears ample room for an idea of law without rules. Which of these answers is correct depends on the type of rules with which we are concerned, and thus turns on a distinction between mandatory rules and rules of a quite different sort.

Although earlier I distinguished rules forbidding behavior from rules requiring it, both types are similar in rendering the covered behavior non-optional. *Permissions*, however, make behavior optional, and are consequently different both from prohibitions and requirements. Yet even the class of permissions can usefully be subdivided. Ordinarily permissions authorize behavior that could have and did pre-exist the permission. When a rule permits an agent to ϕ, it speaks to a situation in which ϕ-ing was a conceptual possibility prior to the grant of permission. We understand perfectly well the idea of crossing the Brooklyn Bridge on foot even if we have no idea whether that activity is permitted or not.

By contrast, another type of permission is partly permissive and partly constitutive (see above, Chapter 1.3), simultaneously creating a *power* and granting explicit permission for its use. Such empowering (or *power-conferring*) rules have recently been analyzed by Hart,[4] Raz,[5] and Kelsen,[6] among others, but the account I offer here is not

[2] On the lack of conceptual or historical necessity of law operating according to general rules, see Kenneth Winston, 'On Treating Like Cases Alike', *passim*.

[3] In *The Morality of Law*, Lon Fuller stresses generality as being essentially definitional of law, but in 'Positivism and Fidelity to Law' he offers a picture of rules (including the example of the statue of the truck) in substantial tension with the one I have been developing here. This appears to represent an inconsistency in Fuller's thought, for he seems unwilling to apply the picture of rules he thinks ought to exist *within* a legal system to those rules that to him *define* a legal system.

[4] H. L. A. Hart, *The Concept of Law*, 26–48, 77–9, 238–40; id., 'Bentham on Legal Powers', *passim*.

[5] Joseph Raz, *Practical Reason and Norms*, 97–106; id. *The Concept of a Legal System*, *passim*; id., 'Normative Powers and Voluntary Obligations', *passim*.

[6] Hans Kelsen, *The Pure Theory of Law*, 145–63; id., *Allgemeine Theorie der Normen*, *passim*. I have profited greatly from Stanley Paulson's analysis of Kelsen in 'An Empowerment Theory of Legal Norms', *passim*.

intended as exegesis. Just as previous accounts of power-conferring rules differ from each other, so too does mine differ from any of them, although my debt to all is plain. But because my account departs from other accounts both in detail and in emphasis, I want to call the rules to which I will refer *jurisdictional* rules.

The rules I identify as jurisdictional owe their existence to the distinction between the creation of jurisdiction and the substance of its exercise. Jurisdictional rules typically grant to some agent or institution the power to make decisions with respect to some category of events. Thus a rule empowering a particular court to resolve custody controversies between residents of a certain geographic area or a rule empowering the referee to decide all disputes in a sporting event are archetypal jurisdictional rules. And such rules are interesting and important because the jurisdiction they grant is largely independent of the extent of substantive control on the exercise of that jurisdiction. We can see this most clearly by considering naked jurisdictional rules, which create jurisdiction but impose essentially no substantive regulative constraint on its exercise. Some court, for example, might be empowered to decide all custody disputes involving parents residing in New Jersey, but authorized then simply to make the best all things considered decision with respect to each of those disputes.

By noting the possibility of naked jursdictional rules, we are able to see the relationship between rules and legal systems in a different light, for often when we imagine there could be no legal system without rules we are thinking not so much of mandatory as of jurisdictional rules. It is hard to conceive of a legal system without jurisdictional rules, since otherwise nothing would establish the *system* in the first place. Even Weber's picture of a totally *ad hoc qadi* justice needs jurisdictional rules, for something must determine that it is the man under the tree and not someone else whose role it is to dispense justice. This much seems obvious, and so we can acknowledge that any legal system would need jurisdictional rules to create and organize the institutions of decision-making. Yet a system constituted and structured by a system of jurisdictional rules could still impose little in the way of substantive constraint on the decisions its decision-makers were expected to reach. Police officers might have the jurisdiction to keep the peace in certain specified areas, but not be further limited in how they ought to do so, and judges might have jurisdiction to settle disputes of a certain kind, but again not be told how those disputes should be resolved.

In these and other cases, the officials would have a Solomonic mandate, with rules existing only to determine who had the authority to do what, but not the substance of how they did it.[7]

Even a system whose rules were exclusively jurisdictional, however, would still present questions about the status of those rules. Specifically, even jurisdictional rules are subject to the mandatory rule/rule of thumb distinction that has dominated much of this book. Any conferral of jurisdiction is itself based on some background justification, some rationale for creating that jurisdiction, and thus there will always be the possibility that a jurisdictional rule will turn out to be under- or over-inclusive with respect to its generating justification. When a case arises in which the grant (or denial) of decision-making jurisdiction appears absurd or at odds with the justification for creating the jurisdiction, the decision-maker is faced with a now-familiar choice: Will the jurisdiction be contracted (or expanded) at that point, or will the explicit grant of jurisdiction control even when it seems best, from the perspective of the jurisdictional rule's justification, that the rule not control? Suppose that some jurisdictional rule, premised on the justification of recognizing special expertise in maritime matters, empowers a tribunal of maritime experts to decide all disputes arising out of events 'on open waters'. Yet were an injured water-skier to make a claim against the manufacturer of the defective water-ski, the rule itself would appear to give the maritime court jurisdiction even though the justification behind the creation of the jurisdiction would appear to indicate the contrary. The resolution of the jurisdictional question would then turn on exactly the same issues

[7] The possibility I raise calls forth Kelsen's distinction between formal and material authorization. My notion of jurisdiction without substantive constraint tracks Kelsen's idea of formal authorization, and my contrasting notion of a substantively constraining mandatory or regulative rule is quite similar to Kelsen's material authorization. See Kelsen, *Pure Theory of Law*, 193–278; Paulson, 'Material and Formal Authorisation in Kelsen's Pure Theory', *passim*.

If pressed too hard, the distinction between the jurisdictional and the substantively constraining mandatory rule collapses. Any substantively constraining mandatory rule could be recast in jurisdictional form, for there is no logical or grammatical difference between authorizing a court to decide all controversies in which the amount at issue is greater than ten thousand dollars and authorizing a court to grant monetary relief whenever it finds that one person has slandered another. Still, there is a way in which the latter rule admittedly incorporates a jurisdictional rule, but in which a more purely jurisdictional rule such as the former can stand on its own without the kind of substantive guidance that we see in the latter. Without claiming, therefore, that there is some logical divide between the two types, I still prefer to rely on a difference in degree that is reflected in common and legal understanding.

that arise when such conflicts occur with respect to mandatory rules.

Thus the questions to be asked about the status of jurisdictional rules are quite similar to those asked about the status of regulative rules. Will the instantiation be treated as at least partly autonomous of its generating justification? Or will jurisdictional instantiations be treated as analogous to rules of thumb, again useful as preliminary guides but not precluding jurisdiction when background justifications or higher order rules indicate its desirability? When this latter alternative is chosen (which it rarely is in most legal systems), the jurisdictional rules are themselves transparent to more fluid conceptions of who should be deciding what. And when the former, rule-based, status of jurisdictional rules prevails, there will be some instances in which jurisdiction will not be exercised despite the fact that the background justifications would indicate that it should. This more rule-based approach to grants of jurisdiction appears to be the more commonly selected alternative, with jurisdictional rules occasionally precluding jurisdiction when the justification behind those rules would allow it, and occasionally requiring jurisdiction when the background justification would prohibit it.[8]

Thus, the distinction between mandatory rules and rules of thumb cuts across the distinction between jurisdictional and substantively regulative rules. Still, concentrating on the distinction between rules that create jurisdiction and rules that indicate outcomes within that jurisdiction enables us usefully to contrast decision-making environments in which the decision-makers operate comparatively freely within a rule-established jurisdiction with those in which the decision-makers are constrained not only with respect to the kinds of issues they decide, but also with respect to the factors they may take account in making that decision. Thus the distinction between naked jurisdictional rules and more substantively constraining alternatives is illustrated by the distinction among: (*a*) a rule granting a judge jurisdiction to decide which of two separated

---

[8] My sense that courts are likely to have a rule-based approach to jurisdictional rules is supported by cases such as *United States* v. *Locke*, 471 US 84 (1985), in which Justice Thurgood Marshall, normally more inclined than other Justices to choose less rule-bound approaches to adjudication, rigidly applied the language of a jurisdictional prerequisite (filing required '*before* December 31') even when it was apparent that a mistake had been made in drafting the legislation.

Even more than with other types of rules, however, jurisdictional rules present a contrast between under- and over-inclusion, with remedying over-inclusion by denying jurisdiction seemingly less an assertion of unjustified power than remedying under-inclusion by claiming jurisdiction.

spouses shall have custody of their child, but requiring only that the judge make the best all things considered decision; (*b*) a rule granting the same jurisdiction, and instructing the judge to award custody to the spouse with the greater financial resources; and (*c*) a rule granting jurisdiction for the purpose of awarding custody to the mother in all instances. All these rules are equivalent in jurisdiction, in the sense that the same disputes between the same individuals are within the jurisdiction in each case, but they differ greatly in the extent to which the content of decisions within that jurisdiction is guided by substantively regulative rules.

There is no doubt that it takes a large array of jurisdictional and other empowering rules to create a legal system, and thus there is no cause to take issue with Hart's conclusion that a legal *system* comes into being upon the merger of primary rules regulating conduct with secondary rules governing the recognition, change, and adjudication of the primary rules.[9] But the import of the distinction between jurisdictional and substantively regulative rules is that legal systems could exist in the Hartian sense and yet still be comprised largely of naked jurisdictional rules with little substantively regulative content. And once we recognize that such a system is both possible and still plausibly considered a legal system, we are able then to focus on the empirical question of the extent of substantively regulative constraint within existing legal systems, and the normative question of the desirability of more or less substantively regulative modes of decision-making within a legal system.

When components of legal systems are largely devoid of rules imposing much substantive regulative constraint on the decision-makers within that system, we say that decision-makers exercise 'discretion', being limited in where they can operate but essentially unlimited in what they did once there. The extent of discretion is a variable, however, and the type of rules employed is usually the vehicle by which a decision-making environment determines how much discretion its decision-makers will have.[10] Will judges or other legal officials be told to make decisions in just *this* way, or will they be substantively unfettered, unleashed by terms such as 'reasonable' or 'appropriate' to decide for themselves just what matters in the

---

[9] Hart, *The Concept of Law*, 77–96.

[10] Commonly that discretion will be granted or limited by the indeterminacy of the rules within the system. See Gidon Gottlieb, *The Logic of Choice*, 91–110; Charles Curtis, 'A Better Theory of Legal Interpretation', *passim* ; Alexsander Peczenik and Jerzy Wróblewski, 'Fuzziness and Transformation'; Frederick Schauer, 'Authority and Indeterminacy', 31–7.

particular case at hand? And even when judges and other legal officials are given narrow and specific prescriptions with which to work, the extent to which those officials are instructed or compelled to treat the prescriptions as opaque mandatory rules rather than transparent rules of thumb will reflect the extent to which the system has chosen to constrain the discretion of its decision-makers.

There is little that can be said acontextually about the desirable level of substantive regulative constraint on the decision-makers in any legal system; or about whether a relative lack of constraint, if thought desirable, should be implemented by the use of indeterminate terms like 'reasonable' or instead by systemic norms treating more determinate norms as being permissibly transparent to their background justifications.[11] Yet now that we have seen that rules serve primarily as vehicles for the allocation of power, we can appreciate that the extent to which decision-makers adopt (or are compelled to adopt) rule-based decision-making modes is likely to embody social judgements about the distribution of jurisdiction. Rules, including legal rules, apportion decision-making authority among various individuals and institutions, reflecting a society's decisions about who will decide what, who is to be trusted and who not, who is to be empowered and who not, whose decisions are to be reviewed and whose are to be final, and who is to give orders and who is to take them.

Because rules allocate power across time by entrenching the categories and generalizations of the past and thus dissipating the power of the present (or by entrenching the categories and generalizations of today against the pressures of tomorrow), the extent of their use also reflects the extent of decisional conservativism within the system. Insofar as legal systems embrace rule-based decision-making, they serve as institutions to preserve the past rather than as vehicles for departure from it. As shown in Chapter 5.5, rules can never allow a decision that could not otherwise be made, but can preclude otherwise eligible and indeed optimal decisions. It may be that such logically suboptimal decision procedures are optimal in reality, yet this is still the optimality of an entrenched past. Entrenching the past may provide the purchase from which political agents can now do what would otherwise be politically or psychologically

---

[11] Note that although constraint can be lessened by one or the other device, it can be imposed only by a conjunction of (at least somewhat) determinate rules and (some) lack of transparency. A determinate rule totally transparent to its background justifications is only as determinate as those justifications.

impossible, but when the circumstances require a departure from the past rather than obeisance to it, a decision-making apparatus operating in rule-based mode will find itself impeded and not empowered.

Thus, to the extent that legal systems embrace rule-based decision-making, they embrace as well those values of intertemporal consistency discussed in the previous chapter—stability for stability's sake, unwillingness to trust decision-makers to depart too drastically from the past, and a conservatism committed to the view that changes from the past are more likely to be for the worse than for the better. I have emphasized in this section that nothing inherent in the idea of a legal system mandates that it serve those values. Insofar as it aims to do so, however, the inculcation of rule-based decision-making is likely to be the implement of that aim, and it should be no surprise that legal systems most bent on preserving what now exists will be those most reliant on rules.

8.2 *The Common Law*

When all or part of a legal system seeks the goals served by rule-based decision-making, it will ordinarily employ and entrench canonically inscribed rules of considerable specificity. Even though a totally complete code of the sort envisaged by Bentham may be an impossibility, foundering on the limitations of language and the phenomenon of open texture, some rules are far more constraining than others. Thus although even an entrenched 'No dogs allowed' rule can be rendered indeterminate in application by cases involving deceased dogs or prairie dogs, such a rule is far more constraining than 'No disturbances'. When rule-based values are thought important, therefore, more constraining (and ordinarily more specific) rules will be selected and entrenched, with the system thereby relinquishing some of its ability to adapt to a changing future in exchange for the virtues of rule-based decision-making.

Often, however, systems professing to prefer rule-based values have chosen as a method of decision-making not the application of entrenched specific and canonically inscribed rules, but rather the system that Bentham so scorned—the common law. Yet from the perspective of the analysis of rules, what are we to make of the common law? Where in our distinction between rule-based and particularistic decision-making are we to fit this institution?

In common-law adjudication, by no means restricted to the legal institutions of 'common-law' systems such as those of the United

States, England, and Australia (and not necessarily exhaustive within those systems), the judicial role is not perceived as primarily involving the application and interpretation of canonical texts containing lists of equally canonical rule-formulations. Instead, common-law judges make decisions by applying legal principles contained in generations of previous judicial opinions, with each of those previous opinions being the written justification and explanation of the decision in a particular lawsuit. As the stock of such opinions increases, certain justifications recur, and certain principles become ossified. The result is the eventual development of an array of general prescriptions, such as 'Contracts must be based on consideration' and 'Those whose wild animals injure others are liable in damages for the injuries caused regardless of fault'. These general prescriptions appear as rules, and in any well-developed common law domain lawyers will have the ability to refer to rules, opinions will cite rules, and treatises will collect rules, even though one could not pick up an authoritative and canonical set of the rules of contract in a way that one could pick up the tax code or the rules of chess. Over time, therefore, there appear to be 'rules' of tort, of contract, of property, and so on, even though the set of such rules nowhere exists in codified canonical form. Moreover, these rules seem not to be simply descriptions of regularities that have emerged from previous particularistic decisions. They are thought to be prescriptive, and common-law judges are thought to be constrained by them.

Nothing in this picture is yet inconsistent with the idea of a rule, for often rules, of which the rules of language and etiquette are common examples, emerge without there being an original canonical rule-formulation. A distinctive feature of the common law, however, apart from the fact that its rules are made by judges and not by legislators, is the status these rules have when confronting the facts of a particular case. It is characteristic of the common law that the rules taken to exist prior to some case, and which would be known to lawyers prior to the case, are subject to modification when the features of the case demand. That is, when it appears to the common law judge that application of what was previously thought to be the rule would be silly, or inconsistent with good policy, or inconsistent with the justifications for having that rule, it is open to that judge to modify the previous rule at the moment of application. The common law process is characterized by the way in which its rules are subject to change in the course of their application, a

phenomenon plainly in tension with the account of rules I have
offered in previous chapters.[12]

Most of the landmarks of common law decision-making demonstrate this feature of treating rules as malleable at the moment of
application. The rules governing liability for defective products in
New York in 1916 were such that a lawyer would be able to say that
liability was imposed only upon those who *sold* such a product.
A manufacturer, not having entered into a transaction with the
ultimate consumer, was not liable even were the consumer to be
injured by a defectively manufactured product. Yet in *MacPherson*
v. *Buick Motor Co.*,[13] Judge Benjamin Cardozo of the New York
Court of Appeals ruled that manufacturers not in 'privity' with the
purchaser could be liable to consumers despite the lack of privity.
Similarly, the contract law of New Jersey in 1960 was generally
understood to be such that a consumer's waiver of an otherwise
applicable warranty was valid unless the waiver had been fraudulently
induced. Yet in that year, in *Henningsen* v. *Bloomfield Motors,
Inc.*,[14] the Supreme Court of New Jersey ruled such waivers void,
even absent fraud, where they were 'unconscionable', and where
the nature of the industry allowed no real opportunity for the
consumer to bargain for different terms.

The key to understanding *MacPherson*, *Henningsen*, and a host
of equally famous decisions lies in the fact that these were not cases
in which there was no rule in place at the time of decision, nor even
cases in which a possibly applicable rule was vague or otherwise
indeterminate. Instead, at the time the judges were called upon to
decide these cases, lawyers within the relevant jurisdictions could
have identified rules that appeared to control the events. We miss
the point if we think of such cases as involving situations unprovided
for by previous law, or as falling within gaps in the previous law, or
as presenting only penumbral applications of existing rules. From
the perspective only of what the rules were then thought to be, these
were not hard cases, but easy ones. In these and countless similar

---

[12] This tension is explained illuminatingly in A. W. B. Simpson, 'The Common
Law and Legal Theory', *passim*. Bentham's conclusions were similar in *A Comment
on the Commentaries* and *Of Laws in General*, but where Bentham was led by those
conclusions to urge the rejection of common law method entirely, Simpson asks us
instead to view the common law as a practice, a practice whose institutions, customs,
sources, and participants provide a degree of stability not provided by the so-called
'rules' of the common law. I explore these themes at greater length in Schauer, 'Is the
Common Law Law?'

[13] 217 NY 382, 111 NE 1050 (1916).   [14] 32 NJ 358, 161 A.2d 69 (1960).

cases, the events were encompassed, immediately prior to the decision, by what at least *appeared* to be a rule. Despite that, however, the circumstances of the particular case, or the judges' perception of a change in the empirical or normative landscape of the world, led those judges to decide the case in a way contrary to that plainly indicated by the prior rule. Thus, decisions like these, which sometimes purport only to be applying the existing rules, are in fact changing those rules in the very process of applying them.

The common law's characteristic lack of canonicity greatly facilitates changing the rules as they are applied. Although lawyers and judges can describe any number of common-law rules, and although both opinions and textbooks can state them in 'black letter' fashion, the rules have no single authoritative formulation, and accordingly the process of applying them does not involve an interpretation of the *text* of the rule. But although this explains why it is comparatively easy for common-law rules to be modified or even discarded in the process of application, it leaves unanswered the larger question of whether the rules of the common law are thus rules at all. There are things the common law undoubtedly refers to as 'rules', but if they are always subject to modification when the circumstances of some case appear to indicate the desirability of a modification, then the normative purchase is provided not by the supposed rule, but rather by whatever factors are used to determine whether a rule should be modified or applied as previously understood.

If what appears to be a rule can thus be modified when its indications are inconsistent with wise policy or the purpose behind the rule, then as we have seen the rule itself furnishes no constraint. If this is so, and this is how Bentham and others have understood the operation of the common-law, then it appears that common-law 'rules' are indeed descriptive rather than prescriptive, functioning merely as a temporary guides. This understanding of the status of common-law rules would be consistent with the fact that when a court refines or even changes a common-law rule in the process of applying it, the society in which it operates does not take the court to have done something illegitimate (although it may think it has done something *wrong*). The norms of practice and behavior constraining the common-law judge do not prohibit as extra-jurisdictional this seemingly rule-free activity, although it is an activity treating one species of legal rule as a descriptive summary of previous decisions rather than a prescriptive guide for future ones. Indeed, the common-law judges who receive the most glory, at least from history, are those like Cardozo, for whom the pre-existing rules seem to act more as opportunity for change than as constraint against it. It thus appears central to the common law that its rule-formulations, whether in a legal treatise, in the discourse of lawyers, or even in a case itself, are treated as contingent and non-canonical.

To understand the common law, therefore, we must focus not on the way the common law allows the filling of gaps, the resolution of difficult cases, or the making of law when no rule appears to control, for such activities are of peripheral importance. What is central to the common law is the way in which what had previously been thought to be the rule is a rule only in a very peculiar sense, for it will be applied to new cases if and only if that application is consistent with the full array of policies and principles that, in a more complex rule system, occupy the same place that justifications occupied in many of our earlier and simpler examples.[15] The common law appears consequently to be decision according to justification rather than decision according to rule. It abounds with rules of thumb, but avoids the use of rules in a strong and constraining sense.[16] Unlike rule-based decision-making, the common law does not view the wrong answer as the inevitable price of invariably crude generalizations. Rather, it treats all generalizations as contingent and perfectible (Fuller talked of the common law as 'working itself pure'), with wrong results representing defects in the system rather than as the inevitable by-products of under- and over-inclusive rules. Common-law rules are ideally neither under- nor over-inclusive, for the areas of conceivable under- or over-inclusion according to some formulation having the status only of a rule of thumb are remediable precisely at the moment of application.

Even if the revisability of common-law rules were no more constrained than I have just portrayed, that lack of constraint would

---

[15] See Melvin Eisenberg, *The Nature of the Common Law*. My reference to 'policies and principles' is in partial agreement with Ronald Dworkin's distinction between the two (*Taking Rights Seriously*, 22–8, 90–100). I agree with the essence of the distinction (or at least agree that it fits with Dworkin's non-consequentialist ethics), but disagree with Dworkin's descriptive claim, that common-law judges ordinarily use only principles and not policies as sources from which they decide when and whether to change existing law rules. I offer no views here on whether Dworkin is correct in maintaining that judges *ought* to be limited to the domain of principle and ought to leave determinations of policy to popularly responsible institutions such as elected legislatures.

[16] Common-law rules come very close to Rawls's summary conception of rules in 'Two Concepts of Rules', emerging as summaries of previous particularistic decisions, and providing no reasons for decision *qua* rules in future cases.

not indicate that the system ought to be condemned. The system would not, however, be one in which the functions associated with rule-based decision-making were very much served. Instead, the common law would be a system in which the advantages of precise application of background justifications were thought to outweigh the disadvantages of a necessarily cruder application of rules. And not only does the common law as it actually exists appear willing to sacrifice some of the goals of predictability and efficiency on the altar of perfectability, but it seems also, much to Bentham's disgust, to be willing to entrust considerable decision-making authority to the judiciary. A cruder rule-based approach would be one in which the power of judges to determine justifications would be more limited, in which people could plan their affairs based on a readily accessible and invariant guide to how those plans will be treated at law, in which the content of the law was more stable, and in which the use of decision-making resources was more efficient.[17] By ameliorating rule-based decision-making, the common law allocates power to its judges, treating the risks consequent to that empowerment as less dangerous than those flowing from the application of crude canonical rules to circumstances their makers might not have imagined and producing results the society might not be willing to tolerate.

This caricatured conception of the common law is not designed to portray accurately the decision-making process of existing common law systems. It is designed, however, to demonstrate the way in which the aspirations of the common law tend away from ruleness, and in which a gain in precisely what makes the common law distinctive is commensurately a loss in what makes rule-based decision-making valuable. At various times systems going by the name 'common law' have been closer or further from the pure common law model I have attempted to sketch. As an interesting historical literature has pointed out,[18] for example, the common law has quite frequently operated in a less instrumental and more formalistic style, treating the extant general understanding of a rule

---

[17] I refer here only to my previously employed conception of efficiency in terms of a frugal use of arguably limited decisional resources. I avoid the question of whether the output of the common law is indeed efficient in a larger sense. On that issue, see, for example, George Priest, 'The Common Law Process and the Selection of Efficient Rules'; Paul Rubin, 'Why is the Common Law Efficient?'

[18] See, for example, M. Horwitz, *The Transformation of American Law, 1780–1860*; R. B. Ferguson, 'The Horwitz Thesis and Common Law Discourse in England', *passim*.

as being at least *presumptively* applicable just because of its existence. In such cases these general understandings, formulated as summaries of the array of earlier decisions, carry normative weight even when their background justifications would not be served, and even when they might be marginally improved by changing them in the process of application. In practice, therefore, common-law rules become encrusted over time, and operate as rules in just the sense in which I use that term in this book. The previous understandings of rules become formulated both in cases and in the professional literature, these formulations (or minor variants on them) become entrenched, and consequently the meaning of that formulation, rather than a case-sensitive application of the justifications lying behind it, determines or at least influences the decision of subsequent cases, such that the seeming desirability of a modification or refinement of the existing rule is no longer a sufficient condition for making the modification or refinement.

When such an understanding of the common law is in force, previously articulated common law rules become sticky, resisting the modification to meet the case at hand that characterizes the common law. Under such circumstances, therefore, some decisions will be made in which the results differ from those that would have been generated absent this stickiness. To the extent that such cases exist, systems depart from a pure rule of thumb model of the common law. We thus see in most actual common law systems a willingness to accept, in traditional rule-like fashion, some number of inferior results in particular cases in exchange for those rule-related values fostered by a stronger conception of rules than the traditional theory of the common law purports to have. Moreover, actual common law systems purport to rely heavily on precedent to supply stability and predictability values. As the following section will show, this is more problematic than the traditional picture of the common law is often willing to acknowledge, but at the very least specific language in previous opinions often also takes on a canonical significance, being treated as itself a rule rather than merely the articulation of the reasons for creating one. Insofar as this phenomenon exists, the language in previous opinions serves to make actual common-law systems somewhat more rule-based in their methods than my earlier and sparser picture would indicate.

Still, although the common law as a system incorporates some number of devices ameliorating the system's tendencies away from rule-based decision-making, it is useful to think of the common law not only as a system but as a method. As a method, it is most associated with comparatively or completely transparent rules of thumb, seeking case-specific optimization rather than rule-based stability. And as a method, the common law is only contingently related to those subjects, such as property, contract, and tort, that in common law countries have been substantially developed by use of that method. It is also a method used to develop the law pursuant to the implicit authorization in broad statutory terms, and it is, according to some, even a method that should influence our understanding of statutes in canonical form.[19]

As a system and not as a method, however, we can see the common law as a decision-making environment in which the methods of the common law are present but not exclusive. Commonly the methods of the common law are tempered in common-law systems by rules, but rules appearing in slightly different form. Given their lack of codes, common-law systems normally find their rules in cases and in professional discourse, and will entrench those rules by understandings that tend to give those rules presumptive albeit not conclusive force. The vehicle for this entrenchment is often thought to be the idea of precedent, and it is to this that I will now turn.

8.3 *The Problem of Precedent*

Because the common law, even in more diluted form, still does not rely on the interpretation of canonical texts, its ruleness must be found elsewhere. Although authoritative descriptive rules in professional discourse may take on prescriptive status, more commonly the rule-based constraint within the common law is grounded in the principle of *precedent*. In dealing both with authoritative interpretations of statutes and with common-law decisions, legal systems characteristically purport to rely on precedent, and frequently justify that reliance by reference to many of the same virtues that are used to justify rule-based decision-making, such as predictability, stability, and decision-maker disability. This suggests that there

---

[19] See especially Guido Calabresi, *A Common Law for the Age of Statutes*. Such a suggestion has the effect of treating those statutes as themselves having at least some of the adaptability in the face of internal failure characteristic of rules of thumb. That approach, apart from any question of its desirability, is certainly plausible, for, as we saw in Chap. 6, specific rule-formulations have the status of rules in a strong sense if and only if a background set of understandings makes them so. Similarly, therefore, a different background set of understandings could make them something else, such as rules of thumb, or rules with at least some potential for simultaneous modification and application.

may be an affinity between rule-based and precedent-based decision-making, an affinity that itself may explain why decision-making systems valuing these traits find a place both for rules and for a strong system of precedent.

But just what is it to rely on precedent?[20] The bare skeleton of an appeal to precedent is easily stated: The previous treatment of occurrence A in manner x constitutes, solely because of its historical pedigree, a reason for treating A in manner x if and when A again occurs. It is important to recognize that although we can use the past for many purposes, not every use of the past involves reliance on precedent. We must, for example, differentiate an argument from precedent from an argument from experience. The first time a child sees a red coil on top of a stove he may touch it, but when he sees the red coil again he knows its dangers and keeps his fingers safely clear. When a physician sees a certain array of symptoms that in the past have indicated typhoid, she will probably diagnose typhoid when those symptoms again appear. Yet although in each of these cases a present array of facts similar to some previous array leads a decision-maker to draw on experience in reaching a conclusion, this process is different from an argument from precedent. When reasoning from experience, the facts and conclusions of the past have no significance apart from what they teach us about the present. The probability that the present will be like the past both determines and exhausts the value of the previous experience. If we believe that the current case ought to be decided differently, no purely precedential residuum remains in the calculus. Moreover, if we now believe that the previous decision was incorrect, we will completely reject the value of the experience. But if we are truly arguing from precedent rather than learning from experience, then the fact that something was decided before gives it present decisional weight despite our current belief that the previous decision was erroneous.

More generally, when the strength of a current conclusion totally stands or falls on arguments for or against that conclusion, there is no appeal to precedent, even if the same conclusion has been reached in the past. If precedent matters, a prior decision now believed erroneous still affects the current decision simply because it is prior, and thus an argument from precedent operates substantially like an argument from rule. Just as an argument from rule gives independent weight to the fact that a result is indicated by that

---

[20] In part of what follows, I recast arguments first made in Schauer, 'Precedent'.

rule, so too does an argument from precedent give independent
weight to the fact that a result resembles one reached in the past. An
argument from precedent is accordingly an argument from authority,
which is why calling a precedent authoritative is so different from
saying that it is persuasive.

What distinguishes reasoning from precedent from reasoning
from rule, however, is the necessity in precedential reasoning of
constructing the generalization/factual predicate that already exists
in the case of a rule. As we have seen, the factual predicate of a rule,
a generalization necessarily encompassing a multiplicity of events,
is part of the rule's canonical form. But where there is only a
previous decision and no rule-formulation, the source of the factual
predicate is obscure, and consequently the manner in which the
previous decision constrains becomes problematic. Consider still
another common-law landmark, *Donoghue* v. *Stevenson*, in which
the House of Lords ruled, as in *MacPherson* v. *Buick*, that the
bottler of a bottle of ginger beer would be liable to the ultimate
consumer of that product where the product was defective, in this
case for containing the remains of a decomposed snail.[21] Now if, as
it is said, this decision is to have precedential effect, what effect will
that be? Suppose a subsequent case presented the question of
liability in the context of a decomposed *spider* in a bottle of
sparkling *water*. Because spiders are not snails, because sparkling
water is not beer, and because the decision in *Donoghue* v. *Stevenson*
was only about a particular event, the court in the spider-in-the-
sparkling-water case must generalize, or construct a factual predicate,
around the result in the snail-in-the-ginger-beer case. The necessity
of generalization is brought about by the fact that the first case did
not involve a category, but was only about one event. *Donoghue* v.
Stevenson did not involve all beverages, or all decomposed animals,
or all of anything else. It was about decomposed snails in ginger
beer, and there is nothing that logically compels the spider-in-the-
sparkling-water case to be treated as similar to and therefore
governed by the snail-in-the-ginger-beer case.[22]

The problem of precedent is thus before us. No two events are
exactly alike, but the idea of precedential constraint presupposes
that a prior decision will control a subsequent set of facts that are
like the first. Yet given the lack of absolute identity, the determinant

[21] [1932] AC 532, 1932 SC (HL) 31.
[22] On the lack of a logical link between one case and another, see Julius Stone,
The Province and Function of Law, 187–9.

of likeness must come from somewhere other than the allegedly constraining decision of particular facts. Under one view, that determinant of likeness, or *rule of relevance*, is supplied by the second court. Because the first (precedent) case contains no generalization, the decision-maker in the second (instant) case creates the generalization *at that time*, in light of the circumstances of the instant case as well as those of the precedent case. Should it turn out that something about the difference between sparkling water and ginger beer was perceived at the time the instant case is decided to be normatively relevant, it is open to the judge to craft a different generalization, one that includes the precedent case but not the instant case.[23] It should be apparent, however, that this process is substantially non-constraining. Any number of generalizations could be constructed that would include the precedent case but not the instant case, or vice versa, and any number could be constructed to include both. As a result, the naked decision in the first case alone, as a set of facts and a result, can after the fact be taken to be an instance of any number of overlapping but non-congruent categories, and thus cannot serve to provide the rule-like constraint on subsequent cases that adherence to precedent is often thought to provide.

This conclusion does not change if there are numerous precedent cases rather than just one. Suppose there is a long history of adulterated product cases involving not only snails and spiders, but chemicals, bacteria, sand, and dirt, and involving not only bottles of beer and sparkling water, but products of all varieties. With such a stock of common-law cases, an observer could, by a process of inductive interpretation, state a legal rule, in the form of 'cases $c(1)$, $c(2)$, . . . $c(n)$ stand for the rule that x', where x has a generalizing factual predicate including $c(1)$ through $c(n)$. As with any inductive process, however, the ability to extract a rule from a series of cases is impeded by the phenomenon of underdetermination. No one rule is uniquely derivable from the series of previous decisions, and thus a multiplicity of extensionally divergent rules would satisfy the constraint of being compatible with all of the members of that

---

[23] On this process, see Edward H. Levi, *An Introduction to Legal Reasoning*, *passim*; Stone, *The Province and Function of Law*, 187–89. A variant asserts that the ability of the decision-maker in the precedent case to determine which facts are material operates as some constraint on the decision-maker in the instant case. Arthur Goodhart, 'Determining the Ratio Decidendi of a Case'. Even this view, however, emphasizes the construction in the latter case rather than the constraint of the earlier. J. L. Montrose, 'The Ratio Decidendi of a Case', 593.

series. As we saw in examining the relevance of Wittgensteinian rule-following considerations to regulative rules (Chapter 4.3), therefore, the ability to identify the rule-based constraint in a series without a formulated generalization is deeply problematic. But again as with any inductive process, the problem of underdetermination does not make induction in reality impossible. It does, however, make the inductive result dependent on contingent values lying outside the particulars around which the inductive generalization is constructed. These values are themselves more or less entrenched, however, and in the context of complex and contested legal events the constraints that make some inductions permissible and others not will rarely be sufficient to prevent a decision-maker from constructing generalizations that would justify either of two mutually exclusive decisions.

Faced with these and related problems, a common view of legal precedent considers the precedent to consist not only of the previous events and a decision, but also of the precedent court's *description* of those facts. Once the description of the facts become part of what the precedent *is*, then it turns out that an argument from precedent is quite similar to an argument from rule.[24] The description of the precedent facts is in reality a generalization, and as a result this articulated description constitutes the factual predicate for a rule. If the precedent court decides the snail-in-the-ginger-beer case *because* harmful substances should not be found in consumer products, and explicitly describes a snail in a bottle of ginger beer as an instance of the category of harmful substances in consumer products, then a subsequent court can take that description as the factual predicate of a rule and decide (and be constrained) accordingly.

Even if there is in the precedent case no explicit statement of the category of which the precedent case is a member, it is likely that the precedent court will indicate its reasons for deciding in one way rather than another. Given that a reason is a reason only because it is logically prior to and broader than the decision that it is a reason for, a reason can be seen as itself a generalization. Consequently a subsequent court can use the reasoning in the precedent case to construct the generalization which in turn will comprise the factual predicate of a potentially constraining rule.[25]

---

[24] A persuasive articulation of this view is Larry Alexander, 'Constrained by Precedent'. For a precursor, see Simpson, 'The Ratio Decidendi of a Case', 415.

[25] The more 'construction' that takes place, however, the more the problem of undetermination intrudes, with extensionally divergent constructions of the same

At times, however, there will be no authoritative characterization, whether direct or through the mediation of a rationale, in the precedent case. This can happen as a consequence of indeterminacy in the language of a judicial opinion, or because there may (both in law and without) be no written opinion at all. Yet even in the absence in the precedent case of an authoritative characterization supplying an authoritative generalization, the constraints of precedent may not be quite as illusory as is often supposed. Even if no two events are exactly alike, and even if nothing in the precedent case mandates the appropriate generalizing category, it is a mistake to assume that the decision-maker in the instant case is largely unconstrained in determining what events are assimilable with what other events. At times, we may be dealing with natural kinds, such that our knowledge of an access to these kinds is likely to create pressures to decide subsequent dog cases in the same way that earlier dog cases were decided just because the category 'dog', being natural, imposes itself to make some assimilations more plausible than others. And even when natural kinds are not involved, or are merely components of more complex events, the categories of assimilation may still be substantially determined by linguistic and cultural determinations largely out of the control of individual decision-makers. Despite obvious differences, we refer to both amateur chess and professional football as 'games', and despite obvious similarities, we have different words for killing deer in the woods of Vermont than we do for killing cows in the stockyards of Omaha. Such extra-legal categories of assimilation have the potential for creating groupings that transcend and intrude into individual decision-making. As a result, insofar as some characterizations of past events flow more easily as a result of their place within an existing linguistic and conceptual structure, it will not necessarily be the case that a previous decision is totally subject to multiple generalizations around it. Although numerous generalizations may be logically possible, linguistic and cultural patterns larger than any one decision-making environment may still make some generalizations much more possible than others. The presence of a live snail in a bottle of ginger beer is logically both an example of an adulterated consumer product and an example of a trapped animal, but in this world the former generalization is culturally, linguistically, and psychologically much easier than the latter. Similarly, government

reasons becoming increasingly possible with an increase in the vagueness or complexity of the reasons articulated in the precedent case.

prohibition of a march by neo-Nazis in the United States is more likely to be taken as an instance of government suppression of political speech than as an instance of action against Nazis, just as exactly the opposite assimilative tendencies might be expected in Germany or Israel. As a result, it may often be the case that the absence of a canonical generalization in the precedent case is not dispositive of the lack of precedential constraint in the instant case, for the decision-maker in the instant case may find that in looking at a previous decision she discovers a factual predicate forming around it purely by virtue of the conceptual apparatus with which she views the world.

Thus, either a canonical description in the precedent case of the facts of that case, or a canonical rationale in the precedent case that can be used to construct a derivitively canonical description, or a seemingly natural category within which the facts of the precedent case fall, may each serve as a generalization from the past, and thus comprise the factual predicate of a rule now to be applied. This itself says nothing about the weight that a precedent-derived rule will have in the decision in the instant case, any more than the formulation of any other rule determines its own weight.[26] It does show, however, that except for the fact that the lack of a canonical formulation of a factual predicate substantially increases the indeterminacy of the rule set forth in the precedent case (an indeterminacy that is compounded when multiple and extensionally divergent precedent cases are available), nothing about precedent-based constraint uniquely differentiates it from rule-based constraint. This leaves a great deal to be said about the status of a precedent-derived rule, but now that we see that such rules are but a subset of rules *simpliciter*, we can assimilate into the ensuing discussion of the weight and status of legal rules all of the issues that might arise with respect to the weight and status of legal precedent.[27]

[26] On precedents as providing reweighting second-order reasons see Stephen Perry, Second-Order Reasons, Uncertainty and Legal Theory', 932–6; id., 'Judicial Obligation, Precedent and the Common Law', *passim*.

[27] The commonplace distinction between *distinguishing* a precedent and *overruling* it tracks the distinction between modifying a rule at the moment of application and repealing it. If the instant case lies outside the factual predicate of the rule constructed from the precedent case, then the precedent case is not a precedent for the instant case. But if the instant case lies within the factual predicate of the rule constructed, yet is distinguished from the precedent case because of differences between the instant and precedent cases not reflected in the previous understanding of what the precedent case was a precedent for, then what is described as distinguishing is exactly like modifying a rule at the moment of application, and so substituting a new rule for the old one.

8.4 *Conflicts of Rules and the Priority of the Local*

The extent to which a legal system is rule-based will thus be largely a function of the weight attributed to canonically formulated rules, professionally understood rules of the common law, and rules that are constructed around prior decisions. Even where that weight is substantial, however, the dominance of rule-based decision-making within the system is far from assured. Only if every event fell under one and only one rule would the status of individual rules *as* rules be a reliable indicator of the extent of rule-based constraint in the system as a whole. Yet in reality this is rarely the case, and more commonly various rules and precedents within a decision-making system will for many cases point in opposite directions. Without any mechanism for dealing with conflicts of rules, no amount of weight attached to any single rule will assure rule-based decision-making, for that weight will frequently be cancelled by a rule of equivalent weight indicating the opposite conclusion.

Thus although in previous sections of this chapter, and indeed throughout this book, I have been looking only at isolated rules, it is time to complicate the picture, for most rule *systems* contain a highly complex array of rules. When a multiplicity of rules are arrayed as a system, the degree of rule-based constraint will often turn out to be more a function of how the various rules relate to each other than of how any one rule operates. This is less a logical claim than an empirical one. Although the phenomenon of open texture ensures that no system can be perpetually immune from conflicts among its rules, rules planned carefully in light of existing knowledge can at least minimize the likelihood of conflict. Yet when rules are drafted not simultaneously but over time by numerous non-co-ordinating drafters, the potential for conflict increases dramatically. As a result, the array of rules comprising the legal system (or any similarly designed rule system) will frequently indicate different and mutually exclusive results for the same event, especially given the fact that events themselves are complex and not simple. When the array of rules is that messy, the hierarchy of these potentially conflicting rules is much more likely than the status of any one rule to determine the extent of rule-based constraint within the system.

The relationship among rules within a rule system can be usefully described in terms of the dimension of *locality*. Consider the difference between two rules, one requiring all drivers to drive safely at all times and another setting a *minimum* speed of 40 miles per hour on a certain stretch of limited-access highway. Although the rules are extensionally divergent, some cases exist which are within the factual predicates of both rules and for which the two rules indicate different and mutually exclusive results. Driving at 40 miles per hour or more might also under some circumstances be unsafe driving. But although many cases can be imagined in which two (or more) potentially conflicting rules are applicable, one of the rules seems *more* applicable, or, to put it better, more *directly* applicable. The rule that is less general, and applicable to a smaller number of events, seems to be more applicable to the events to which it does apply. The rule that includes the smaller number of events in addition to the event at issue seems in some way to be closer to that event, and thus this rule can be called the more *local* rule.[28]

The dimension of locality explains many of the tensions that arise in systems of rules. It is logically possible but rare in practice for two rules of equivalent locality to conflict. Rules specifying a maximum speed of 40 miles per hour rarely govern the same stretch of highway as do those specifying a minimum speed of 45. Far more common are conflicts between rules located different distances from the particular event under consideration. *Riggs* v. *Palmer*,[29] immortalized by Ronald Dworkin,[30] is as good an example as any. In *Riggs* a testator had in his will named his grandson as beneficiary, and the grandson thereafter attempted to accelerate the receipt of his legacy by murdering his grandfather. When the legacy was challenged in court, the grandson relied on the Statute of Wills, which at the time provided, in essence, that one named in a will shall inherit in accordance with its terms.[31] The challengers, however, relied successfully on a less local but still applicable rule, one prohibiting people from profiting by their own wrongs.

---

[28] The dimension I refer to as 'locality' is quite similar to that of generality. '[A] principle p1 is more general than another principle p2 if and only if it is analytically true that to break p2 is, in virtue of that fact, to break p1, but the converse is not analytically true', R. M. Hare, 'Principles', 3. Yet unlike Hare's account of generality, my notion of locality allows for one rule being more local than another rule which goes in a different direction. Under my account, a 'no vehicles in the park' rule, based on safety, is more locally applicable to some vehicle in the park situation than is a 'be polite' rule, even though it is not necessarily the case that to bring a vehicle into the park is to be impolite.

[29] 115 NY 506, 22 NE 188 (1889).

[30] Ronald Dworkin, *Taking Rights Seriously*, 23; id., *Law's Empire*, 15–20.

[31] See Charles Silver, 'Elmer's Case', 383.

The decision in *Riggs* therefore represents the resolution of a normative conflict by giving the more distant rule a priority over the more local. Insofar as less local rules such as the 'no man shall profit from his own wrong' rule involved in *Riggs* are likely to be less specific, more global, and in some way more fundamental, such an approach to normative conflict is hardly illogical. A priority of the more fundamental (even if more distant) over the more local, however, will diminish the constraints in any system using that mechanism for resolving normative conflict. Given that rules are instantiations of their justifications, one way of viewing the conflict between the local and the distant is as a conflict between the result generated by the rule and the result generated by direct application of the less local but still applicable justification. In a complex normative system, however, local rules are likely to conflict not only vertically with the results indicated by *their* generating justifications, but also horizontally (or perhaps diagonally) with the justifications lying elsewhere in the system. The Statute of Wills, which served as the rule allowing the named beneficiary—the grandson—to inherit in *Riggs*, is not the instantiation of the principle that no one shall profit from his own wrong. The two lie along different axes. But a norm of decision permitting (or even requiring) the decision-maker to prefer the more distant rule is but an extension of a norm permitting that decision-maker to prefer the rule's own generating justification to the rule itself. If rule-based constraint is diminished insofar as rules are defeasible in the service of their own justifications, as I have argued at length throughout this book, then, *a fortiori*, that constraint is diminished to the extent that the most local rule is defeasible even in the service of justifications lying elsewhere within the system.

Conversely, the power of rules is increased within a rule system to the extent that rules have a *local priority*, both over their own justifications and over other more distant rules within the system. When the priority of a specifically applicable rule generates the outcome consistent with that rule even when other rules within the system would say otherwise, and even when a decision-maker taking everything into account would choose a result other than that indicated by the most local rule, decision-makers constrained by that priority will be in some cases precluded from reaching the best result. Thus, for rules to operate *as rules* within a system of rules, it is not enough that they must be treated as entrenched with respect to their own generating justifications. They must be treated as entrenchèd with respect to other rules as well, and it is that relationship that the idea of local priority seeks to capture.

Local priority need not be absolute to be a priority, any more than rules need be absolute in order to be rules. But given that existing legal systems are (contingently) such that events will frequently be conflictingly controlled by rules more and less locally applicable, *some* degree of local priority is necessary to preserve in those systems a modicum of rule-based decision-making. Commonly that priority exists only as a presumption, subject to being overcome in particularly exigent cases such as *Riggs*. That the Statute of Wills operates in this presumptive but not absolute way, for example, is demonstrated by the fact that many unworthy beneficiaries not as spectacularly unworthy as the grandson in *Riggs* do inherit according to the terms of the will, although they might not if a rule such as 'no man may profit from his own wrong' were to be applied directly to their conduct. Thus the local priority can be overridden, but the fact that it takes more to override the local priority in the name of another rule than would be necessary to apply the other rule in the absence of the local priority is reflected in the set of cases, such as those involving slightly unworthy beneficiaries, for which the overridable priority is not in fact overridden. Such outcomes indicate that at least presumptive priority is commonly granted to the most locally applicable rule, a status that appears minimally necessary for rules existing within rule systems to do the work that is expected of them.

8.5 *The Realist Challenge*

But is all this illusory? Does all the talk of rules and presumptions actually make a difference? No discussion of rule systems in law, and indeed no discussion of rules at all, would be complete without dealing with that series of sceptical challenges to rule-based decision-making called *American Legal Realism*, or, more commonly, simply *Legal Realism*. Legal Realism has nothing whatsoever do to with metaphysical or ethical realism, or with any other philosophical position commonly referred to as 'realist'. Indeed, in important ways Legal Realism is the polar opposite of such positions, for Legal Realism argues that legal decision-makers are largely unconstrained by forces external to their own decision-making preferences.[32] The Legal Realists, of whom Jerome Frank and Karl Llewellyn were the

---

[32] See Jules Coleman, 'Negative and Positive Positivism', 147–8.

most prominent,[33] challenged the ability of rules to constrain choice, especially judicial choice, in the way that the traditional account of rules supposes. The Realists believed that decision-makers, especially judges deciding hard cases, initially make an 'all things considered' judgement about who ought to win. That preliminary judgement, taking into account moral, political, economic, and psychological factors, is not arbitrary, but is particularistic in focusing on the optimal result *for this case*. Having made that decision, the decision-maker, the Realists contend, *then* rationalizes the decision in terms of some legal rule. To the Legal Realist, rules serve not as sources of *ex ante* guidance, but as vehicles of *ex post* legitimation of decisions reached without regard for the rules.

The Realists recognized that some amount of legitimizing was necessary. They did not see legal decision-makers as tyrants able to rely on 'because I said so' to justify whatever they wished. Rather, the Realists acknowledged that legal decision-makers ordinarily operate in a social and political milieu in which they are compelled to support their decisions with a publicly plausible justification. But although Realism recognizes the necessity of a plausible public justification referring to existing legal rules, it argues as well that when faced with a decision-making occasion, the judge can rationalize any number of conflicting decisions. If this is so, none of those rule-rationalized choices commands its priority over any other, and the choice among rule-rationalizable outcomes will be based on non-rule-based, or all-things-considered, grounds. The notion of a rule as a constraint on decision thus evaporates, with references to rules serving only to mask what is in reality particularistic decision-making.

The Realist picture of decision-making may seem an implausible account of a wide variety of decision-making situations. Our daily encounters with rules, legal and otherwise, belie the claim that we can do whatever we wish and find some legal rule to support our actions. There appear to be no rules rationalizing the conclusions that someone may serve three four-year terms as President of the United States, that English law permits a father to marry his natural daughter, or that a person failing to pay her income taxes by the

[33] See Jerome Frank, *Law and the Modern Mind*; Karl Llewellyn, *The Bramble Bush*; id., *Jurisprudence: Realism in Theory and Practice*. Among the more useful secondary accounts are Laura Kalman, *Legal Realism at Yale*; Wilfred Rumble, *American Legal Realism*; William Twining, *Karl Llewellyn and the Realist Movement*. Contemporary manifestations include Duncan Kennedy, 'Freedom and Constraint in Adjudication: Toward a Critical Phenomenology of Judging'.

appointed time shall under Norwegian law be put to death, any more than there is a rule in contract bridge allowing a player to bid two spades after his opponent has made a legal bid of three hearts. No Realist has seriously claimed that rules are *so* illusory that a decision-maker desiring one of these outcomes could reach it and rationalize that conclusion, for any sophisticated version of Realism recognizes that insofar as anyone sought such results, they would likely note the futility of litigation and the issue would simply never arise. The corollary of this, however, is that the cases that do arise occur largely within the domain of events that two parties deem worth litigating. Given this constraint on the array of occasions for judicial decision, the plausibility of the Realist challenge increases dramatically, for now we are looking at a domain of decisional occasions selected at least in part for their difficulty.[34] Thus if we assume that litigants are statistically unlikely to litigate a plainly specious claim, the array of decisional opportunities confronting a judge will be a self-selected group of cases in which a plausible rule-based argument can be made on both sides of the issue.[35]

With respect to this limited array of cases the Realist challenge appears most powerful, for now that challenge can be reformulated to maintain that with respect to any decision in which two parties can urge a non-frivolous result, judges can (and do) decide on the basis of factors external to the rules they purportedly apply, using rules only to rationalize results reached on non-rule-based grounds. Moreover, it appears that the likelihood of legally justifying both of two mutually exclusive results is dramatically increased by the ability of the decision-maker to rely on different features of the same event. We have seen that sometimes several conflicting rules (possibly at different distances from the event) will apply to the same description of the same event. More commonly, however, conflicts among rules will arise as a product of the way in which any complex event can be characterized in various ways. Even if it is rare for a legal system simultaneously to require and to prohibit the same conduct, it is not so rare for a legal system to have rules simultaneously requiring x and prohibiting y. Insofar as some number of complex events contain both x and y properties, there-fore, the alternative characterizations produce the same effect that

---

[34] On the empirical basis for the claim that disputes wind up in court in proportion to their legal difficulty, see George Priest and William Klein, 'The Selection of Disputes for Litigation', *passim*.

[35] I explore this issue at length in Schauer, 'Judging in a Corner of the Law'.

would be produced had the legal system contained a rule both requiring and prohibiting x (or y).[36]

That the Realist challenge is both coherent and plausible, however, is not sufficient to prove it. If the challenge is only that people are likely to litigate cases not resolved by a system of rules, and that in *those* cases either of two (or more) mutually exclusive results can be justified according to some rule, it approaches being true by definition, saying only that rules do not guide the decisions they either do not address or do not resolve.[37] But the Realist claim is stronger, purporting also to describe cases that rules do literally address. Here part of the claim is based on the existence of rules sufficiently indeterminate to make them tolerant of widely divergent specifications. Suppose some rule required a judge to resolve all disputes so as best to protect human dignity and rights. And then suppose the judge were asked to decide whether to punish a person who publicly and erroneously (but in good faith) impugned the honesty of another. Insofar as it is possible to justify either result (liability or non-liability for the impugner) as promoting human dignity and rights, depending on how one evaluates the competing rights to speak and to a good reputation, it is clear that the rule itself does not bear the laboring oar in pointing to one result rather than the other. The concern of the Realists was that this fact was often obscured in the language of judicial justification, with judges often pretending that it was the rule rather than something else that determined the outcome.

More commonly Realism seizes upon cases involving potentially conflicting rules within a rule system. When a rule system contains rules of equivalent locality, or contains no priority rules preferring the local to the distant, or contains an array of rules often able to justify opposite results depending on the characterization of a single event, decision-makers will often be able to justify by reference to a rule either of two (or more) incompatible results. These possibilities provide the foundation of the Realist challenge, which can now be seen as an empirical claim about the propensity of any rule system to fail to provide rule-based guidance for the events that it purports to cover.

In fact the Realist challenge is empirical in two ways. First, it is a

---

[36] Among the earliest sources of this argument is F. Geny, *Méthode D'Interprétation et Sources en Droit Privé Positif, passim.*

[37] Making this definitionally true claim may be important if people deny the phenomenon of choice within the universe of close cases. See Schauer, 'Formalism'.

contingent but not a necessary truth that rule systems have a multitude of actually or potentially conflicting norms. We know that the phenomenon of open texture assures that rule systems cannot guarantee perpetual avoidance of conflict, especially when complex events allow their inclusion under multiple rules.[38] And we know that litigation incentives are such that a formal adjudicative system would see a concentration of open-texture cases. But even so the Realist challenge would be largely epiphenomenal for a rule system designed with the express purpose of minimizing to the greatest extent conflict between rules for all foreseeable events. No existing legal system, however, has been designed with such singleness of purpose, and consequently the availability of rules to justify inconsistent results is a frequent albeit contingent fact of existing legal systems, although the extent of the phenomenon varies from system to system.

In addition, the Realist challenge makes an empirical claim about the psychology of the judge and about most judges' self-understandings of their roles. Assuming the availability of multiple and apparently conflicting justificatory rules, a decision-maker is faced with two alternatives. She can decide on the basis of factors other than those rules, and then employ the congenial rules to justify a decision reached on other grounds. Or she can wrestle with the rules, attempting to find some reconciliation or interpretation or priority that will eliminate what at first looked like a conflict between opposing rules. Although the Realists assumed the former, yet other perspectives on judicial decision-making, most notably that of Ronald Dworkin, assume just the opposite, and assume that a judge faced with seemingly conflicting rules will take that as an opportunity for deeper reflection rather than for departure from the domain of the rule system. Although resolving this dispute about

[38] This is a logical necessity, a function of the way in which the terms of the legal system are themselves open-textured, and thus always potentially vague. Yet this logical possibility need not loom as large as often supposed. Any rule system could contain a default (or closure) rule providing that any event not encompassed by the existing rules was to be treated in some particular way. For example, a legal system could contain a rule providing that no liability could be imposed unless the grounds for liability were apparent in the existing set of legal rules. Although this would not eliminate the potential vagueness that could come from new events lying on the edge of what was previously thought clear, it would eliminate much of the difficulty ordinarily presented by the occurrence of events not then dealt with by existing rules. It is only because the legal system seeks to regulate all human conduct (see below, Chap. 9.3), and only because it is unwilling to tolerate the consequences of such a default rule in doing so, that hitherto unexpected events create the legal problems that they do.

the psychology and self-understanding of the judge is empirical, there is no reason to suppose that the answer is consistent across the domain of decision-makers. Where the decision-maker has strong views, whether on morals, politics, personality, or economics, and where the case implicates those views, then the former mode may prevail, with the moral, political, psychological, or economic view dominating the desire to work out the best internally coherent answer. But where the decision-maker is more agnostic, either generally or about the issues presented in the particular case, an account premised on the desire of judges always to interpose their own views may misrepresent the phenomenology of judging.

The plausibility of the Realist challenge consequently hinges on empirical conclusions about the structure of a rule system and about judicial self-understanding (or judicial ability to act on some self-understanding). The Realist empirical conclusions are at least plausible, and in many decision-making environments may well be correct, although I can hardly go further here. We can now see, however, that the Realist challenge is but an application of a point discussed earlier. Because rules operate within a framework that determines the status of those rules, and because that framework is likely to be substantially political, social, economic, and psychological, the status of a rule in the decisional process of any decision-maker, or a population of decision-makers, is not something that can be determined solely by analysing the concept of a rule. That analysis can explain what happens when decision-makers take rules seriously. It cannot explain if and when they do so.

8.6 *Presumptive Positivism*

The discussion of canonical rules, common-law rules, precedent, and local priority has stressed the way in which each of these features of legal decision-making contributes to the extent of rule-based constraint in the system. Commonly these constraints will be presumptive rather than absolute, thereby providing some constraint while allowing for the possibility of override in particularly exigent circumstances. When rules or their equivalents function in this presumptive manner, the values served by rules are promoted but tempered by the way in which presumptions, as discussed in Chapter 5.3, allow a decision-maker to retain the ability to glimpse at the full array of available factors to determine if this is a case in which those factors might provide a reason of such exceptional strength as to provide a stronger reason for overcoming the exclusion of those

factors than the rule provides for the exclusion itself. If this normatively appealing picture of the role of rules is also descriptively
accurate for many legal systems, it provides for us a new way of
looking at an old issue.

For generations legal theorists have been debating the conceptual
validity, descriptive accuracy, and normative desirability of a perspective on law known as *positivism*, which under one view is the
systemic embodiment of a rule-based perspective on normative
systems. Discussions of legal positivism often counterpoise that
perspective with one known as 'natural law', and the central tenet of
positivism is consequently taken to be its denial of any necessary
connection between law and morality. From Austin and Bentham
to Hart and Kelsen to MacCormick and Raz, prominent positivists
have offered a perspective on legal systems that maintains that the
identification of a legal norm, and the designation of it as legal, are
logically independent of the substantive moral content of that
norm. At this point, however, confusion sets in unless we distinguish
two quite different conceptions of positivism.

One conception of positivism, traceable to Kelsen and recently
offered in different versions by Jules Coleman,[39] David Lyons,[40]
and Philip Soper,[41] denies that positivism is a descriptive claim, and
maintains instead that it is a conceptual claim about the idea of law,
such that what is or is not law in a community is a social fact about
that community. Under this view, what Coleman calls 'the separability
thesis', positivism is correct as long as a community *could* establish
as law a set of norms or decision-making process not dependent for
its status as law on its moral correctness. 'The separability thesis is
the claim that there exists at least one conceivable rule of recognition
(and therefore one possible legal system) that does not specify truth
as a moral principle among the truth conditions for any proposition
of law'. But pursuant to this account of positivism a community
could also establish as its law not only a set of norms dependent on
moral correctness, but could even make its set of legal norms totally
congruent with its set of moral norms. As long as the determination
is made by the community, as long as it is a question itself of social
fact, then there remains no *necessary* connection between law and
morality.

---

[39] Coleman, 'Negative and Positive Positivism'.
[40] David Lyons, 'Principles, Positivism, and Legal Theory'.
[41] Philip Soper, 'Legal Theory and the Obligation of the Judge: The Hart/
Dworkin Dispute'.

This conceptual account of positivism may well be correct, and in fact I believe it is, but whether it is or not has very little connection with an account of rules. If positivism maintains only that what is law and what is not is determined by social fact and not necessarily by moral argument, then similarly a community decision to take as its law the *ad hoc* decisions of one person would also be sufficient for it to be so. And if such an extreme version of rule-free decision-making satisfies the conditions for law, then it is clear that nothing about rules has much bearing one way or another on the soundness of the positivist thesis as a non-descriptive metaphysical or conceptual account of the nature of law.

Under another understanding of positivism, however, one defended (in a more extreme form than is relevant here) by Raz[42] and attacked by Dworkin, positivism is a descriptive claim about extensional divergence between a community's law and its morality, such that for positivism to be descriptively correct the rule of recognition in any community (if the descriptive claim is taken to be universal) or some community (if the descriptive claim is only about one community) must demarcate that community's law from its morality. Under this view (and I have no cause here to argue which view is a better account of positivism), one seeing positivism as descriptive rather than conceptual account, a community whose law and morality are congruent is not a community whose legal system is accurately *described* as positivistic.

From the perspective of this understanding of what positivism purports to claim, positivism is descriptively accurate in any community in which the set of legal norms is not congruent with the set of moral norms. Now, however, the emphasis on morality is distracting. In this descriptive rather than conceptual debate about positivism, morality is but an example of a larger universe of the 'non-legal'. Although those who subscribe to this version of what questions positivism seeks to address and what answers it gives to them do maintain that the core of positivism consists of its denial of a conceptual or necessary connection between the status of a rule as a rule of law and the moral desirability of that rule, they would, if asked, maintain with equivalent fervor the denial of a conceptual connection between the status of a rule as a rule of law and, say, its political feasibility, its aesthetic or literary appeal, or its economic viability. Just as this understanding of positivism maintains that a

---

[42] Raz, *The Authority of Law*, 37–52.

morally iniquitous law can still be a law, so too does it (or would it) maintain that both economically silly and politically disastrous laws are still laws.

Little point would be served here by trying to resolve the debate between which of these accounts of positivism is sounder. I want to assume the soundness of the latter account of what positivism claims (which is not to assume that the claim is correct), but that is consistent with the former account, addressing a quite different question, also being sound. But nothing here turns on the assumption, and readers who resist it can substitute a word other than 'positivism' for the claim of extensional divergence that grounds what is to follow. Still, under the assumption that positivism is about the *idea* of recognition (rather than 'rule' of recognition, which may impose an unnecessary constraint) in the Hartian sense, the heart of positivism lies not in something special about the law/morality distinction, but in the concept of *systemic isolation*. To the positivist there can be systems whose norms are identified by reference to some identifier that can distinguish *legal* norms from other norms, such as those of politics, morality, economics, or etiquette. This identifier, which Hart refers to as the 'rule of recognition' and Dworkin labels a 'pedigree', picks out legal norms from the universe of norms, and thus provides a test for legal validity. If a norm is so selected, it is a valid legal norm, notwithstanding its moral repugnance, economic inconsistency, or political folly.

Once we see that positivism is about normative systems smaller than and distinguishable from the entire normative universe, we can agree that a positivist system is in many respects the systemic analogue of a rule.[43] Just as rules commit decision-making to a truncated array of relevant decisional factors, so too does positivism commit decision-making to a truncated array of norms. And just as this narrowing of the potentially relevant may in the case of individual rules generate an answer that is, all things considered, the wrong answer, so too may decision-making solely according to the norms picked out by the rule of recognition be the wrong answer from the perspective of the background justifications for the legal system as a whole. A positivist view of a legal system takes the legal system as a

---

[43] We might think of the idea of a 'closed system', but this idea should be taken with caution. As Kelsen properly insisted, there is no reason to believe that a closed system of legal norms need constitute the exclusive source of decisional guidance within the legal system. Moreover, as Kelsen also teaches us, distinguishing legal from non-legal norms does not entail the conclusion that legal norms can be applied to particular cases without the use of extra-legal considerations.

whole to be the instantiation of its background justification (justice, or order, or whatever), and, in rule-like fashion, treats that instantiation as entrenched against efforts to view it as merely transparent to the justifications for the system itself.

We are now in a position to understand Ronald Dworkin's powerful attack on positivism. If we look at real legal systems, he claims, we often see that the results indicated by application of the pedigreed rule are morally, socially, economically, or politically undesirable. Consider again *Riggs* v. *Palmer*, the case of the murdering heir. *Riggs*, to repeat, was not a hard case in the sense of presenting events not covered by existing rules. The existing rules, rules whose validity could be ascertained by recourse to a Hartian rule of recognition, *did* provide an answer.[44] It was just that that answer was morally uncomfortable, and what positivism cannot explain is when and how, as in *Riggs*, the answer generated by positivism is rejected by recourse to norms not themselves identified or identifiable by a rule of recognition. Positivism, of course, does not maintain a strong thesis of exclusivity. Nothing about positivism compels the idea that only legally pedigreed rules should guide judicial decisions. But positivism does seem committed to the weaker thesis that *if* there is a legally pedigreed rule that applies to the case at hand, then it should be employed to produce the result. If legal decision-makers may disregard the result generated by the legally recognized rule, then there seems little point in the idea of a rule of recognition at all.

But even this view might be stronger than positivism needs. That is, it could be said that what happened in *Riggs* was simply that non-legal norms trumped the legal, in the same way that positivist theory allows the citizen to refuse to obey morally reprehensible laws. Positivism is about legal validity and not about ultimate action, and nothing in positivism commits any decision-maker, including a judge in a court of law, to treating positivistic norms as the exclusive input into decision-making.

Such a solution to *Riggs*, however logically impeccable it might be, would seem to the Dworkinian as experientially impoverished. If it turns out that judges, the archetypal legal actors, are with some frequency deciding cases according to norms other than legal norms, than what purpose is served by identifying the subset that we would call 'legal'?[45]

---

[44] See Sanford Levinson, 'Taking Law Seriously', 1087.

[45] At this point, the difference in focus between Dworkin and the positivists

Some defenders of positivism have attempted to respond to Dworkin's challenge in a different way, noting the way in which the trumping norm in *Riggs*, that no man may profit from his own wrong, is itself a legal norm, pedigreed as valid in its own right by a rule of recognition.[46] If that is so, then nothing about *Riggs* calls positivism into question, and *Riggs* is but an example of the fact that the rule of recognition may recognize rules of priority allowing such general and distant rules (what Dworkin calls 'principles') to trump less general and more locally applicable rules.

Yet even this response can be met by cases such as *Henningsen* v. *Bloomfield Motors*. What makes *Henningsen* important is not that it too, as in *Riggs*, set aside what seemed prior to the case to be the answer generated by the positivistically recognized rules. What cases like *Henningsen* show us is that no answer generated by the set of positivistically pedigreed norms is immune from rejection in the service of norms not so pedigreed. However possible it might be to argue that *Riggs* set aside the positive law in the name of other positive law, the same cannot be said of *Henningsen*, where the positive law was set aside in the name of moral and social principles not previously incorporated within the legal system. And if positive law is always capable of being set aside in the name of non-pedigreed values, then even a decision not to set aside the positive law involves a decision, *en passant*, that the positive law is consistent with those larger values.[47] The result of this, a result inconsistent with the positivist picture, is that legal results are *always* a function not only of pedigreed norms, but of non-pedigreed and non-pedigreeable ones as well.[48]

becomes crucial. Many positivists see themselves as primarily concerned with the normal operation of legal rules in everyday life, and if that perspective says little about the role of the judge in morally or politically or even legally hard cases, it is only minor cause for concern. Yet Dworkin, seeing law largely through the eyes of the judge, needs to treat as central what most positivists view as peripheral.

[46] For this variety of defense of positivism, see Coleman, 'Negative and Positive Positivism', *passim*; Neil MacCormick, *Legal Reasoning and Legal Theory*, 229–74; Rolf Sartorius, 'Social Policy and Judicial Legislation', *passim*; Silver, 'Elmer's Case', 387–99; Richard Tur, 'Positivism, Principles, and Rules', *passim*.

[47] On this point, see *Law's Empire*, 350–4, and Melvin Eisenberg, *The Nature of the Common Law*, 2–3, 146–61.

[48] Insofar as *Henningsen* stands instead for the proposition that in some systems judges are unlimited in the norms they may use in making their decisions, then an account of judicial decision-making may be positivistic in the first (conceptual) sense but not in the second (descriptive) sense, for now from the perspective of the judge there is no systemic isolation and no rule of recognition distinguishing legitimate legal inputs into judicial decision-making from any other inputs.

Riggs, *Henningsen*, and related cases cannot be taken to be have refuted positivism, however, but only to have refuted the proposition that positivism accurately describes the legal system of the United States or the legal system of any other country in which similar examples can be found. Imagine a system, however, in which (*a*) a master rule of recognition pedigreed a limited number of rules; (*b*) all decision-makers within the system were instructed to make decisions according to and only according to those pedigreed rules; and (*c*) a default (or closure) rule specified the result to be reached in all cases not covered by one of the pedigreed rules. In such a system, a positivistic explanation appears to be sound, and we can thus see that positivism as a descriptive thesis is flawed not conceptually (unless taken to be a claim about all legal systems, rather than about possible legal systems), but only empirically. Few legal systems resemble this stylized model, but there is no logical reason why they could not.

That real systems have departed from this model should come as no surprise. It is characteristic of legal systems that the matters with which they deal are important, in a way that the rule systems of chess and cricket are not. The outcome of a legal decision may make a litigant a prince or a pauper, famous or infamous, a success or a failure. And when the litigants for whom such consequences attach are standing before the legal decision-maker, the pressure to reach the correct result, rather than the substantively incorrect result generated by faithful application of the rules, is likely to be enormous. Moreover, law does not just stand there to be watched. We expect people to obey its mandates, even when they disagree. In some systems, most notably and most extremely the United States, the system is also entrusted with the power to make decisions with profound moral, political, and economic effects. Is it any wonder, then, that such a system would be uncomfortable with a decision, however justified by reference only to a particular rule, that seemed incorrect in light of all morally, socially, and politically relevant considerations? And if a society desires a system in which respect and accuracy are more important than predictability, stability, or even decision-maker disability, then might not the virtues of ruleness be sacrificed with some frequency to the goals of reaching the best answer?

Yet even within a system recognizing that the large and distant must occasionally trump the small and local, the virtues associated with rules seem still to persist. We cannot and do not expect individuals incessantly to be calculating the likelihood that 55 miles per hour may under some circumstances mean something else. Or maybe we do expect citizens to engage in such calculations, but we are confident that these calculations will be so intuitive and usually so coincident with the locally generated answer that the calculating citizen need not be paralysed by uncertainty.

This confidence exists, however, precisely because the local does have a priority. That priority is not absolute, as cases such as *Riggs* and *Henningsen* show us, but it can be and is a priority none the less. And if in fact there is a priority for the result generated by a limited and pedigreeable set of rules, what emerges is a system that might best be described as *presumptive positivism*. Such a theory would explain not only why Riggs's grandson did not inherit, but also why a host of almost but not quite as unworthy beneficiaries *do* inherit. It could explain not only why the document that Henningsen and Bloomfield Motors signed did not control when Henningsen brought suit, but also why what people sign most often does control. And more broadly, it would explain why lawyers and judges devote so much time to learning and referring to legal rules. Were those rules to be but one type of a much larger array of types of considerations to be considered in a more holistic decisional mode, we would be at a loss to explain the proportional dominance of those rules in legal decision-making, and puzzled about the justification for institutions such as law schools, bar examinations, and the West Publishing Company.

Thus, presumptive positivism is a descriptive claim about the status of a set of pedigreed norms within the universe of reasons for decision employed by the decision-makers within some legal system. In saying that this pedigreed set has presumptive but not absolute force, I do not mean to rely on the strictly epistemic sense of 'presumptive' that one finds, for example, in the law of evidence. Often when we employ a presumption, we presume the existence of some fact from the existence of some other fact, and thus the existence of the presumed fact is a product of uncertainty about the actual state of affairs. Presumptions, like the presumption of innocence or the presumption of paternity, serve primarily as substantively skewed accommodations to epistemic uncertainty.

By contrast, my use of 'presumptive' refers generally to the force possessed by a rules, and more specifically to a degree of force such that the rule is to be applied unless particularly exigent reasons can be supplied for not applying it. When used this way, there is nothing necessarily epistemic about the idea of a presumption, and the idea is only a way of describing a degree of strong but overridable priority within a normative universe in which conflicting norms might produce mutually exclusive results. We might prefer the norms emanating from one source to those emanating from another for epistemic reasons, but the same preference might instead emerge from any of a number of non-epistemic reasons for allocating jurisdiction in one way rather than another. When, for example, in American constitutional law a distinction drawn by government on the basis of race is taken to be unconstitutional unless the state can show a 'compelling interest' in drawing such a distinction, the status of the racial distinction can properly be described as 'presumptively unconstitutional', despite the fact that the reasons for creating that status are not epistemic. It is not that the state is taken to know less about some factual matter, but rather that various non-epistemic considerations make some governmental decisions impermissible (rather than erroneous) except in the gravest of emergencies.

A similar notion of presumptiveness undergirds presumptive positivism. Presumptive positivism is a way of describing the interplay between a pedigreed subset of rules and the full (and non-pedigreeable) normative universe, such that the former is treated by certain decision-makers as presumptively controlling in this not-necessarily-epistemic sense of presumptive. As a result, these decision-makers override a rule within the pedigreed subset not when they believe that the rule has produced an erroneous or suboptimal result in this case, no matter how well grounded that belief, but instead when, and only when, the reasons for overriding are perceived by the decision-maker to be particularly strong.

I cannot here prove the descriptive accuracy of presumptive positivism, for such a claim would require empirical identification not only of those instances in which the presumption was over-ridden, but also of the statistical claim that usually the presumptive rules do control. It is worthwhile, however, pointing out (and connecting this discussion with that in Chapter 5.3 explaining my differences with Raz on whether there can be a non-absolute exclusion) that a psychological claim about presumptions does undergird the perspective I offer here. The best way to demonstrate that is by illustrating the plausibility of the opposite assumption. This opposite psychological assumption, one implicit in Raz's claim that exclusionary reasons are necessarily non-overridable, maintains that the very idea of a rebuttable presumption, however logically impeccable it might be, is phenomenologically fallacious. In order for a presumption ever to be rebutted (or overridden), the argument goes, the potentially rebutting considerations must be investigated not only in those cases in which rebuttal in fact takes place, but in every case. How other than by examining the potentially rebutting factors in every case can we determine if they are strong enough in this case? If that is so, the argument continues, then a claim about presumptiveness involves a claim that decision-makers, having 'peeked' beneath the curtain that is the presumptive rule, might then still be able to put down that curtain and ignore the potentially overriding factor in all cases in which it was not overly strong. And it is exactly that ability, to ignore what one already knows, that the sceptic doubts.

Against this, I have nothing to offer but a contrary possibility. This possibility maintains that decision-makers can tell the difference between a factor that would control were the decision process particularized and a factor that does not control because of the presumption or burden of persuasion that prevails in a particular decisional environment. If juries can acquit in those cases in which they believe the defendant guilty but do not believe that the prosecution has proved that fact beyond a reasonable doubt, then other decision-makers might similarly find in favor of a presumptively controlling but ideally non-controlling rule in cases in which the overriding factor was weak. If that is so, then we can reconcile the opposing observations in the dispute about positivism. On the one hand, positivists observe that most of the things people call laws exist in a moderately limited collection of books, that lawyers refer to a moderately limited collection of sources with remarkable frequency, and that it does not seem all that difficult in most easy cases to figure out what the law requires. But in other cases, Dworkin and others observe, norms that in no way constitute such a closed set seem to control, even when a norm that is legal in the narrow sense goes in the opposite direction. But if presumptive positivism is correct, then both observations are correct. In most cases, the result generated by the most locally applicable and pedigreed rule controls. But in every case that rule will be tested against a larger and unpedigreeable set of considerations, and the rule will be set aside when the result it indicates is egregiously at odds with the result that is indicated by this larger and more morally acceptable set of values. Whether we call this array of overriding factors 'law' or not is a dispute that is to some extent terminological.

It is also a dispute, however, that goes to the rhetoric of legality, to the extent to which legal decision-makers relying on a non-pedigreeable universe of social norms shall when doing so be buttressed by the connotations of deduction, constraint, and limited domain suggested by the word 'law'. I will explore this question no further here, and conclude this chapter only with the descriptive assertion that presumptive positivism may be the most accurate picture of the place of rules within many modern legal systems.

9
THE INTERPRETATION
OF RULES

9.1 *The Occasions of Interpretation*

Rules are normally unobtrusive, doing much of their work without inducing conscious interpretive doubt in their addressees. We may not like to stop at 'Stop' signs, pay our income taxes, refrain from smoking at the dinner table, or wear clothes we find uncomfortable, but we understand what is required of us and commonly act accordingly. In such cases we think of rules as being *applied*, and to speak of the 'application of a rule' ordinarily presupposes a comparatively routine enterprise. Sometimes, however, things are not this easy, and we are unable quickly and easily to determine just what it is that the rule wants us to do. Then we say that the rule is in need of *interpretation*, and ordinary talk appears to reserve the word 'interpretation' for those cases in which there seems to be a problem.

In this respect, common linguistic usage is potentially misleading, for *every* application of a rule is also an interpretation.[1] When I read 'No Dogs Allowed' as indicating that no dogs are allowed, and when I understand the non-allowance of dogs to prohibit me from bringing Angus into this restaurant at this time, I engage in interpretive tasks that for different people in this world, or for people in different worlds, might be performed differently. Still, we ordinarily do not think of these tasks as involving interpretation, for there is a sense in which to interpret a text or a rule is to deal with a *quandary*, to *struggle* with a situation in which rules, usually sluggish creatures,

---

[1] 'When you come tomorrow, bring my football boots. Also, if humanly possible, Irish water spaniel. Urgent. Regards. Tuppy.'
'What do you make of that, Jeeves?'
'As I interpret the document, sir, Mr Glossop wishes you, when you come tomorrow, to bring his football boots. Also, if humanly possible, an Irish water spaniel. He hints that the matter is urgent, and sends his regards.'
'Yes, that's how I read it, too. . . .'
P. G. Wodehouse, *The Ordeal of Young Tuppy*, quoted in Simon Blackburn, *Spreading the Word*, 3.

become more obtrusive when normally reflexive interpretive questions become harder. On these occasions, unlike on many others, we are uncertain about just what it is that a rule requires of us.[2]

Questions about the interpretation of rules, therefore, turn out to be questions about how hard cases should be decided. Yet even though recasting the question in this way draws on a useful distinction between those rules that speak clearly to us and those that do not, there is a risk that formulating the issue in this way is question-begging. Interpretation may be what we do when we face a hard case, but the very question of what constitutes a hard case is problematic. Our first task in thinking about interpretation, consequently, is to consider the *occasions* of interpretation. Only after we have some sense of what makes a hard case hard can we approach the question of how those hard cases should be resolved.

When I talk of 'resolving' a hard case, I do not refer to what an agent should, all things considered, *do*. Rather, I am concerned with how the indications of a rule should be understood. Suppose, having just come from the taxidermist, I arrive at the restaurant with the stuffed, preserved, and mounted carcass of my recently deceased pet bulldog. My first question is whether this 'No Dogs Allowed' rule even applies at all, for the stuffed dog is at best a penumbral application of 'dog'. But if I determine that the rule *does* apply, that does not compel the conclusion that I should, all things considered, stay away from the restaurant, nor does it compel the conclusion that the proprietor, all things considered, should refuse me entry.

I have assumed in this example that the rule resides in the meaning of one canonically inscribed rule-formulation, and the interpretive difficulty arises just because it is unclear what the word 'dog' *means* in this context. But it is not always so clear just what the rule *is*. What if the sign had been partially obliterated, reading, 'No #(/g#\ Allowed'? Were that the case, I would even before determining what the rule means have had to determine what the rule *says* ('No Dogs Allowed' or 'No Cigars Allowed', or something else), and this too is an interpretive question.

More realistically, it may be unclear what the rule is, or what it

---

[2] My conclusions about the distinction between application and interpretation are consistent with Colin McGinn's understanding of Wittgenstein as contrasting the *active* process of interpretation with the *passive* act of literal seeing. *Wittgenstein on Meaning*, 15–16. See also Marcelo Dascal and Jerzy Wróblewski, 'Transparency and Doubt', *passim*.

says, not because language has been physically obliterated, but because there is no single canonical formulation to which we can point. We have seen that common-law rules often operate in rule-like fashion, but locating the rule is frequently difficult. One version may exist in a judicial opinion, another in a legal treatise, and a third in a law journal article by an eminent author. In such cases, the first interpretive hurdle is finding the rule, for we cannot interpret what we cannot find. Similar problems arise when rules are perceived to reside in whole or in part at the level of purpose or first-order justification. It may be difficult to determine what the justification for some rule-formulation is, and if it is the justification and not the formulation that constitutes the rule (see above, Chapters 4.5 and 5.1), we face interpretive difficulties at the outset.

Even when we have located the rule, interpretive problems may still arise. Under one view, a troublesome case—an interpretive occasion in the 'hard case' sense of interpretation—exists whenever the result generated by a rule is, all things considered, problematic. From this perspective, an 'easy' or 'clear' case is one in which there is not only a plain answer on the basis of the materials comprising the rule itself, but in which that plain answer is otherwise, all things considered, acceptable. As should be obvious by now, however, such an approach (questions of presumption aside) turns out to collapse the idea of a rule entirely, for it dissolves the indications of the rule into the question of what decision should be made on the basis of the full array of justifications, at one or several levels higher than that of the rule itself, existing in the entire decisional environment.

There are times when the work of Ronald Dworkin seems susceptible to such an 'interpretation'. Recall from Chapter 8 *Riggs* v. *Palmer*, where the apparently clear Statute of Wills seemed to allow a grandson who had murdered his grandfather to inherit just as the grandson would have inherited had his grandfather died of natural causes. It is crucial to understanding the idea of a hard case, as well as to understanding Dworkin's attack on legal positivism, that we recognize that the events involved in *Riggs* fell rather plainly within the linguistic grasp of the most locally applicable rule, the Statute of Wills. Dworkin's descriptive claim is that the fact of an event being within the language of the most locally applicable rule is not dispositive of the result that a court would or should reach in deciding what to do in that case.[3] Although *Riggs* was thus in one

---

[3] See esp. Ronald Dworkin, *Law's Empire*, 15–53, 114–50.

sense an easy case, it becomes hard precisely because the result generated by the most locally applicable rule is socially, politically, or morally *hard* to swallow. In those circumstances, Dworkin properly observes, American practice, and less pervasively English practice,[4] empowers the judge to treat the most locally applicable rule as being other than conclusive, subject to override or revision on the basis of those factors that made the locally easy case hard in the first instance.

But note that this procedure, perhaps as politically and morally desirable as it is descriptively accurate, casts into serious question the status as a rule of what appears to be the most locally applicable rule. In order for the rule not to collapse into the array of justifications that made us worry about the result, in order for the rule not to be superfluous by generating a set of results extensionally equivalent to those that would have been generated without the rule, the rule *qua* rule must, as we have seen, have at least some degree of presumptive force, some degree of resistance. If it does, then there will be a non-empty set of cases in which the rule will generate results that might have been otherwise without the rule, even if there are also cases in which the presumption is overcome or the resistance penetrated. But if the rule supplies no resistance when all things considered it appears to indicate the wrong result, then the rule exists only in form and not in effect.

It is not clear just how much resistance rules have in Dworkin's interpretive model. His very focus on principles being extracted or constructed from previous rules, and even more his occasional references to 'gravitational force',[5] may indicate that his vision is closer to the picture I am painting than I may have suggested. Yet none of his numerous examples are ones in which the most locally applicable rule generates a result that would not be reached by application of that rule's (or the system of which it is a member's) background principles, and thus it is unclear whether there is room in Dworkin's approach for a strong form of rule-based decision-making.[6] Insofar as there is not, however, then his approach seems

---

[4] On the difference in practices on this point, see P. S. Atiyah and R. S. Summers, *Form and Substance in Anglo-American Law*, *passim*.

[5] Dworkin, *Taking Rights Seriously*, 111–15. Also relevant is Dworkin's discussion of 'local priority' in *Law's Empire*, 250–4, 400–7. Although Dworkin is speaking of the priority among different departments of law, the same idea is applicable to the rules within a single department.

[6] On the way in which Dworkin appears to collapse the idea of a rule by requiring that it be interpreted in the morally and politically best way on this occasion, see

less accurate as a description even of American legal practice. As noted in Chapter 8, unworthy beneficiaries who are not as unworthy as the grandson in *Riggs* v. *Palmer* do inherit with some frequency, even in circumstances in which they could accurately be described as wrongdoers. This is strong evidence for the proposition that one of the features of American law is the way in which the strictures of the most locally applicable rule do produce results that would otherwise be different. The most locally applicable rule does not always control, as *Riggs* and countless other cases indicate, but this indicates only that presumptive rather than conclusive positivism is the best account of the role of rules in the American and many other legal systems.

This digression about Dworkin illustrates the difficulties involved in trying to determine just what is a hard case, in the sense of presenting a decision-maker with an interpretive quandary. If we define as hard cases even those in which a clear rule produces an uncomfortable result, then easy cases are only those in which the result indicated by the rule is consistent with the best, all things considered, result. This obviously will not do, for it again collapses a rule into its justification. Now it may be that the justification is itself the rule, for we know now that a rule may be located somewhere other than in a canonical formulation. In some decision-making environments the rule may consist of some combination of formulation and first-order justification, or some combination of formulation and original intent, or something else. But whatever or wherever it is, *that* rule will have a core and a penumbra, with interpretive problems, as we have defined them, existing only in the penumbra and not in the core. Thus, identifying the occasions of interpretation requires identifying the hard cases, and that task is parasitic on a theory of both what makes a hard case hard and an easy case easy. And this is in turn a function of what data—rule-formulation, original intent, purpose, or whatever—constitute the rule. Only when we have a picture of what data generate a decision can we understand when that data is clear and when it is not.[7] Still, it appears that Dworkin's arguably accurate portrayal of American legal practice merges the question of what to do with that of how to

---

Larry Alexander, 'Striking Back at the Empire', 424–5; Frederick Schauer, 'The Jurisprudence of Reasons', *passim*.

[7] I use 'data' to describe the items plausibly relevant in determining what the law is, without begging the question by referring to those items as 'rules' or 'law'. The idea I have in mind is close to Ruth Gavison's 'first stage law' in 'Comment'.

determine what a rule *means*. If what a rule means just *is* what we should do, then the two questions collapse into each other. But if this account is false, and if consequently rules themselves are not irrelevant in a given decisional environment, then quandaries about what to do, which we *might* call 'interpretive', are not the same as quandaries about what a rule *means*, which we should certainly call 'interpretive'.

9.2 *Hart and Fuller Revisited*

This same confusion between what a rule indicates and what a judge ought to *do* (or even what a legal system ought to do) pervades the renowned debate between H. L. A. Hart and Lon Fuller.[8] When Fuller raised as a counterexample the statue of the vehicle that was to be erected in the park (see above, Chapter 4.5), or when he similarly asked whether a 'No sleeping in the station' rule was to be applied to a tired businessman who had briefly nodded off while waiting for his train, he took himself to be challenging the very possibility of a rule having a clear instance apart from the application of its *purpose* in the circumstances and context of a particular application.

It is more than plausible that a legal system would want to take as its rules some combination of the meaning of a rule-formulation and the locatable purpose lying behind that formulation. Thus, a rule in such a system might very well just *be* the meaning of the formulation if and only if the result indicated by the formulation were consistent with the result indicated by the rule's justification. But, as I have stressed throughout this book, such a rule is extensionally equivalent to the justification being the rule itself. There is nothing incoherent about this, for rules can exist at levels other than that of canonically articulated rule-formulations. Still, this only pushes the problem to a different remove, for there still might be cases, as we have seen, in which the result indicated both by the formulation and its justification would still differ from the result indicated by the even deeper justification behind *that* justification. Consider not only the Olympic champion, but also a case in which the same businessman, having missed the last train, takes off his shoes, lies down on his coat, and proceeds seriously to sleep while awaiting the first train the next morning. Under these circumstances, the justification for the rule, prohibiting people from using the station as a substitute for a home

---

[8] H. L. A. Hart, 'Positivism and the Separation of Law and Morals'; Lon Fuller, 'Positivism and Fidelity to Law: A Reply to Professor Hart'.

or a hotel, might be served by prohibition, but it is possible that the justification behind *that* justification, dealing with archetypal cases of vagrants, would not be served by applying even the first-order justification and sanctioning the businessman. If under these circumstances the rule-when-consistent-with-its justification *is* applied, even when it is inconsistent with *its* justification, we have merely discovered that there *are* rules within the system. The rules, however, reside in the entrenched first-order justification rather than in an inscribed rule-formulation.

Thus, unless we embrace an implausible particularist theory of meaning, under which the notion of meaning collapses into what a decision-maker in a particular environment should do on a particular occasion (see above, Chapter 4.1), it appears that Hart was correct. There *are* core meanings of rules (clear cases under the rule), even though they may not always be congruent with the core meaning of the ordinary language of the rule's canonical formulation. There are also, of course, the cases that Hart referred to as penumbral (Are bicycles or baby carriages to be considered to be vehicles?), in which interpretation in a different sense is required.[9]

This suggests that Hart need not have conceded even as much as he subsequently did to Fuller.[10] In acknowledging the function of purpose in constituting the very idea of the rule itself, Hart too was incorporating what is but a contingent choice made by most contemporary legal systems. Consider in this regard some other famous examples of cases in which the literal application of a rule generated what was undeniably an absurd result. One is the case imagined by Pufendorf, in which a Bolognese surgeon performing emergency surgery was prosecuted, under a law plainly designed to prevent dueling and public fighting, for 'letting blood in the streets'.[11] Another is the fictional *R. v. Ojibway*, in which the provisions of a mythical Small Birds Act defined as a small bird any small animal covered with feathers and having two legs.[12] This definition, however, turned out to encompass not only small birds, but also a pony with a down pillow on its back, the result of which was that the

---

[9] Note also Bertrand Russell, 'Vagueness', 87: 'All words are attributable without doubt over a certain area, but become questionable within a penumbra, outside which they are again certainly not attributable.'

[10] Hart, *Essays in Jurisprudence and Philosophy*, 8, 106.

[11] S. Pufendorf, *De Jure Naturae et Gentium Libri Octo*, quoted in *United States* v. *Kirby*, 74 US (7 Wall.) 482, 487 (1968).

[12] H. Pomerantz and S. Breslin, 'Judicial Humour—Construction of a Statute', 138.

pony's owner, who had killed the pony to relieve it from the pain of a broken leg, was properly convicted for violating the law prohibiting the killing of small birds.[13]

These cases, along with Fuller's statue and many that are real rather than fictional, are designed to show the absurdity of literal application of rule-formulations. It is important to distinguish, however, the absurdity of the result from the conceptual possibility of under- and over-inclusive rules. The results in these cases may be distasteful, but the fact that I find anchovies distasteful does not lead me to question their existence. Still, an intolerance for absurdity has produced a legal environment in which judges are commonly *empowered* to set aside the result indicated by the most locally applicable rule-formulation when that result would be absurd. But that approach, treating the justification and not the formulation as the rule, is contingent and not necessary. Moreover, it is by no means clear that the seemingly distasteful alternative has nothing to be said for it. Wary of empowering judges to determine purpose (consider the instructions given to police officers on what to tell a suspect when that suspect is arrested), some system might instruct judges simply to apply the rule, even if the result seemed to them inconsistent with its purpose, or even if the result seemed to them absurd. Such an approach would reflect a decision to prefer the occasional wrong or even preposterous result to a regime in which judges were empowered to search for purpose or preposterousness, for it might be that such empowerment was thought to present a risk of error or variance of decision even more harmful than the tolerance of occasional absurd results. The question, therefore, is not only whether a result is absurd, but whether decision-makers should have the jurisdiction to determine which results are absurd and which not. When so recast, the argument for what is often pejoratively referred to as 'formalism' may still not be persuasive, but is far from absurd.

Were such an approach adopted in some legal system, that system might (but only might) have less of a claim on the obedience of its addressees. It would certainly reduce the intellectual appeal of being a judge. Yet neither of these consequences need be dispositive, and neither suggests that it is conceptually impossible to have such a system. What we see, therefore, is a persistent tendency, especially in judge-centred legal theorizing, to take the contingent empower-

---

[13] Note that ponies have two legs—and more.

ment of judges as demonstrating the incompatibility of the idea of a rule with the tolerance of an absurd result. But exactly the opposite is the case, for the very idea of rule-based decision-making entails the acceptance of some number of suboptimal results in the area of under- or over-inclusiveness.

Absurd outcomes, consequently, are but the extreme manifestation of a central feature of the idea of a rule. It may sometimes be desirable to avoid the recalcitrant experiences thrown up by any rule, but the compulsion to avoid the wrong answers plainly generated by plainly applicable rules is quite distinct from the occasions on which we are unsure of what a rule seems to require. The debate about the nature of a rule, therefore, including the debate between Hart and Fuller about what to do in the area of rule's under- and over-inclusiveness, is in the final analysis not very pertinent to quite different questions about interpreting rules when they are unclear.

9.3 *Rules and Reality*

Before turning to questions about the resolution of hard cases, however, it is necessary to consider one further attempt to conflate the questions of what a rule requires with what, all things considered, a decision-maker ought to decide. This position, to which I have alluded earlier (Chapter 4.1), is chararacterized as an application of realist semantics to questions about the interpretation of rules, and from a different starting point again seeks to call into question the idea of a comparatively context-independent core meaning for any rule. As with the views of Fuller and Dworkin, this view challenges the notion that there are easy cases under a rule, and consequently challenges as well the notion of a hard case, for the idea of a hard case is coherent only against a background understanding of rules in which there are cases that are easy.

The position to which I refer is one most prominently associated with Michael Moore, although it has been carried on by Leo Katz, David Brink, and some number of others.[14] All purport to base their inspiration on semantic perspectives commonly associated with, among others, Saul Kripke, Keith Donnellan, and Hilary Putnam. Under that perspective, or so its translators suppose, language is essentially transparent, being but the contingent marker

---

[14] See Michael Moore, 'A Natural Law Theory of Interpretation'; id., 'The Semantics of Judging'. See also Leo Katz, *Bad Acts and Guilty Minds*; David Brink, 'Legal Theory, Legal Interpretation, and Judicial Review'; id., 'Semantics and Legal Interpretation (Further Thoughts)'.

for a deeper reality. In an interesting way, therefore, realist semantics is to conventionalist semantics as rules of thumb are to mandatory rules. If it therefore turns out that our understanding of the underlying phenomenon that language reflects changes, then the meaning of the language changes as well, not as a causal consequence but as a logically necessary corollary to the change in understanding itself.

The implications of this perspective for our understanding of rules are intriguing. Using Putnam's example, if our understanding of the nature of water were to change, then the meaning of the word 'water' would change as well, and then the meaning of any rule whose factual predicate included 'water' would change commensurately. Moore and others maintain, therefore, that rules must be understood in accordance with this transparency thesis, so that those who interpret rules are not only warranted in looking beneath them, but are obliged to do so.

But even supposing Kripke, Putnam, and their philosophical compatriots to be correct, what is it that language is transparent *to*? According to the standard version of the theory, certain words are transparent to the actual kind (or artefact) itself, as currently understood by the best available theory of just what water *is*. Yet it is an unwarranted leap from the currently understood best theory of what water *is* to what some decision-maker would want to do with this water at this time. That is, nothing in realist semantics necessitates (or even tolerates) a particularist view of language, and even though a linguistic community's view of what 'water' stands for may change as its view of what water is changes, it does not follow that there is not, for a particular linguistic community at a particular time, some comparatively acontextual conception of what the word 'water' means. And as long as this is the case, then nothing we have concluded changes, for it always remains possible for the application of that meaning to generate a result other than that generated by direct application of the justifications behind the rule of which that meaning is a component part.

But, the proponents say, what about terms with moral content, such as 'death' or 'careless'? Here it appears as if that moral component is part of the meaning of the term, and surely it would be immoral to rely on a conventional definition of 'death' if doing so would produce an immoral result. Yet that tack denies the possibility of a rule-based morality. Even words with moral content have referential capacities, and that reference can be to something other than the optimal result in *this* case. Were it otherwise, then the idea of morality would become essentially particularistic, with no moral term or phrase or sentence having the ability to say anything except 'make the best decision right now all things considered'.[15] If all of moral decision were necessarily particularistic, the constraint of rules would indeed collapse, at least in the context of morally loaded terms, but the source of that conclusion seems odd. I can fully acknowledge changing conceptions of death, as well as the inextricable moral component in the definition of the word 'death', without acknowledging that the only answer to the question 'Is she dead?' is 'Why do you want to know and what turns on it?'

It is now clear that the realist programme works only if the semantic theory on which it is based incorporates a theory of optimal particularistic decision-making. That is, the purported application of realist semantics as a challenge to a conventional account of rules (and Brink, among others, puts it in just these terms) is successful only if rules *mean* just what the best moral decision in any particular case would be. But unless we are to lose the concept of meaning entirely, or unless the entire position is now restricted to a (relatively) small number of morally loaded terms with little conventional meaning,[16] this view of language as being congruent with the best particularistic decision under the circumstances seems scarcely comprehensible.[17]

If restricted to a set of terms much smaller than the universe of language, the position under discussion becomes much more plausible. Suppose we are in the legal system, and we are dealing with terms such as 'assumpsit' or 'habeas corpus' or 'bill of attainder' or 'real party in interest'.[18] These terms, technical to the core, have no meaning apart from their systemic legal meaning. Consequently, it would be much more plausible for those terms to have meanings that incorporated the goals and aspirations of the system of which

[15] On these issues, the discussion above of the asymmetry of authority (Chap. 6.4) is relevant in explaining why a rule-based morality may make more or less sense depending on the standpoint of evaluation.

[16] This qualification appears implicitly in Brink's more recent 'Semantics and Legal Interpretation (Further Thoughts)'.

[17] In 'Defeasibility and Meaning', G. P. Baker recognizes the tension I am describing, and hints that the idea of defeasibility hinges either on a rejection of standard accounts of meaning or on a willingness to collapse a theory of meaning into a theory of speech acts. I believe him right on both counts, although I am less sanguine about the possibility of developing a theory of meaning that will rescue the idea of defeasibility.

[18] And perhaps also with American constitutional terms such as 'equal protection of the laws', 'due process of law', and 'the freedom of speech'.

they were a part. In that case, *if* one of the aspirations of the system were the avoidance of absurdity, then a rule incorporating the term 'habeas corpus' would be incapable unless misinterpreted of generating an absurd result, because the avoidance of absurdity in the particular case was built into the meaning of the term itself.

But the question-beggingness of this approach ought to be apparent. As we have seen, it may not be absurd for a system to accept some number of absurd outcomes in individual cases. Any system sensitive to questions of allocation of power and institutional design might at least consider as plausible a more strongly rule-based system that acknowledged the possibility of absurd results, but acknowledged as well that it was willing to accept those absurd results as the lesser of the possible decisional evils.

This is not to say that such a system would be better than one less tolerant of absurdity or suboptimality in individual cases. It is to say, however, that the realist idea turns out to be strikingly similar to Fuller's, for both take the definition of terms to be coextensive with the goals of the system in which those terms are used, and both, at least in their extreme manifestations, take the definition of terms also to be coextensive with the best particular decisions reached on particular occasions within that system. Insofar as this approach is applied to terms with an existence outside the system, it appears incoherent. And insofar as it is applied to terms existing only within the system, it turns out that the argument amounts to a quite plausible but hardly conceptually necessary theory of adjudication masquerading as a theory of meaning.

9.4 *Purpose and Intention in the Interpretation of Rules*

Although the route has been circuitous, we are back where we were at the beginning of this chapter. We have seen that under any plausible and non-question-begging conception of a rule, there will be some cases plainly encompassed by the rule, some plainly not encompassed by the rule, and some whose coverage is doubtful. I will repeat that this is compatible with any conception of what (or where) the rule *is*. If the rule is some canonical formulation, then some cases will be plainly covered by that formulation, some plainly not, and some whose coverage is doubtful. Similarly, if the rule is some justification or set of justifications, then there will once again be an array of cases plainly within *that* rule, some without, and some on the borderline. Only if the notion of a rule is coextensive with a totally particularized determination, in which case there is no notion of a rule at all, will there not be an array of plainly in, plainly out, and doubtful cases.

Thus, we are now in a position to think about the central interpretive question. Just how should rules be interpreted in doubtful cases, regardless of what the components of the rule are? A common answer to this question is that such doubts should be resolved by consulting the original intentions of those who wrote the rule. These intentions, it is said, are the necessary source of decision-making guidance when the otherwise available guidance of the rule itself fails.

The recourse to original intent cannot plausibly be taken as a linguistic necessity. Even those most wedded to an intentionalist theory of meaning do not hold that the meaning of a term just *is* that intention.[19] Were that the case, then it would be impossible to explain how it is that the words used were able to give the listener any clues as to what the speaker intended to say.

Once we recognize that language has meaning independent of what its initial users (or inscribers) intended to say,[20] we can see that there is nothing necessary about the recourse to original intent. If meaning has run out, and we are faced with a linguistically hard case, then nothing about the nature of meaning suggests that we must then ask the 'What would James Madison have thought about this?' question. We might *want* to ask that question, but to do so would require a substantive determination of why the rules were taken to exist in the first instance.

Take, for example, the (comparatively) well-accepted proposition that where statutory language has run out, the original intentions of the body that enacted the legislation are to be taken as dispositive. Let us assume, controversially, that collective bodies such as legislatures can have intentions. Still, the existence of that intention does not mandate its use. To use these intentions is to view

---

[19] I am thinking here of H. P. Grice, 'Meaning'; id., 'Utterer's Meaning and Intentions'; Stephen Schiffer, *Meaning*.

[20] Rules persist over time, and so do their formulations. This leads to a problem about how we should understand the language in which a rule is formulated. Even apart from questions of intent, should the language mean what it would have meant at the time the rule was written, or should the language mean what it means now in this linguistic community, even if that is different from the meaning it had when the rule was written? The answer can be determined only by reference to the values that inform the internalization of the rule. Although any internalization takes place *now*, the internalization of now could (but need not) incorporate the meaning of some time in the past.

legislation on a command model,[21] much as we view the relationship between private and sergeant. When we consider the relationship between private and sergeant, we recognize that the relationship
of authority (perhaps itself established by other rules) puts the
private in a position of being under an obligation to comply with the
wishes of the sergeant. As soon as this is our model, we can
understand why the puzzled private, on some occasion insufficiently
guided by the instructions actually issued by the sergeant, would
resort to other evidence to determine what the sergeant would have
wished done under these circumstances.

Here, and elsewhere, the recourse to original intentions is compelled by the substantive nature of the relationship. Given that the
very point of a will, for example, is to allow the owner of property to
dispose of it upon her death *as she wishes*, we can understand why
reference to the intent of the testator would be the natural course
when the instructions contained in the will itself were indeterminate.
Similarly, it is not difficult to understand the impetus behind the so-
called 'subjective' theory of contracts, pursuant to which external
evidence of the intentions of the contracting parties is available to
fill out the terms of an agreement when the contractual terms
contained in the document itself do not dictate a clear answer to
some interpretive question.

In other contexts, however, the recourse to original intent seems
less compelled by the nature of the enterprise. When some situation
arises in which an interpreter is unsure of what the rules of baseball
or bridge require, the importance of trying to ascertain from
extrinsic evidence what Abner Doubleday or Cornelius Vanderbilt
thought or would have thought about the situation seems attenuated.
We think that the recourse to original intent is as odd for bridge or
baseball as it is natural for wills or contracts because our understanding of what bridge is about is an understanding describable
without reference to the creators of the game. Bridge would be just
as much fun (for those of us who think it fun) had the rules been
discovered under a cabbage leaf. Only where the intentions of the
drafter of a rule are part of what the activity of following those rules
is all about might reference to original intent in cases of interpretive
difficulty be necessary.

As a result, we can also see why the question of original authorial
intent with reference to the rules in the Bible, in the Koran, or in the

---

[21] See Richard Posner, 'Legal Formalism, Legal Realism, and the Interpretation
of Statutes and the Constitution'.

Talmud is a question neither of normative theory nor of philosophy of language, but of theology. Similarly, the question of original authorial intent with respect to legal interpretation is once again a question of substantive jurisprudence, by which I mean it is a question answerable by, and only by, a theory of what law is and what law does. If, for example, law just *is* about continuity, about binding the future by current legislative decisions, and about following the orders of human commanders,[22] then it is hardly surprising that recourse to original intent would be valued, for under this picture of law those who created the laws at some point in the past are more than mere scriveners, they are the law-givers who must be obeyed, just as today's legislatures are the lawgivers who must be obeyed tomorrow.

Conversely, if we look at law differently, as a set of rules that, whoever drafted them, are the rules that *we* accept today and that *we* choose to employ now to co-ordinate our social existence, then nothing about the use of legislative intentions to solve interpretive problems follows from the fact that some human beings at some time were primarily responsible for first putting the canonical forms of these rules into the law-books. Under this latter picture, the source of guidance in cases of indeterminacy remains open, a question for those who now live under the rules to answer in terms of who they wish to empower to fill the gaps occasioned by indeterminacy. If a society fears granting too much power to those with authority to fill those gaps, most notably judges, it may still choose to compel those judges to follow historical intentions. Here, however, the recourse to original intent is less the product of the theoretical significance of original intent than of its instrumental utility as constrainer. From this perspective the instrument of constraint could be something else, such as a default rule providing that in cases of legal doubt the proponent of the legal claim should lose. For when the use of original intent is in the service of constraint *qua* constraint rather than in the service of a substantive theory of authority,[23] original intent becomes little more than a technique, among others, that might serve this purpose.

---

[22] Dworkin's efforts to demonstrate the difficulties of divining original intent, *Law's Empire*, 53–76, are necessary for him precisely because his is a substantive theory of the nature of law that would seem to make the intentions of prior members of the community relevant. Under a different theory of law, there would be no suggestion that original intent was important, and thus no need to demonstrate that it is difficult to ascertain.

[23] This is not to say that there could not be a substantive theory of constraint.

9.5 *Interpretation and Discretion*

It follows that there may be circumstances in which the absence of clear guidance from existing rules need not be taken to be an occasion for imposing additional constraints on interpreters. In those circumstances we acknowledge that when rules run out interpreters have *discretion*. Yet the identification of an area of discretion does not answer any of our questions. It just presents them. Just what *is* discretion, and under what circumstances might it be wise to grant it?

People commonly speak of 'unfettered discretion', but the phrase is redundant. Discretion just *is* freedom from otherwise plausible fetters. As constraint is imposed then discretion diminishes *pro tanto*. When we think of interpretation in terms of problems arising when we are unsure whether a rule applies, we often presuppose this model of discretion, and many of those who have written about rules often explicitly incorporate it. Sometimes we see references to an 'interstitial' rule-making responsibility that is triggered when the constraint of rules runs out, and some refer to 'gaps' arising in rule systems, gaps it is the task of the interpreter to fill. Kelsen's image of a 'frame without a picture' captures what many people think, for that metaphor offers the model of a painter free to paint whatever she wishes on the canvas as long as the boundaries established by the frame are respected.[24]

Yet here there seems to be confusion, for identifying the decision-making freedom that remains after rules have done their work is different from attempting to determine what the rules say in the first instance. The question of what is to be done in the interstices between rules is not the same as the question of where those interstices are located.

Thus, when a rule first appears unclear, it seems unimpeachable to look initially to the justifications lying behind the rule. Although it may be unclear whether a stuffed dog is a dog, the unclarity evaporates once we recognize that the justification behind the 'No dogs allowed' rule pertains to excluding from the restaurant those agents likely by their annoying behavior to interfere with the dining

---

[24] This model of interpretation is articulated in Aleksander Peczenik and Jerzy Wróblewski, 'Fuzziness and Transformation'. See also Gidon Gottlieb, *The Logic of Choice*, 91–100; Charles Curtis, 'A Better Theory of Legal Interpretation', *passim*; Lawrence M. Friedman, 'Law and Its Language', 572–3; Frederick Schauer, 'Authority and Indeterminacy', *passim*.

pleasure of others in the restaurant. Whatever might be said about stuffed dogs, there is no disputing their inability to run around, bark, or eat food scraps off the floor. Thus, although we have seen that it is inconsistent with the virtues commonly thought to come from rule-based decision-making to permit a justification to *trump* the rule, it does not follow that the justification should be invisible when we are unsure of what the rule means, and thus what behavior it restricts.

However often the recourse to justification will solve an otherwise difficult case, the difficulty will sometimes remain even after the justification has been consulted. Not only are we sometimes unsure of whether a rule applies, but we are also frequently unsure of whether its purpose applies (even when we know what the purpose is). Suppose we were to conclude that a stuffed dog, perhaps a dog and perhaps not, might or might not annoy other patrons in the restaurant, in part because, however docile or quiet a stuffed dog might be, it still is not what most people wish to see when dining. The exclusion of the stuffed dog might or might not serve the purpose behind the rule. We are just not sure.

Here, it seems again plausible to retreat to justification, in this case to the second-order justification lying behind the first-order justification. It might be, for example, that the justification of preventing annoyance to patrons was itself the instantiation of a justification of maximizing the dining pleasure of those patrons. Were that the case, we (the hypothetical interpreters) might wish to exclude the stuffed dog, on the theory that although it is unclear whether the stuffed dog would be annoying, it is much clearer that the presence of a stuffed dog could hardly increase the dining enjoyment of anyone in the restaurant other than the stuffed dog's owner.

This purpose-oriented picture of interpretation appears to leave no room for *gaps*. Although the identification of purpose may be difficult and even controversial, the idea of a gap still seems a poor characterization for what is going on even when we are unsure about what a rule's purpose requires. Consider again the 'No Vehicles in the Park' regulation. When the question arises whether a bicycle is a vehicle, there might, when the first-order justification is consulted, be some doubt about whether the purpose behind the rule was to minimize noise or to promote pedestrian safety. Under the former the bicycle is allowed in the park, but under the latter it is excluded. In order to resolve this difficulty, we might expect the interpreter to go to the second-order justification. Suppose, however, that this next level of inquiry reveals merely a desire to maximize the pleasure of the residents of the town in which the park is located. We are now in doubt, and the task before us is far from easy, as a practical matter generating a multiplicity of answers among a multiplicity of interpreters. Yet those interpreters are still on a path that started at the rule itself, and the destination might be different than if the interpreter had started from somewhere else.

If we are thinking about just one regulative rule, therefore, it seems hard to generate the idea of a gap. The failure of the 'No Dogs Allowed' rule to exclude men without neckties is hardly a 'gap' in the rule, and it is peculiar to think of every instance of non-coverage of a rule as a gap. Moreover, even the failure of the 'No Dogs Allowed' rule to exclude bears or rowdy children is a 'gap' only if, as we have seen, it is the justification and not the instantiation that is the rule. If bears and rowdy children are excluded, then 'No Dogs Allowed' just is not, and never was, a *rule*. Consequently, if one rule cannot generate the idea of a gap, and if indeterminacies at the edge of that rule (the Case of the Stuffed Dog, for example) can be resolved by a process that goes from and through the rule itself, it is equally difficult to locate any room for what might be called 'discretion' in any strong sense of that word.

The situation looks different, however, if instead of considering only one rule we look to and assume a *comprehensive* rule system. When I say comprehensive I do not mean closed, as with the rules of chess. Rather I intend to refer to a system, such as the common law in common law countries, that aspires to determine all controversies. That does not mean, of course, that everyone who brings a lawsuit will win. It does mean, however, that the system seeks to provide an answer for every case in which two citizens have grievances. Under this approach, therefore, there is no such thing as a situation falling totally outside the rule system, anymore than, to use Dworkin's example, there are serves in tennis that are neither in nor out.[25]

When a rule system has such comprehensive ambitions, there

---

[25] Dworkin, *A Matter of Principle*, 119–45. Dworkin makes a similar point in his discussion of the Tal–Fischer chess match. *Taking Rights Seriously*, 101–5. Fischer's smiling at Tal, an activity hitherto uncovered by the rules of chess, is a hard case just because the rules of chess purport to cover anything that happens between players during a match. On the comprehensive pretensions of legal rules, see Jonathan Cohen, 'Theory and Definition in Jurisprudence', 223–7.

may indeed be gaps, for every event is expected to have a rule-generated result. Suppose our restaurant purports to have a comprehensive rule system dealing with all cases in which any prospective patron approaches the restaurant door. From this perspective, there ought to be a resolution of every case in which someone seeks to come into the restaurant with anything. We might imagine a rather complex list of prohibitions, pursuant to which dogs, men without neckties and jackets, and children under 6 years old were excluded. Now suppose again that a patron arrives with pet bear in tow. No specific prohibition excludes the bear, so we might think that the non-prohibition of bears allows the bear entrance. That would be the result if the rule system were taken to be comprehensive, *and* if the system were held to contain a default rule specifying the result for any case not specifically enumerated. *If* the rules of the restaurant implicitly provided that anything not prohibited were permitted, then the bear would be permitted, and there would be nothing close or hard or interpretive about the matter. Similarly, if the rules of chess specified that players could do anything not specifically prohibited, then Fischer's smiling at Tal would be permitted, and again nothing about the case could be said to be 'hard'.

We are now approaching an understanding of our problem. Gaps are exclusively a product of the conjunction of two distinct conditions, existing only within systems purporting to be comprehensive, *and* which provide no default (or closure) rule for unprovided cases. If there is no default rule within a system, as there is not within chess for activities taking place within a match but not covered by the rules, and there is not for the common law system, then the response to a case presented but not covered by the system is 'We'll see'. Understanding the existence of gaps within a legal system, therefore, is a function of law (or at least the common law) *not* containing a rule providing that the plaintiff loses if she cannot rely on a pre-existing cause of action. If the plaintiff has a grievance, this becomes a legally cognizable event even if there is no extant rule granting relief in cases of that kind.

When a gap does exist, under such conditions of comprehensive systemic aspirations coupled with the absence of a default rule, two different approaches are imaginable. Under one, the existing rules provide no purchase for the now-necessary rule-making, and the interpreter making a decision for the new case will decide what, all things considered, ought to be done. Under the other, most prominently associated with Dworkin,[26] the interpreter views the existing rule system as a potentially coherent array of rules, and decides the new case in the way that will best fit with and carry on the enterprise established by the existing rule system.

It is not at all clear, however, that the two approaches are truly different. Let us look more closely at the two models, one which we can call 'legislative', in that it sees the interpreter as performing a role guided by the same considerations that guided the original maker of the rule, and the other, which we can call 'interpretive', asking the interpreter to supplement the rule solely by reference to those rules that already exist within the applicable rule system. Under the interpretive model, given that by stipulation the purpose behind the original rule is unable to provide an answer, the interpreter must reach that decision most coherent with the existing 'data'. But this process runs into the problem of underdetermination. No one explanation, theory, or story will uniquely fit the existing rules and decisions under them. The interpreter must then, among all of the interpretations that fit the existing rule system, pick among them on the basis of some factor other than one uniquely derivable from that system.[27] In order to do this, the interpreter, if rational, will then make the decision that is best, all things considered, where 'all things considered' is based on just what it is that the system is designed to accomplish.

Under the legislative model, where again by stipulation any notion of a purpose behind a particular rule has been exhausted as a source of decisional guidance, the newly empowered legislator must make the best decision, again 'all things considered'. Given that we can expect even the original rule-maker to have taken into account the very reasons for having this rule system, it appears that the interpreter operating in the legislative mode will be basing the decision of the same factors used by the interpretive interpreter to choose among competing coherent theories.

Note that the similarity we have located is a similarity rather than true extensional equivalence. Under the legislative model it would be open to the interpreter to choose an interpretation that did not fit well with the existing system and its purposes, an option not open to

---

[26] Dworkin's vision is one in which the task of interpretation is pervasive and not interstitial. Consequently, we might describe this perspective as Dworkinian but not as Dworkin's.

[27] See Lawrence Alexander and Michael Bayles, 'Hercules or Proteus: The Many Theses of Ronald Dworkin'; Marsha Hanen, 'Justification as Coherence'.

the interpretive interpreter. But it is hard to imagine any rule system that would give its interpreters, where they are different from its rule-makers, the power when faced with an interpretive dilemma to reach a decision departing drastically from the existing presuppositions of the entire system. And as long as we are not dealing with such a system, one which takes the fortuity of the previously unprovided for case as a warrant for the interpreter to change the nature of the system, then it appears that the legislative interpreter will engage in a process similar to that pursued by the interpretive interpreter.

All of the foregoing, however, assumes that we are dealing with difficult cases arising on the edges of *regulative* rules. Where we are dealing with jurisdictional rather than regulative rules, however, the picture appears different. To say that the 'No Dogs Allowed' rule is jurisdictional is odd, although the rule does empower its applier to determine what a dog is. In most cases, however, this determination will already have been made by the linguistic community. But when the rule looks different, and prohibits the denial of 'equal protection of the laws', or 'contracts, combinations, and conspiracies in restraint of trade', or 'conduct unbecoming a gentle-man', or 'unsportsmanlike conduct', the rule has a dominant juris-dictional or empowering facet conjoined with its regulative side, for *every* application requires the applier to make the linguistically (and perhaps socially) undetermined determination of what conduct is 'unequal', 'in restraint of trade', 'unbecoming a gentleman', or 'unsportsmanlike'.

In such cases, it seems circular to hold that the determination of the meaning of these empowering terms is to be made by reference to existing rules within the system, for one of the rules of the system is that these determinations are to be made by the interpreter. In this case it is difficult even to conceive of these as hard cases in the interpretive sense. It is exactly the purpose of such rules to em-power the interpreters to work out the results on the basis of factors not themselves contained in the rule, and thus an interpreter engaging in that task is doing something different than is forced into an interpretive act by the limitations of language, by the limitations of the foresight of the rule-maker, or by the ineliminable factor of open texture. When we see the interpreter forced into interpretation by one of these factors, we can understand why interpretation ought to be modest, avoiding taking the fortuitous case as occasion for altering the nature of the rule. But when the rule itself requires at its core that interpreters make determinations not themselves determined by the rule, shackling the interpreter to other rules seems self-defeating, for to take an empowering rule as subject to the disempowering constraints of other rules is to take empowerment as necessarily subject to disempowerment.

This is not to say that some system might not prefer such a course. It is to say, however, that to require an empowered interpreter to be restricted is compelled by the idea of a rule or by the idea of a rule system. Instead, it is consistent with the idea of rules as tools for serving certain purposes in certain parts of society. Consequently, without a substantive theory of what a decisional environment is designed to *do*, we cannot know what kinds of rules, if any, it would want to have. A rule-based decision is acontextual, but the determination of whether a decisional environment should employ acontextual decision-making is a decision that cannot itself be made acontextually.

10
EPILOGUE
THE SILENT VIRTUES

So what?

The picture of rule-bound adjudication that has emerged in this book appears at first glance strikingly unimportant. I have made much of the recalcitrant experience, the occasion on which the instantiation of a justification turns out to ill-serve its generating justification. But surely such cases are rare. Most commonly, the application of a rule will be consistent with its justification. Applying the rule to a particular case will yield results identical to those that would have resulted from direct application of the justification itself. Thus, the instances on which I have focused seem to be marginal, conceivably interesting but statistically inconsequential. And if the recalcitrant experience—the case that demonstrates extensional divergence between rule and justification—is such an uncommon occurrence, then does much really turn on whether any system chooses to make its decisions according to the picture I have painted of rule-based decision-making?

In part, the importance of the seemingly unimportant resides in the intersection between the complexity of life and the necessary limitations of the mind. It is not just, as Gregory Trianosky reminds us, that 'ordinary people just can't keep all the distinctions, caveats, and exceptions straight in their heads'.[1] Rather, rule-based decision-making is premised in part on the belief that none of us, ordinary or not, have the mental capacity incessantly to consider all of the things that an 'all things considered' decision-making model requires of us. If we are not to be paralysed by uncertainty, and stumble into numerous errors just because we have too little time to consider too much, we must often simplify our thought processes, using a form of decision-making that limits us to the consideration of a manageable array of factors.

Rules, as we have seen, serve this life-simplifying purpose,

---

[1] Gregory Trianosky, 'Rule-Utilitarianism and the Slippery Slope', 421.

operating in a way captured as well by IBM as by any philosopher when it proclaimed in an advertisement that its purpose was to build 'machines to work so that people can think'. Rules also serve this agenda-simplifying or desk-clearing function, taking much off the agenda so that what remains can be dealt with with the care and detail it deserves. In this respect, rules have silent virtues, for often we are able to do what we can precisely because rules free us from having to do anything else. Thus, although a regulatory rule may seem to bite only when the results it indicates diverge from the results that would have been indicated by direct application of its background justifications, that account is phenomenologically misleading. Even if the rule demonstrates its extensional divergence in only one case out of a thousand, and in the other 999 appears to do exactly what the justification would have done without the rule, the rule's import lies in just the way in which it frees its addressees from determining whether this is the one case in which the results would have been different. Only because of the rule is the addressee freed from looking behind the rule *in every case*, and thus the rule, extensionally divergent in one case out of a thousand, influences the nature of the decision-making process in the other 999 as well.

Even when rules are presumptive rather than absolute, a similar phenomenology applies, although plainly in a tempered form. When a rule has but presumptive force, its addressee must inspect a wider range of factors than those encompassed by the rule's factual predicate, for otherwise there is no way to determine whether this is one of the cases in which the reason provided by the rule is outweighed by other reasons. Still, there are degrees of intensiveness of that inspection. It is one thing to inspect the world on the assumption that everything in it is part of the decision, and it is another thing to inspect the same world on the quite different assumption that something in it might but probably will not be relevant to the decision to be made. The latter process is more of a *glimpse* than any kind of careful scrutiny, and rules may exert their focusing function by determining what shall be examined with care and what shall only be glimpsed. And although the glimpse may in some cases indicate some reason to examine more closely that which was just glimpsed, the rules have their force in the way in which, in every case, they justify a much more casual examination than would otherwise have been the case.

To some extent these tasks may be performed by rules of thumb rather than by rules that themselves provide reasons for action *qua* rules. But as we saw in Chapter 5.7, the decision-simplifying and desk-clearing functions can be served only by rules having at least some modicum of evidentiary force. Only if a rule at least elevates the burden of justification necessary to take an action inconsistent with its indications can it have any effect, including a decision-simplifying one, on decision-makers. And when even rules that can be set aside for internal failure do elevate this burden of justification, they cease to be the weightless rules of thumb imagined by those whose references to rules of thumb are invariably prefaced with 'mere', and they then operate in substantially the same way as do those rules whose lack of transparency to their background justifications is more obvious.

Even more importantly, however, truly transparent rules of thumb fail to capture the role of rules in allocating power, in making the jurisdictional determinations that are essential in any complex and multi-membered society. Although the bite of a rule may be most obvious only in the odd case in which the existence of a rule makes a difference to the outcome, taking the statistically rare recalcitrant experience to be the whole story is to miss the point of rules. When a decision-maker makes a decision based on only a limited number of factors, that decision-maker is operating in a world in which rules have allocated the determination of other factors to someone else or to some other person or institution. Even when they do not indicate a decision other than the one that would have been reached without them, rules operate as perhaps the most important tool for the division of decisional labor.

These jurisdictional functions may appear within agents as well as among them. The lesson of the Grand Inquisitor may be seen as a lesson about intra-personal agendas, and about the difficulties involved in having too many choices. When with respect to some decisions that affect me I defer to others, and thus alienate some of my freedom, I may be acting merely to concentrate and thus accentuate my freedom in other areas. When as I respect the rules that give some of my power to others, and as I make rules for my own behavior, I often do so in the service of the psychological impossibility of treating my life as a series of constant and unbounded choices. If I thus relinquish some of my ability to make choices I might otherwise have been able to make, I in so doing make a rational decision not to make decisions about every detail of every moment of my life

Thus, the essence of rule-based decision-making lies in the concept of jurisdiction, for rules, which narrow the range of factors to be considered by particular decision-makers, establish and constrain the jurisdiction of those decision-makers. For all the assistance that has been given to our understanding of rules by those who have thought about the role of rules in moral decision-making, that perspective has its limitations. The gains in understanding emanating out of that important body of thought are limited by its general unwillingness to look at rules from other than the standpoint of the moral agent, ultimately responsible for her own moral decisions, attempting to decide what to do. When making moral decisions, however, all moral agents are jurisdictionally equivalent, for it seems almost inconsistent with the very idea of morality to say that some decision with moral implications is none of my business.

Yet from any other standpoint, 'That's none of my business!' depicts a large part of our complex and multi-jurisdictional world. People serve different functions, have different abilities, live in different places, have different allegiances, belong to different groups, and in numerous other ways occupy a world in which allocation of authority among people, groups, and institutions is a necessary way of life. These jurisdiction-allocating determinations need not be considered morally sterile. We remain in need of a moral theory of jurisdictional separation, focusing on questions other than the question of what one autonomous and anonymous moral agent should do.

But even apart from the moral component of jurisdictional separation, such division of responsibilities pervades our prudential and our pragmatic existence. There may be little of moral interest in whether an umpire should allow four strikes to an especially worthy batter, but these kinds of decisions, decisions about who should have the power to decide what, are still central to almost every facet of communal life. Rules, telling agents what they should do and thus what they should not, are the implements by which roles are established and power is allocated, and they serve this function not only in those cases in which an agent makes a decision that that agent would have reached even by considering factors that are in some other agent's jurisdiction. Rules, therefore, are instrumentalities not only of power, but of restraint. They are the devices of arrogance, but they are also the devices of modesty. Insofar as rules are the frequently undesirable justifications for the denial by agents of ultimate reponsibility for what they do, they are at best a mixed blessing. But insofar as rules are the frequently desirable devices for limiting jurisdiction and thus of limiting power, and insofar as they are the also frequently desirable devices for allocating responsibility in a complex world, their force is felt not only in the odd case, but in every case. It is not just that these virtues of rules are frequently unnoticed and are thus silent. Rather, it is the very silence itself, the ability to take things off the agenda as well as to put them on, that explains much of what is valuable about rules.

BIBLIOGRAPHY

ADAMS, ROBERT MERRIHEW, 'Motive Utilitarianism', *Journal of Philosophy*, 73 (1976), 467–81.

ALEXANDER, LARRY, 'Pursuing the Good—Indirectly', *Ethics*, 95 (1985), 315–32.

—— 'Striking Back at the Empire: A Brief Survey of Problems in Dworkin's Theory of Law', *Law and Philosophy*, 6 (1987), 419–38.

—— 'Constrained By Precedent', *Southern California Law Review*, 63 (1989), 1–64.

—— 'Law and Exclusionary Reasons', *Philosophical Topics*, 18 (1990), 5–22.

—— and BAYLES, MICHAEL, 'Hercules or Proteus? The Many Theses of Ronald Dworkin', *Social Theory and Practice*, 5 (1980), 267–303.

ALSTON, WILLIAM P., 'Meaning and Use', *Philosophical Quarterly*, 13 (1963), 107–24.

ANSCOMBE, G. E. M., 'Wittgenstein on Rules and Private Language', reviewing *Wittgenstein: On Rules and Private Language*, by Saul Kripke, *Ethics*, 95 (1985), 342–52.

ATIYAH, P. S., and SUMMERS, R. S., *Form and Substance in Anglo-American Law: A Comparative Study in Legal Reasoning, Legal Theory and Legal Institutions* (Oxford: Clarendon Press, 1987).

AUSTIN, J. L. *How to Do Things With Words*, 2nd edn., J. O. Urmson and Marina Sbisà (eds.) (Cambridge, Massachusetts: Harvard University Press, 1975).

—— 'Other Minds', in *Philosophical Papers*, 3rd edn., J. O. Urmson and G. J. Warnock (eds.) (Oxford: Oxford University Press, 1979), 76–116.

AUSTIN, JOHN, *The Province of Jurisprudence Determined and The Uses of the Study of Jurisprudence*, with Introduction by H. L. A. Hart (New York: Noonday Press, 1954).

BAKER, G. P., 'Defeasibility and Meaning', in P. M. S. Hacker and J. Raz (eds.) *Law, Morality, and Society: Essays in Honour of H. L. A. Hart* (Oxford: Clarendon Press, 1977), 26–57.

—— 'Following Wittgenstein: Some Signposts for *Philosophical Investigations* §§ 143–242', in Steven H. Holtzman and Christopher M. Leich (eds.) *Wittgenstein: to Follow a Rule* (London: Routledge & Kegan Paul Ltd., 1981), 31–71.

—— and HACKER, P. M. S., *Scepticism, Rules and Language* (Oxford: Basil Blackwell, 1984).

—— —— *Frege: Logical Excavations* (Oxford: Basil Blackwell, 1984).

—— —— *Wittgenstein: Understanding and Meaning (An Analytical Commentary on the* Philosophical Investigations, *Volume 1)* (Oxford: Basil Blackwell, 1980).

—— —— *Wittgenstein: Rules, Grammar and Necessity (An Analytical Commentary on the* Philosophical Investigations, *Volume 2)* (Oxford: Basil Blackwell, 1985).

BAR-HILLEL, YEHOSHUA, 'Indexical Expressions', *Mind*, 63 (1954), 359–79.

BAYLES, MICHAEL D., 'Coercive Offers and Public Benefits' *The Personalist*, 55 (1974), 139–44.

—— 'Mid-Level Principles and Justification', in J. Roland Pennock and John W. Chapman (eds.), *Justification* (NOMOS XXVIII), (New York: New York University Press, 1986), 49–67.

—— (ed.) *Contemporary Utilitarianism* (Garden City, New York: Doubleday & Company, Inc., 1968).

BENDITT, THEODORE, 'Threats and Offers', *Personalist*, 58 (1977), 382–4.

BENTHAM, JEREMY, *Of Laws in General*, H. L. A. Hart (ed.) (London: Athlone Press, 1970).

BLACK, MAX, 'The Analysis of Rules', in *Models and Metaphors* (Ithaca, New York: Cornell University Press, 1962), 95–139.

BLACKBURN, SIMON, *Spreading the Word: Groundings in the Philosophy of Language* (Oxford: Clarendon Press, 1984).

BOYLE, JAMES, 'The Politics of Reason: Critical Legal Theory and Local Social Thought', *University of Pennsylvania Law Review*, 133 (1985), 685–780.

BRANDT, RICHARD B., *Ethical Theory: The Problems of Normative and Critical Ethics* (Englewood Cliffs, New Jersey: Prentice-Hall, Inc., 1959).

—— 'Toward a Credible Form of Utilitarianism', in Hector-Neri Castañeda and George Nakhnikian (eds.), *Morality and the Language of Conduct* (Detroit: Wayne State University Press, 1963), 107–43 (also in Bayles, *Contemporary Utilitarianism*).

—— 'Fairness to Indirect Optimific Theories of Ethics', *Ethics*, 98 (1988), 341–60.

BRILMAYER, R. LEA, *Justifying International Acts* (Ithaca, New York: Cornell University Press, 1989).

BRINK, DAVID O., 'Legal Theory, Legal Interpretation, and Judicial Review'. *Philosophy & Public Affairs*, 17 (1988), 105–48.

—— 'Semantics and Legal Interpretation (Further Thoughts)', *Canadian Journal of Law and Jurisprudence*, 2 (1989), 181–91.

BURTON, STEVEN, *An Introduction to Law and Legal Reasoning* (Boston: Little, Brown & Co., 1984).

CALABRESI, GUIDO, *A Common Law for the Age of Statutes* (Cambridge, Mass.: Harvard University Press, 1982).

CAMPBELL, RICHMOND and LANNING, SNOWDEN (eds.), *Paradoxes of Rationality and Cooperation: Prisoner's Dilemma and Newcomb's Problem* (Vancouver: University of British Columbia Press, 1985).

CARTWRIGHT, NANCY, 'Causal Laws and Effective Strategies', *Nous*, 13 (1979), 419–37.

CATON, CHARLES E., 'Introduction', in Caton (ed.), *Philosophy and Ordinary Language* (Urbana, Illinois: University of Illinois Press, 1963), v–xii.

CHRISTIE, GEORGE, C., *Law, Norms and Authority* (London: Gerald Duckworth and Co., Ltd., 1982):

COHEN, JONATHAN, 'Theory and Definition in Jurisprudence', *Proceedings of the Aristotelian Society* (Suppl.), 29 (1955), 213–38.

COLEMAN, JULES, 'Negative and Positive Positivism', *Journal of Legal Studies*, 11 (1982), 139–62.

CORNELL, DRUCILLA, 'Institutionalization of Meaning, Recollective Imagination, and the Potential for Transformative Legal Interpretation', *University of Pennsylvania Law Review*, 136 (1988), 1135–229.

COVAL, S. C., and SMITH, J. C., *Law and its Presuppositions: Actions, Agents and Rules* (London: Routledge & Kegan Paul, 1986).

CURTIS, CHARLES P., 'A Better Theory of Legal Interpretation', *Vanderbilt Law Review*, 3 (1950), 404–37.

DARWALL, STEVEN, *Impartial Reason* (Ithaca, New York: Cornell University Press, 1983).

DASCAL, MARCELO and WRÓBLEWSKI, JERZY, 'Transparency and Doubt: Understanding and Interpretation in Pragmatics and in Law', *Law and Philosophy*, 7 (1988), 203–24.

DAVIDSON, DONALD, 'Actions, Reasons, and Causes', in *Essays on Actions and Events* (Oxford: Clarendon Press, 1980), 3–19.

DETMOLD, M. J., *The Unity of Law and Morality: A Refutation of Legal Positivism* (London: Routledge & Kegan Paul, 1984).

DIGGS, B. J., 'Rules and Utilitarianism', *American Philosophical Quarterly*, 1 (1964), 32–44 (also in Bayles, *Contemporary Utilitarianism*).

DONELLAN, KEITH S., 'Reference and Definite Descriptions', *Philosophical Review*, 75 (1966), 281–304.

DUHEM, PIERRE MAURICE MARIE, *The Aim and Structure of Physical Theory*, P. P. Wiener (trans.) (Princeton: Princeton University Press, 1954).

DUMMETT, MICHAEL, *The Interpretation of Frege's Philosophy* (London: Gerald Duckworth & Company Ltd., 1981).

DWORKIN, RONALD, *Taking Rights Seriously* (Cambridge, Mass.: Harvard University Press, 1977).

—— *A Matter of Principle* (Cambridge, Mass.: Harvard University Press, 1985).

—— *Law's Empire*. Cambridge, Mass.: Harvard University Press, 1986.

EELS, ELLERY, 'Probabilistic Causal Interaction', *Philosophy of Science*, 53 (1986), 52–64.

EISENBERG, MELVIN A., *The Nature of the Common Law* (Cambridge, Mass.: Harvard University Press, 1988).

EMMET, DOROTHY, *Rules, Roles and Relations* (London: Macmillan, 1966).

EZORSKY, GERTRUDE, Review of Lyons, *The Forms and Limits of Utilitarianism. Journal of Philosophy*, 65 (1968), 533–44.

FARBER, DANIEL and FRICKEY, PHILIP, 'Practical Reason and the First Amendment', *UCLA Law Review*, 34 (1982), 1615–56.

FERGUSON, R. B., 'The Horwitz Thesis and Common Law Discourse in England', *Oxford Journal of Legal Studies*, 3 (1983), 34–58.

FINNIS, JOHN, 'The Authority of Law in the Predicament of Contemporary Social Theory', *Notre Dame Journal of Law, Ethics & Public Policy*, 1 (1984), 115–37.

—— 'On Reason and Authority in *Law's Empire*', *Law and Philosophy*, 6 (1987), 357–80.

FLATHMAN, RICHARD, *Political Obligation* (London: Croom Helm, 1973).

FOGELIN, ROBERT, *Wittgenstein* (London: Routledge & Kegan Paul Ltd., 1976).

FRANK, JEROME, *Law and the Modern Mind* (New York: Brentano's, 1930).

FREGE, GOTTLOB, *The Foundations of Arithmetic: A Logico-Mathematical Enquiry into the Concept of Number*, J. L. Austin, (trans.) 2nd rev. edn. (Oxford: Basil Blackwell, 1959).

FRIED, CHARLES, 'Two Concepts of Interests: Some Reflections on the Supreme Court's Balancing Test', *Harvard Law Review*, 76 (1963), 755–78.

FRIEDMAN, LAWRENCE M., 'Law and Its Language', *George Washington Law Review*, 33 (1964), 563–79.

FULLER, LON L., 'Positivism and Fidelity to Law—A Reply to Professor Hart', *Harvard Law Review*, 71 (1958), 630–72.

—— *The Morality of Law*, rev. edn. (New Haven: Yale University Press, 1969).

GANS, CHAIM, 'Mandatory Rules and Exclusionary Reasons', *Philosophia*, 15 (1986), 373–94.

GARVER, NEWTON, 'Rules', in *The Encyclopedia of Philosophy*, vol. 7 (New York: Macmillan Publishing Co., Inc., 1967), 231–3.

GARVEY, JOHN, 'Freedom and Equality in the Religion Clauses', *The Supreme Court Review*, (1981), 193–221.

GAUTHIER, DAVID, *Practical Reasoning: The Structure and Formulation of Prudential and Moral Arguments and their Exemplification in Discourse* (Oxford: Clarendon Press, 1963).

—— *Morals By Agreement* (Oxford: Clarendon Press, 1986).

GAVISON, RUTH, 'Comment', in Ruth Gavison (ed.), *Issues in Contemporary*

Legal Philosophy: The Influence of H. L. A. Hart (Oxford: Clarendon Press, 1987), 21–34.

GEWIRTH, ALAN, 'Are There Any Absolute Rights?', *Philosophical Quarterly*, 31 (1981), 1–16.

GILLIGAN, CAROL, *In a Different Voice: Psychological Theory and Women's Development* (Cambridge, Mass.: Harvard University Press, 1982).

GLOVER, TRUDY, 'What's Wrong with Slippery Slope Arguments?', *Canadian Journal of Philosophy*, 12 (1982), 303–16.

GOLDMAN, HOLLY S., 'David Lyons on Utilitarian Generalization', *Philosophical Studies*, 26 (1974), 77–95.

GOMBRICH, E. H., 'The Logic of Vanity Fair: Alternatives to Historicism in the Study of Fashions, Style and Taste', in Paul Arthur Schlipp (ed.), *The Philosophy of Karl Popper*, 2 (La Salle, Illinois: Open Court Publishing Co., 1974), 925–57.

GOOD, I. J., 'A Causal Calculus (I) & (II)', *British Journal for the Philosophy of Science*, vol. 11 (1961), 305–18; vol. 12 (1961), 43–51.

GOODHART, ARTHUR L., 'Determining the Ratio Decidendi of a Case', *Yale Law Journal*, 40 (1930), 161–83.

—— 'The Ratio Decidendi of a Case', *Modern Law Review*, 22 (1959), 117–24.

GOTTLIEB, GIDON, *The Logic of Choice* (London: George Allen and Unwin., 1968).

GREEN, LESLIE, 'Law, Co-ordination and the Common Good', *Oxford Journal of Legal Studies*, 3 (1983), 299–324.

GREENAWALT, KENT, *Conflicts of Law and Morality* (Oxford: Clarendon Press, 1987).

GRICE, H. P., 'Meaning', *Philosophical Review*, 66 (1957), 377–88.

—— 'Utterer's Meaning, Sentence-Meaning, and Word-Meaning', *Foundations of Language*, 4 (1968), 225–42.

HANEN, MARSHA, 'Justification as Coherence', in M. A. Stewart (ed.), *Law, Morality and Rights* (Dordrecht, Netherlands: Reidel, 1983), 67–92.

HARE, R. M., *The Language of Morals* (Oxford: Clarendon Press, 1952).

—— *Freedom and Reason* (Oxford: Oxford University Press, 1963).

—— 'Principles', *Proceedings of the Aristotelian Society*, 73 (1972–3), 1–18.

—— *Moral Thinking: Its Levels, Method and Point* (Oxford: Clarendon Press, 1981).

HARRIS, J. W., *Law and Legal Science: An Inquiry into the Concepts Legal Rule and Legal System* (Oxford: Clarendon Press, 1979).

HARRISON, JONATHAN, 'Utilitarianism, Universalisation, and Our Duty to Be Just', *Proceedings of the Aristotelian Society*, 53 (1952–3), 105–34 (also in Bayles, *Contemporary Utilitarianism*).

HART, H. L. A., 'Positivism and the Separation of Law and Morals',

Harvard Law Review, 71 (1958), 593–629 (also in Hart, *Essays in Jurisprudence and Philosophy*).

—— *The Concept of Law* (Oxford: Clarendon Press, 1961).

—— 'Bentham on Legal Powers', *Yale Law Journal*, 81 (1972), 799–822.

—— *Essays on Bentham: Jurisprudence and Political Theory* (Oxford: Clarendon Press, 1982).

—— 'Definition and Theory in Jurisprudence', in *Essays in Jurisprudence and Philosophy* (Oxford: Clarendon Press, 1983), 21–48.

—— *Essays in Jurisprudence and Philosophy* (Oxford: Clarendon Press, 1983).

HEINER, RONALD A., 'Imperfect Decision and the Law: On the Evolution of Legal Precedent and Rules', *The Journal of Legal Studies*, 15 (1986), 227–61.

HELD, VIRGINIA, 'Coercion and Coercive Offers', in J. Roland Pennock and John W. Chapman (eds.), *Coercion* (NOMOS XIV) (Chicago: Aldine-Atherton, 1972), 49–62.

HILPINEN, RISTO, 'Normative Conflicts and Legal Reasoning', in Eugenio Bulygin *et al.* (eds.), *Man, Law, and the Modern Forms of Life* (Dordrecht, Netherlands: D. Reidel, 1985), 191–208.

—— 'Conflict and Change in Norm Systems', in Åke Frandberg and Mark Van Hoecke (eds.), *The Structure of Law* (vol. 14, Skrifter fran Juridiska Fakulteten i Uppsala), (Uppsala, Sweden: Iustus Forlag, 1987), 37–49.

HINTIKKA, JAAKKO, 'On the Incommensurability of Theories', *Philosophy of Science*, 55 (1988), 25–38.

HOLDCROFT, DAVID, *Words and Deeds: Problems in the Theory of Speech Acts* (Oxford: Clarendon Press, 1978).

HOLMES, STEPHEN, 'Gag Rules, or the Politics of Omission', in Jon Elster and Rune Slagstad (eds.), *Constitutionalism and Democracy* (Cambridge: Cambridge University Press, 1988), 3–42.

HONORÉ, A. M., 'Real Laws', in P. M. S. Hacker and J. Raz (eds.), *Law, Morality and Society: Essays in Honour of H. L. A. Hart* (Oxford: Clarendon Press, 1977), 99–118.

HORWICH, PAUL, 'On Calculating the Utility of Acts', *Philosophical Studies*, 25 (1974), 21–31.

HORWITZ, MORTON, *The Transformation of American Law, 1780–1860* (Cambridge, Mass.: Harvard University Press, 1977).

JAMES, WILLIAM, *Pragmatism: A New Name for Some Old Ways of Thinking* and *The Meaning of Truth: A Sequel to Pragmatism* (Cambridge, Mass.: Harvard University Press, 1978).

JIWEI, CI, 'The Logic of the Generality of Moral Principles', *Philosophical Quarterly*, 38 (1988), 305–15.

KALMAN, LAURA, *Legal Realism at Yale, 1927–1960* (Chapel Hill, North Carolina: University of North Carolina Press, 1986).

KATZ, JERROLD, 'Literal Meaning and Logical Theory', *Journal of Philosophy*, 78 (1981), 203–33.

KATZ, LEO, *Bad Acts and Guilty Minds: Conundrums of the Criminal Law*. (Chicago: The University of Chicago Press, 1988).

KAVKA, GREGORY, 'Extensional Equivalence and Utilitarian Generalization', *Theoria*, 41 (1975), 125–47.

KELSEN, HANS, *Pure Theory of Law*, 2nd edn. Max Knight (trans.), (Berkeley: University of California Press, 1967).

—— *Allgemeine Theorie der Normen*. K. Ringhofer and R. Walter (eds.), (Vienna: Manz, 1979).

KENNEDY, DUNCAN, 'Legal Formality', *Journal of Legal Studies*, 2 (1973), 351–98.

—— 'Form and Substance in Private Law Adjudication', *Harvard Law Review*, 89 (1976), 1685–778.

KRATOCHWIL, FRIEDRICH, *Rules, Norms, and Decisions: On the Conditions of Practical and Legal Reasoning in International Relations and Domestic Affairs* (Cambridge: Cambridge University Press, 1989).

KRIPKE, SAUL A., *Naming and Necessity* (Cambridge, Mass.: Harvard University Press, 1980).

—— *Wittgenstein on Rules and Private Language: An Elementary Exposition* (Cambridge, Mass.: Harvard University Press, 1982).

LEIBNIZ, GOTTFRIED WILHELM, *Discourse on Metaphysics*, in *Philosophical Papers and Letters*. L. Loemke (ed.) 2nd edn. (Dordrecht, Holland: D. Reidel Publishing Company, 1970).

LEONARDI, PAOLO, Review of *Skepticism, Rules & Language*, by G. P. Baker and P. M. S. Hacker. *Nous*, 22 (1988), 618–24.

LEVINSON, SANFORD, 'Taking Law Seriously: Reflections on "Thinking Like a Lawyer"', *Stanford Law Review*, 30 (1978), 1071–109.

—— 'Who is a Jew(ish Justice)?', *Cardozo Law Review*, 10 (1989), 2359–70.

LEVI, EDWARD H., *An Introduction to Legal Reasoning* (Chicago: University of Chicago Press, 1949).

LEWIS, DAVID K., *Convention: A Philosophical Study* (Cambridge, Mass.: Harvard University Press, 1969).

—— 'Scorekeeping in a Language Game', in *Philosophical Papers: Volume I* (New York: Oxford University Press, 1983), 233–49.

LINDBLOM, CHARLES E., 'The Science of Muddling Through', *Public Administration Review*, 19 (1959), 79–88.

—— *The Intelligence of Democracy* (New York: Macmillan, 1965).

LINSKY, LEONARD, *Names and Descriptions* (Chicago: University of Chicago Press, 1977).

LLEWELLYN, KARL NICKERSON, *The Bramble Bush: Some Lectures on Law and its Study* (New York: Columbia University School of Law, 1930).

—— *Jurisprudence: Realism in Theory and Practice* (Chicago: University of Chicago Press, 1962).

LYONS, DANIEL, 'Welcome Threats and Coercive Offers', *Philosophy*, 50 (1975), 425–36.

Lyons, David, *Forms and Limits of Utilitarianism* (Oxford: Clarendon Press, 1965).
—— 'Principles, Positivism, and Legal Theory', *Yale Law Journal*, 87 (1977), 415–36.
MacCormick, Neil, *Legal Reasoning and Legal Theory* (Oxford: Clarendon Press, 1978).
—— *H. L. A. Hart* (London: Edward Arnold, 1981).
McGinn, Colin, *Wittgenstein on Meaning: An Interpretation and Evaluation* (Oxford: Basil Blackwell Ltd., 1984).
March, James G. and Herbert A. Simon, *Organizations* (New York: John Wiley, 1958).
—— 'Bounded Rationality, Ambiguity, and the Engineering of Choice', *Bell Journal of Economics*, 9 (1978), 587–608.
Margalit, Avishai, 'Open Texture', in Avishai Margalit (ed.), *Meaning and Use* (Amsterdam: D. Reidel, 1981), 141–52.
Michelman, Frank, 'Traces of Self-Government', *Harvard Law Review*, 100 (1986), 4–53,
Minow, Martha, 'Justice Engendered', *Harvard Law Review*, 101 (1987), 10–95.
Moles, Robert N., *Definition and Rule in Legal Theory: A Reassessment of H. L. A. Hart and the Positivist Tradition* (Oxford: Basil Blackwell, 1987).
Montrose, J. L., 'Ratio Decidendi and the House of Lords', *Modern Law Review*, 20 (1957), 124–30.
—— 'The Ratio Decidendi of a Case', *Modern Law Review*, 20 (1957), 587–95.
Moore, G. E., *Principia Ethica* (Cambridge: Cambridge University Press, 1903).
Moore, Michael, 'The Semantics of Judging', *Southern California Law Review*, 54 (1981), 151–294.
—— 'A Natural Law Theory of Interpretation', *Southern California Law Review*, 58 (1985), 277–398.
—— 'Authority, Law, and Razian Reasons', *Southern California Law Review*, 62 (1989), 827–96.
Nagel, Thomas, *The Possibility of Altruism* (Oxford: Clarendon Press, 1970).
Nozick, Robert, 'Moral Complications and Moral Structures', *Natural Law Forum*, 13 (1968), 1–50.
Papineau, David, 'Probabilities and Causes', *The Journal of Philosophy*, 82 (1985), 57–74.
Paulson, Stanley L., 'Material and Formal Authorisation in Kelsen's Pure Theory', *Cambridge Law Journal*, 39 (1980), 172–93.
—— 'An Empowerment Theory of Legal Norms', *Ratio Juris*, 1 (1988), 58–72.
Peczenik, Aleksander and Wróblewski, Jerzy, 'Fuzziness and Trans-

formation: Towards Explaining Legal Reasoning', *Theoria*, 51 (1985), 24–44.

PERRY, STEPHEN R., 'Judicial Obligation, Precedent and the Common Law', *Oxford Journal of Legal Studies*, 7 (1987), 215–32.

—— 'Second-Order Reasons, Uncertainty and Legal Theory', *Southern California Law Review*, 62 (1989), 913–94.

PETTIT, PHILIP and BRENNAN, GEOFFREY, 'Restrictive Consequentialism', *Australasian Journal of Philosophy*, 64 (1986), 438–55.

POMERANTZ, H. and BRESLIN, S., 'Judicial Humour—Construction of a Statute', *Criminal Law Quarterly*, 8 (1966), 137–9.

POSNER, RICHARD, 'Legal Formalism, Legal Realism, and the Interpretation of Statutes and the Constitution', *Case Western Reserve University Law Review*, 37 (1986), 179–217.

POSTEMA, GERALD, 'Coordination and Convention at the Foundations of Law', *Journal of Legal Studies*, 11 (1982), 165–203.

—— *Bentham and the Common Law Tradition* (Oxford: Clarendon Press, 1986).

PRIEST, GEORGE L., 'The Common Law and the Selection of Efficient Rules', *Journal of Legal Studies*, 6 (1977), 65–82.

—— and KLEIN, WILLIAM, 'The Selection of Disputes for Litigation', *Journal of Legal Studies*, 13 (1984), 1–23.

PUTNAM, HILARY, *Mind, Language and Reality* (Philosophical Papers, vol. 2), (Cambridge: Cambridge University Press, 1975).

QUINE, WILLARD VAN ORMAN, *Word and Object* (Cambridge, Massachusetts: MIT Press, 1960).

QUINTON, ANTHONY, *Utilitarian Ethics* (London: Macmillan, 1973).

RADIN, MARGARET JANE, 'Mid-Level Principles and Non-Ideal Justification', in J. Roland Pennock and John W. Chapman (eds.), *Justification* (NOMOS XXVIII), (New York: New York University Press, 1986), 33–48.

RAWLS, JOHN, 'Two Concepts of Rules', *Philosophical Review*, 64 (1955), 3–32 (also in Bayles, *Contemporary Utilitarianism*).

—— *A Theory of Justice* (Cambridge, Mass.: Harvard University Press, 1973).

RAZ, JOSEPH, *The Concept of a Legal System* (Oxford: Clarendon Press, 1970).

—— 'Legal Principles and the Limits of Law', *Yale Law Journal*, 81 (1972), 823–54.

—— 'Normative Powers and Voluntary Obligations', *Proceedings of the Aristotelian Society*, 46 Supp. (1972), 79–102.

—— 'Reasons for Action, Decisions and Norms', *Mind*, 83 (1975), 481–99.

—— *Practical Reason and Norms* (London: Hutchinson & Sons, Ltd., 1975).

—— 'Introduction', in Joseph Raz (ed.), *Practical Reasoning* (Oxford: Oxford University Press, 1978), 1–17.

—— *The Authority of Law: Essays on Law and Morality* (Oxford: Clarendon Press, 1979).

—— 'Legal Principles and the Limits of Law'. (rev. version), in Marshall Cohen (ed.), *Ronald Dworkin and Contemporary Jurisprudence* (Totowa, New Jersey: Rowman & Allanheld, 1983), 73–87.

—— 'The Obligation to Obey: Revision and Tradition', *Notre Dame Journal of Law, Ethics & Public Policy*, 1 (1984), 139–55.

—— *The Morality of Freedom* (Oxford: Clarendon Press, 1986).

—— 'Facing Up: A Reply', *Southern California Law Review*, 62 (1989), 1153–235.

REGAN, DONALD H., *Utilitarianism and Co-operation* (Oxford: Clarendon Press, 1980).

—— 'Law's Halo', in Jules Coleman and Ellen Frankel Paul (eds.), *Philosophy and Law* (Oxford: Basil Blackwell (for the Social Philosophy and Policy Center), 1987), 15–30.

—— 'Authority and Value: Reflections on Raz's *Morality of Freedom*', *Southern California Law Review*, 62 (1989), 995–1095.

—— 'Reasons, Authority, and the Meaning of "Obey": Further Thoughts on Raz and Obedience to Law', *Canadian Journal of Law and Jurisprudence*, 3 (1990), 3–28.

REYNOLDS, NOEL, 'Law as Convention', *Ratio juris*, 2 (1989), 105–20.

RICHARDS, DAVID A. J., *A Theory of Reasons for Action* (Oxford: Clarendon Press, 1971).

ROSEN, DEBORAH, 'In Defence of a Probabilistic Theory of Causality', *Philosophy of Science*, 45 (1978), 604–13.

ROSS, ALF, *Directives and Norms* (London: Routledge & Kegan Paul Ltd., 1968).

ROSS, W. D., *The Right and the Good* (Oxford: Clarendon Press, 1930).

RUBIN, PAUL H., 'Why is the Common Law Efficient?', *Journal of Legal Studies*, 6 (1977), 51–63.

RUMBLE, WILFRED E., *American Legal Realism: Skepticism, Reform, and the Judicial Process* (Ithaca, New York: Cornell University Press, 1968).

RUSSELL, BERTRAND, 'Vagueness', *Australasian Journal of Psychology and Philosophy*, 1 (1923), 84–92.

SALMON, WESLEY, 'Probabilistic Causality', *Pacific Philosophical Quarterly*, 61 (1980), 50–74.

SARTORIUS, ROLF, 'Social Policy and Judicial Legislation', *American Philosophical Quarterly*, 8 (1971), 151–69.

SCHAUER, FREDERICK, 'Slippery Slopes', *Harvard Law Review*, 99 (1985), 361–83.

—— 'The Jurisprudence of Reasons', reviewing *Law's Empire*, by Ronald Dworkin. *Michigan Law Review*, 85 (1987), 847–70.

—— 'Precedent', *Stanford Law Review*, 39 (1987), 571–605.

—— 'Authority and Indeterminacy', in J. Roland Pennock and John

W. Chapman (eds.), *Authority Revisited* (NOMOS XXIX), (New York: New York University Press, 1987), 28–38.

—— 'Formalism', *Yale Law Journal*, 97 (1988), 509–48.

—— 'Judging in a Corner of the Law, *Southern California Law Review*, 61 (1988), 1717–33.

—— 'Is the Common Law Law?', reviewing *The Nature of the Common Law*, by Melvin A. Eisenberg. *California Law Review*, 77 (1989), 455–71.

SCHELLING, THOMAS C., *The Strategy of Conflict* (Cambridge, Mass.: Harvard University Press, 1960).

—— 'Enforcing Rules on Oneself', *Journal of Law, Economics, and Organization*, 1 (1985), 357–74.

SCHIFFER, STEPHEN, *Meaning* (Oxford: Clarendon Press, 1972).

SEARLE, JOHN R., *Speech Acts: An Essay in the Philosophy of Language* (Cambridge: Cambridge University Press, 1969).

—— '*Prima Facie* Obligations', in Joseph Raz (ed.), *Practical Reasoning* (Oxford: Oxford University Press, 1978), 81–90.

—— 'Literal Meaning', *Erkenntnis*, 13 (1978), 207–24, repr. in John Searle, *Expression and Meaning* (Cambridge: Cambridge University Press, 1979), 117–36.

—— *Intentionality: An Essay in the Philosophy of Mind* (Cambridge: Cambridge University Press, 1983).

—— *Minds, Brains and Science* (Cambridge, Mass.: Harvard University Press, 1984).

SHKLAR, JUDITH N., *Legalism: Law, Morals, and Political Trials* (Cambridge, Mass.: Harvard University Press, 1964).

SHWAYDER, DAVID, *The Stratification of Behaviour: A System of Definitions Propounded and Defended* (London: Routledge & Kegan Paul Ltd., 1965).

SILVER, CHARLES, 'Elmer's Case: A Legal Positivist Replies to Dworkin', *Law and Philosophy*, 6 (1987), 381–99.

SILVERSTEIN, HARRY S., 'Simple and General Utilitarianism', *The Philosophical Review*, 83 (1974), 339–63.

SIMMONS, A. JOHN, *Moral Principles and Political Obligations* (Princeton: Princeton University Press, 1979).

SIMON, HERBERT A., *Models of Man* (New York: John Wiley, 1957).

SIMPSON, A. W. B.,'The Ratio Decidendi of a Case', *Modern Law Review*, 20 (1957), 413–15.

—— 'The Ratio Decidendi of a Case', *Modern Law Review*, 21 (1958), 155–60.

—— 'The Common Law and Legal Theory', in A. W. B. Simpson (ed.) *Oxford Essays in Jurisprudence* (2nd ser.), (Oxford: Clarendon Press, 1973), 77–99, and also (in rev. form) in William Twining (ed.), *Legal Theory and Common Law* (Oxford: Basil Blackwell, 1986), 8–25.

SINGER, MARCUS G., *Generalization in Ethics: An Essay in the Logic of Ethics, with the Rudiments of a System of Moral Philosophy* (New York: Alfred A. Knopf, Inc., 1961).

SLOTE, MICHAEL, *Beyond Optimizing: A Study of Rational Choice* (Cambridge, Mass.: Harvard University Press, 1989).

SMART, J. J. C., 'Extreme and Restricted Utilitarianism', *Philosophical Quarterly*, 6 (1956), 344–54 (also, in revised form, in Bayles, *Contemporary Utilitarianism*).

SMITH, M. B. E., 'Is There a Prima Facie Obligation to Obey the Law?', *Yale Law Journal*, 82 (1973), 950–76.

SOBEL, J. HOWARD, 'Utilitarianisms: Simple and General', *Inquiry*, 13 (1970), 394–449.

SOBER, ELLIOTT, 'Apportioning Causal Responsibility', *The Journal of Philosophy*, 85 (1988), 303–18.

SOPER, PHILIP, *A Theory of Law* (Cambridge, Mass.: Harvard University Press, 1984).

—— 'Legal Theory and the Obligation of the Judge: The Hart/Dworkin Dispute', *Michigan Law Review*, 75 (1977), 511–42.

STOCK, GUY, 'Leibniz and Kripke's Sceptical Paradox', *Philosophical Quarterly*, 38 (1988), 326–9.

STONE, JULIUS, *The Province and Function of Law* (London: Stevens & Sons Limited, 1947).

STOUT, A. K., 'But Suppose Everyone Did the Same', *Australasian Journal of Philosophy*, 32 (1954), 1–29.

STRAWSON, P. F., 'On Referring', *Mind*, 59 (1950), 320–44.

SUPPES, PATRICK, *A Probabilistic Theory of Causality* (Amsterdam: North Holland Publishing Company, 1970).

SUSSKIND, RICHARD E., *Expert Systems in Law: A Jurisprudential Inquiry* (Oxford: Clarendon Press, 1987).

TAPPER, COLIN, 'A Note on Principles', *Modern Law Review*, 34 (1971), 628–34.

THOMSON, JUDITH, 'Some Ruminations on Rights', *Arizona Law Review*, 19 (1977), 45–60.

TRIANOSKY, GREGORY, 'Rule-Utilitarianism and the Slippery Slope', *Journal of Philosophy*, 75 (1978), 414–24.

TUR, RICHARD, 'Positivism, Principles, and Rules', in Ellspeth Attwooll (ed.), *Perspectives on Jurisprudence* (Glasgow: University of Glasgow Press, 1977), 42–78.

TWINING, WILLIAM, *Karl Llewellyn and the Realist Movement* (London: Weidenfeld & Nicolson, 1973).

—— and MIERS, DAVID, *How To Do Things With Rules: A Primer of Interpretation*, 2nd edn. (London: Wiedenfeld & Nicolson, 1982).

ULLMAN-MARGALIT, EDNA., *The Emergence of Norms* (Oxford: Clarendon Press, 1977).

ULLMAN-MARGALIT, EDNA., 'On Presumption', *Journal of Philosophy*, 80 (1983), 143–63.

—— and MARGALIT, AVISHAI, 'Analyticity by Way of Presumption', *Canadian Journal of Philosophy*, 12 (1982), 435–52.

URMSON, J. 'The Interpretation of the Moral Philosophy of J. S. Mill', *Philosophical Quarterly*, 3 (1953), 3–39 (also in Bayles, *Contemporary Utilitarianism*).

—— 'Moore's Utilitarianism', in Alice Ambrose and Morris Lazerowitz (eds.), *G. E. Moore: Essays in Retrospect* (London: George Allen & Unwin, Ltd., 1970), 343–9.

VON WRIGHT, GEORG HENRIK, *Norm and Action: A Logical Enquiry* (London: Routledge & Kegan Paul, 1963).

—— —— 'The Foundation of Norms and Normative Statements', in *Practical Reason* (Ithaca, New York: Cornell University Press, 1983), 67–82.

—— —— 'On the Logic of Norms and Actions', in *Practical Reason* (Ithaca, New York: Cornell University Press, 1983), 100–29.

WAISMANN, FRIEDRICH, 'Verifiability', in A. G. N. Flew (ed.), *Logic and Language: First Series* (Oxford: Basil Blackwell, 1951), 117–44.

WARNOCK, G. J., *The Object of Morality* (London: Methuen & Co. Ltd., 1971).

WASSERSTROM, RICHARD A., *The Judicial Decision: Toward a Theory of Legal Justification* (Stanford: Stanford University Press, 1961).

WERTHEIMER, ALAN, *Coercion* (Princeton: Princeton University Press, 1987).

WESTEN, PETER, ' "Freedom" and "Coercion"—Virtue Words and Vice Words', *Duke Law Journal*, (1985), 541–93.

WHITEHEAD, ALFRED NORTH, *An Introduction to Mathematics* (New York: Oxford University Press, 1958).

WHITT, L. A., 'Acceptance and the Problem of Slippery-Slope Insensitivity in Rule-Utilitarianism', *Dialogue*, 23 (1984), 649–59.

WINCH, PETER, *The Idea of a Social Science and its Relation to Philosophy* (London: Routledge & Kegan Paul, 1958).

WINSTON, KENNETH W., 'On Treating Like Cases Alike' *California Law Review*, 62 (1977), 1–39.

—— Book Review of Robert S. Summers, *Lon L. Fuller. Ethics*, 95 (1985), 751–5.

WITTGENSTEIN, LUDWIG, *Philosophical Investigations*, 3rd edn. G. E. M. Anscombe (trans.), (New York: Macmillan Publishing Co., Inc., 1958).

—— *Remarks on the Foundations of Mathematics*, rev. edn., G. H. von Wright, R. Rhees, G. E. M. Anscombe (eds.), G. E. M. Anscombe (trans.), (Cambridge, Mass.: MIT Press, 1978).

WOLFF, ROBERT PAUL, *In Defense of Anarchism* (New York: Harper & Row, 1970).

WOOZLEY, A. D., Book Review of David Lyons, *Forms and Limits of Utilitarianism*. *Philosophical Quarterly*, 17 (1967), 183–4.

WRIGHT, CRISPIN, *Wittgenstein on the Foundations of Mathematics* (Cambridge, Mass.: Harvard University Press, 1980).

YABLO, STEPHEN, 'Identity, Essence, and Indiscernability', *Journal of Philosophy*, 84 (1987), 293–314.

ZIFF, PAUL, *Semantic Analysis* (Ithaca, New York: Cornell University Press, 1960).

—— 'On H.P. Grice's Account of Meaning', *Analysis*, 28 (1967), 1–8.

INDEX

250   INDEX